For Taliya and Selena. My light, my truth, my forever. My daughters!

FIXED

MOSES SWAIBU

FIXED

MY SECRET LIFE
AS A MATCH FIXER

First published in the UK in 2025 by Blink Publishing
An imprint of Bonnier Books UK
5th Floor, HYLO,
103–105 Bunhill Row,
London, EC1Y 8LZ

A CIP catalogue of this book is available from the British Library.

Hardback – 9781789468441

Also available as an ebook and an audiobook

1 3 5 7 9 10 8 6 4 2

Designed by Envy Design Ltd
Printed and bound in Great Britain by Clays Ltd, Elcograf S.p.A.

The authorised representative in the EEA is
Bonnier Books UK (Ireland) Limited.
Registered office address: Floor 3, Block 3, Miesian Plaza,
Dublin 2, D02 Y754, Ireland
compliance@bonnierbooks.ie

www.bonnierbooks.co.uk

CONTENTS

CHAPTER 1

GAME OVER

Tuesday, 26 November 2013: Streatham, London

Sometimes I think: *Imagine if I'd stayed at home that night?* I would have got away with the whole thing. Millions in my back pocket, not a single detective or law enforcement officer in sight. Not even close.

I need to regain control of the situation and collect my compensation.

My former teammates, Delroy Facey and Michael 'Boats' Boateng, along with Del's new match-fixing connections, Chann Sankaran and Krishna Ganeshan, have wasted my time and energy right up until this point.

Boats has turned into a little Judas. I suspect he's been lying to me. What was once love, friendship and genuine care for each other has suddenly turned into an uneasy feeling of betrayal.

During my peak period at Bromley FC, Boats was aware fixing was going on, but he didn't know it was me. He knew how big it was because throughout that whole 2012/13 season in the Conference South, there were whispers in every changing room.

It was in the air. There was a time when players in every team in that league wanted a piece of the action.

People would say, 'Hey, have you heard about that fixing stuff or the betting stuff?'

Each time, I was like, 'Nah.'

Now Boats knows it was me, and he's keen to step up and step up quickly – a little too quickly for his capabilities. He wants to take the flame I've given him and prove himself to his social circle that he can become that guy. Become me.

I've been teasing the idea of match fixing to Boats for months. Sometimes when we spoke after games, I told him exactly how it all works and how I got into it. I've been inadvertently preparing him for a takeover. If he's going to fix a game, this is what it should look like.

He's the only reason I joined Whitehawk FC, my last ever club. And since I've recently quit playing football and fixing matches, I have a plan in place for Boats to take over the Conference South and become my heir apparent. I'll train him to inherit the position of power I held last season and pass the match-fixing baton on to him. The groomed becomes the groomer.

I can't hide it from him any more – he knows the truth about how I was running my match-fixing operation and he wants in.

Plus, I owe Boats a big favour.

He was the one who passed the finance on my Mercedes after I got knocked back for a bad credit rating. An unpaid mobile phone bill from a trip to Miami three years ago, a holiday to celebrate my twenty-first birthday, came back to haunt me.

Last month, Boats called in that favour. When I originally got my car, all he asked for in return was a pair of £100 Nike

Air Force 1s . . . I couldn't believe it. I thought he was joking but then he reaffirmed it. A £40k car in exchange for a 100 quid pair of trainers. I remember saying to him at the time: 'Anything you need, just let me know and I'll sort it out.'

Now he needs money to pay off loans – five grand to be precise. Boats drives a modest Smart car, humble enough for someone so innocent and pure of heart. One recent Saturday evening I had to collect match-fixing cash from a casino and, when I met Boats after, I pulled £3,000 from my bag. I tell him to keep it; no need to pay me back. His eyes opened so wide I had to laugh. That was the moment his head was turned.

I tell Del that it's Boats who's going to take the reins. His introduction to match fixing will be to organise with Chann and Krishna to fix an upcoming Conference South fixture – Arlesey Town v Whitehawk, Boats's current club. In the build-up to the fix, Boats fails to tell me about the meeting he had with the fixers in Croydon. He deceived me.

I want to know how this appointment went down, so I call him.

'Boats, where were you?'

'East Croydon.' He's strangely quiet.

'Who was at the meeting?'

'The fixers and an investor.' His voice sounds different.

'How much money did they give you?'

Silence.

'What colour was the investor?'

'White.'

I hang up. I'm raging. No way in a million years would you find a white British man sitting in front of you talking about match fixing.

Boats also tells me he took along his best friend Hakeem. WTF? How stupid can you be? Why didn't he tell me all this before he went?

This phone call sends shock waves through my body. I'm reacting on emotion. I always use burner phones to send text messages. For the first time, I text him on my personal mobile: 'Be careful who you meet, bro.'

In my eyes he's committed the biggest sin: he's gone behind my back. He's not telling me the truth. I heard it in his voice, and I felt his nervous energy on the phone. He's trying to play me out of the new match-fixing business I'm setting up.

Maybe betrayal was inevitable? So is revenge. Now it's time for payback.

* * *

This morning, Chann sent me text messages with two images – both are of large bundles of banknotes. His way of confirming that he's secured the investment to start a brand-new match-fixing enterprise. The first photo is my 'pocket money' for tonight's meeting.

Before any match is fixed or agreed in principle there's always a standard fee, just for showing up – the 'pocket money'. The amount on offer determines how serious or sophisticated the major match-fixing syndicates can be. The Russians, the Chinese and now the Singaporeans all use different means of inducement for bait. What whet my appetite for tonight is the chance to execute a final master plan before I decide on my next move.

My brain is working on overdrive, spinning with a thousand thoughts. At times I feel like we've gone deep into injury time, after the game is already over.

Chann said the second photo is £60k. I tell him, 'I can easily show you at least a million pounds.' It's turning into a game of 'Who's got the biggest dick on WhatsApp?'!

The money is in place, so I tell Del my game plan. It's all mapped out in my mind. The light-bulb moment I've been waiting for has finally arrived.

In order to teach Boats a lesson, I contact Chann directly and tell him and Krishna to meet me in London that night – I've invited them to join me at the AFC Wimbledon v Dagenham & Redbridge game and present Chann with a new proposition, separate from Saturday's planned Whitehawk fix: I say I can fix tonight's match – I've secured players on both teams to be in on the fix – and that I can give them the correct result so they can alert their syndicate bosses to place bets on Asian betting websites.

In the process, I'll take £5k pocket money just for showing up and for providing them with a pathway into fixing English football matches. The catch is that tonight's match won't be fixed. I have no idea what the final score will be. It's all a bluff. Let's test how serious Delroy's new match fixers are. I'll show Boats how it's done, teach him not to go behind my back and at the same time pocket some easy money.

* * *

I put my baby daughter down to bed, tell my girlfriend Crystal I'll be back in time for her famous chicken curry and then hop in the car with my best mate Benji Kudjodji at the wheel. I lost my driving licence at the start of the year. A six-month ban for a mix-up with my insurance.

I've got a Mercedes-Benz SLK 250 CDI: my cocaine-white

Batmobile. Black leather seats. Classic SLK retractable hard roof. Plus, a built-in panoramic roof. Some days I used to just sit in the car and look up at the pan roof, push the button and watch it glide off.

This is the first time Benji has driven my car. With everything else that's going down, I need someone I can trust. I've known him since primary school, two ten-year-olds bonding over a shared love of football on the back seats of the 289 bus in Croydon.

Benji knows nothing. How could he? He's never been part of any plan. It doesn't occur to me to tell him what's *really* going on. If I did, I'd have to go right back to the beginning . . . but time is of the essence. Tonight is simple for me: go to the game, get the money and back home in time for my curry.

As our friendship grew into our teens, me and Benji played for the same schools district team together. He was one of the best strikers for his age group in the whole borough of Croydon. Then he was with me throughout my time at Crystal Palace Academy.

After all these years, he's never changed. If I had to pick one friend I could trust with my life, it would be Benji.

'Ay, B, are you ready for the game?' I half-shout above the music.

'Yeah, man.' He flashes that big Benji smile. I can't tell him I'm not remotely interested in watching this football match. My focus is elsewhere.

We're off to watch a London derby: AFC Wimbledon v Dagenham & Redbridge at Kingsmeadow Stadium, Kingston upon Thames. English League Two.

The drive to the ground is full of laughter and memories

but I'm trapped in my thoughts, preoccupied with my plan. I think how quickly I've risen through the ranks of match fixing this year.

I enjoy reminiscing with my best mate, but my mind is in a darker place. The money I've been making is fuelling my paranoia. It's really messing with my head. I can't sleep at night. I can't keep up with all this activity and all the demands being made on me. I sit at home feeling empty. Nobody knows what I'm doing or what I'm a part of. The one significant difference in my life is my baby daughter, Taliya, born in March this year.

But what's the next chapter of my life gonna be? I'd recently retired from playing football. I was out. So far out I didn't even want to see a ball or watch football – live or on TV. This is the stage I'm at. For the first time in my life, I'm giving up the one thing that saved me.

At the same time I hung up my boots, I quit match fixing, a decision I've been beating myself up about these past few months. I'm torn. There are still so many options. I've amassed a lot of money – my mountain of savings, my stockpile of cash. But it feels like everything has come to a standstill. Taliya's mum, Crystal, my childhood sweetheart, has no idea where my mind is at. Or that there's a cool million of my match-fixing earnings packed into a room in a Chinese takeaway in Dalston, in the East End of London, less than an hour away from where we live together in Streatham. The match fixer's secret ATM.

I'm getting more and more paranoid about the money I've accumulated, not only for myself but for the syndicate too. I've never had to think about what I'm going to do with my life. What's next. Football *is* my life. You never think it's going to end. Especially not aged twenty-four.

I force myself to do what I always do when I'm stuck between a rock and a hard place: flip into football mode. I'm the former Young Player of the Year at Crystal Palace, ex-captain of Lincoln City FC. I'm a born leader.

I recently quit working for a match-fixing organisation, but I'm still toying with several ideas: continue to expand with rapid growth and similar structure to my ex-boss, Tan; become my own bookmaker; or go abroad and build an even bigger empire. Tan is the head of the Chinese syndicate I had been fixing for. He's five feet nothing, loves puffing on endless cigarettes and doesn't speak a word of English. He describes himself as 'the Boss of all Bosses'. He has a passion and greed for fixing and making money that is completely at odds with his appearance. It got me thinking, *Could I be my own big boss?* I've established a pool of players, ready and hungry to make money. I know safe locations and drop-off points to distribute the funds. I've even got the distribution access for payments with twenty-four-hour guarantees and an international corridor between Europe and the UK. The odds and markets I can achieve will give me an almost 99.9 per cent return.

'*You know what,*' I say to myself. '*Why don't I start my own operation? I can become my own big boss. I'll be at the top of the food chain.*'

Teams are ready to be acquired through betting sponsorship, players are ready to infiltrate. I have it all mapped out and I'm right in the middle of it all as a major player.

* * *

I'm in touch with Del again for the first time in nearly three years, since around the time I left Lincoln, at the end of January 2011.

Back when he and a mysterious Russian guy had first tempted me to get into match fixing with €60k in cash in a duffel bag in a hotel room in Northampton.

Last season I was at Bromley and Del is up north. He gets wind of something tasty going on in the Conference South. So, he calls me:

'Yo, Mo, what's going on, man? Remember that *thing*?'

And obviously I know what that *thing* is. The Northampton hotel room *thing*.

'Yeah, man.'

He says, 'What's happening down there? I hear people are making a killing.'

I was like, 'Yeah, man, I hear the same thing. If I find out anything, I'll let you know.'

He had no clue that I was running the show.

Then he calls again and I tell him, 'Look, bro, I'm out but I know someone that can maybe take over, so let me connect both of you.'

This is my formal introduction of Boats to Delroy.

Then Del starts telling me he's got new investors. He puts me in touch with the two match fixers, Chann and Krishna. They're coming down from Manchester *today*. Things are accelerating. Del texted me last week: 'They're in, bro, for Saturday's game'.

As I mentioned, Saturday's game is Arlesey Town FC v Whitehawk FC, in the Conference South. Boats's first fix. Just over three weeks ago, I was playing centre half for Whitehawk. It came off the back of my three-month deal at Sutton United running out, a moment where I thought I'd never kick a ball again. Early retirement is a ticking time bomb; it's just a matter of when it goes off.

Then Boats lured me back. He's at non-league Whitehawk and kept pestering me to come and play for them. He gave me Darren Freeman's number, his Gaffer. Darren said he rated me and asked if my reluctance to sign was down to the paltry wages. I can hardly tell him I've got money, almost a million pounds. The truth is I had zero motivation to keep playing. But I signed anyway for the sake of Boats. We had a plan.

Four games in and I lost heart again. I walked off the pitch at half-time with Whitehawk one-up against Gosport Borough. I don't come back for the second half. As far as I was concerned my career ended that day in Brighton. It's the second time I've retired in the space of two months. This time it feels permanent.

I'm no longer playing for Whitehawk, but I'm still involved with their performance on the pitch – albeit in a completely different capacity. Del has asked me to put up some players for Saturday's match. Normally you need five in your pocket to fix a match. The match fixers want to meet the players in Manchester. Not possible, I say. The solution? Send photos to them but not of the actual players – snaps of my Monday night five-a-side team. A crack outfit. Half the Whitehawk team are black, my fives team are all black. These guys will never know the difference. Let's see how serious they are.

This is the breakdown. Del wants a piece of the action. He's desperate. I'm out so I recommend Boats. Del connects us with the fixers, Chann and Krishna. They're in Manchester meeting the new investors. Chann sends me photos of the money. He says they'll be on a train to London today. I suggest five players to Del, but they don't play for Whitehawk. It's my Monday night fives team. Boats is in on the Whitehawk fix but he doesn't know I've got tickets for Chann and Krishna for tonight's AFC Wimbledon v Dagenham & Redbridge game. I've told the fixers my prediction. It's a bluff. This match won't be fixed. I'm just pretending to test that they're real. And to teach Boats a lesson for not being transparent and get 'pocket money' compensation for showing up. I'm taking a big risk. Let's see how it pans out.

Right up until the point yesterday when Boats goes all quiet and starts acting funny on the phone about the meeting, I'm getting a sickly feeling in my stomach. Boats, you're almost like my little brother. Not in a violent way, not in a way I'm gonna harm you – but, bro, I must teach you a cold lesson in life. You don't turn your back and be this low.

* * *

We've got a personal interest in the Dagenham team. Their left back has sorted me out with four free tickets. I know him from growing up – he's a Southwark boy – and he's always played football. Whenever I was back in London we used to play street football with other pros in between training with our clubs. He got me a trial at Dagenham in the summer of 2011 after I left Lincoln.

I tell Benji we're meeting two guys I know. I said I'd get them into the game. No explanation needed.

Approaching Malden Junction, we hear the distinctive murmur of football fans for the first time. It grows gradually louder as we hang a right towards Kingston Road past streams of supporters walking to the ground. I can smell hamburgers and hot dogs and fried onions from the fast-food wagons. Fans mill about outside singing and chanting. There's that familiar pre-match tension in the air.

It's a sensory overload. But I can't stop thinking about Boats. He wants to be seen. He wants to be heard. I've got a nasty pent-up anger growing inside me. Who does Boats think he is? He can never *be* me. I'm gonna take the money. Show him how it's done.

'Yo, Ben, park here, bro.' I point to an empty space facing the exit. I've played at Kingsmeadow Stadium before, so I know the shortest routes out of the ground. But this isn't a game of football for me. My only interest is more power, more money. Get in and get out as quickly as possible. I tell Crystal before we leave: 'I'll be back in time for dinner.'

We park up and go to meet my 'acquaintances', Chann and Krishna, outside the main stand. It's Little and Large. 'Little' is Chann, a skinny, ratty-looking man in a black Manchester United tracksuit top. He can't stop talking, in a thick Southeast Asian accent. Broken English. Shifty. Someone you can't trust. 'Large' (Krishna) is shabbily dressed, overweight, hardly says a word.

Chann says, 'So you're Jon Gotti?' Jon Gotti is my Skype pseudonym.

When I was young, I watched a film called *City of God*. He gives me the exact look as Li'l Zé in the scene where he meets his rival for the first time.

I cut him off. 'Where's the money?'

'It's in the bag.'

'OK, cool, let's go and pick up the tickets.'

This guy isn't a match fixer. That much quickly becomes clear to me. He might think he is, but he doesn't know what he's doing. I can see the nervousness in his eyes and sense it in his voice. I've met plenty of match fixers in my time and Chann Sankaran doesn't strike me as one.

By the time we get inside, the players are out on the pitch

for the pre-match warm-up. A blanket of cold mist hovers over the ground. The atmosphere is building. It's three quarters full, a healthy attendance of around 4,000. It only goes to show the passion for football in the UK, even at this relatively low level. Nearly 4000 people have left their homes and travelled here in the wind and rain to witness the great unscripted drama that only sport can offer.

There was a time when I would have shared the excitement the supporters felt as they hurried along the streets towards the ground and jostled with each other going through the turnstiles. As a boyhood Arsenal fan, football meant everything to me. The emotional highs and lows of victory or defeat would last all week before the next match came around, offering another chance to see the likes of Dennis Bergkamp, Patrick Vieira and Thierry Henry show off their dazzling skills.

But me, Chann and Krishna are here for a very different reason. We're here because I've told them I can fix this match. Luckily, my former teammate spots us in the stand and waves. An innocent wave from a friend to a friend. But with underlying meaning for me. I make sure Chann and Krishna see me returning the gesture. This is the common match-fixing signal. I turn to Chann: 'Hey, look, they know all about what's happening and what the fix is.' I can see that they fall for it. This subtle acknowledgement from a player settles their nerves. It convinces them that I'm for real.

The game is barely five minutes old when I turn to Chann again: 'Look, I need the money. Otherwise, this game isn't going to happen and I don't mind going home right now.' As half-time approaches, he passes it to me and I'm like, 'No, no, no . . . not here. Let's go outside.'

I already sense it's unlikely I'll work with these guys again, but I figure it's still worth finding out more about Chann. So I start quizzing him. Does he have any reach in the English game? Is he already in contact with any teams or players? Is he trying to establish links with anyone except me?

For those unfamiliar with the structure of English football, the top tier is the world-famous Premier League, one of the richest leagues in any sport anywhere on the planet. Players are paid astronomical sums by their clubs and it's extremely difficult – though not impossible – for match fixers to corrupt them. Below the Premier League comes the three divisions of the English Football League, today called the Championship, League One and League Two. At the time I was playing, the average salary in Leagues One and Two would have been around £40,000 to £60,000 a year, while most players in the Premier League were earning at least that every week.

The next rung down is the highest level of the non-League game – the National League, which has beneath it the regional divisions of the National League North and South. In my day, these divisions were called the Conference and the Conference North and South. Not all players at this level are full-time; many are poorly paid, contracts are short or non-existent and job security is low. This makes it fertile ground for match fixers to exploit. The higher the division, the greater the betting volume. The greater the betting volume, the greater the ability for match-fixing syndicates to disguise their bets and therefore the greater the opportunity to bet big and win big. Thus, the Football League is a more attractive proposition than the Conference.

Chann and Krishna and their gang are keen to operate at

either level and I'm pretty sure they know they won't be able to do so effectively without going through me.

I'd told Chann I could ensure tonight's match would finish 1-0 to Wimbledon. It was a lie. I had no ability to fix this match. As I mentioned, the money he's got for me isn't for fixing the game, it's just for agreeing to meet. But his syndicate are still intrigued to see if I'm capable of pulling off what I've claimed I could.

Me and Chann leave the ground. Benji and Krishna stay on to watch the rest of the game.

The turnstiles click as we exit the away end through Gate C.

Click. 'Look, where's the money, man?'

Click. 'I don't think this game is fixed. You're lying to me.'

Click. 'Five grand, right?'

Chann looks at me but says nothing.

Click. 'Listen, give me the fucking money.'

Click. Click. Click.

I try to impress on him that I would never have agreed to this meeting for less than five thousand pounds. He's not listening. He hands me an envelope. It feels light. I unzip my bag and stuff the money inside.

We walk round the corner into a nearby Indian restaurant. The Dal Handi is a shabby little twenty-seater curry house, mainly used for takeaways. Business is slow on a wet Tuesday night. A perfect spot to talk undisturbed. We sit down at a random table.

Chann's non-stop, hyperactive chat has me on edge. He shows me betting stuff on his phone – how they put on the bet and how they get paid out, and what betting companies they use on the black market. I'm only half paying attention to him. My spider - senses is on red alert.

I get up from the table and go to the toilet to count the money. I lock the cubicle, flush the loo and start thumbing through the wad of notes. The money feels clean. Too clean. Once money is handled you can almost figure out how many hands it's passed through. This money feels untouched.

There's only three thousand pounds here. I count it again to make sure. He's two grand short. My mind is racing. I'd never known a match fixer to quibble over a couple of grand. This is buttons compared to what we can make together.

Back at the table and Chann won't stop banging on about his boss. It's all Wilson this and Wilson that. How much money this guy Wilson has made match fixing. He does a Google search on his phone and shows me a photo of an Asian guy in his late forties. Wilson Raj Perumal? The name rings a bell. I know about him through the match-fixing grapevine, from the English boys who went to Australia to fix games. Does this joker really have direct access to one of the so-called Kelong Kings, meaning 'Kings of Cheating'? My ex-boss Dan Tan Seet Eng is one of a trio of Singaporean match fixers notorious for conceiving and planning to manipulate football matches all over the world. Wilson Raj Perumal and Rajendran 'Pal' Kurusamy are the other two.

This is Wilson's trusted lieutenant? One of the three ringleaders of global match fixing is sending this guy payments? Chann keeps calling Wilson the 'boss of bosses'. He's acting like some kind of fan boy. Or, more accurately, a stalker.

'He's probably not who you think he is,' I tell him. 'Anyway, he's not the boss of what is currently happening here. I am.'

He starts talking even louder about what will happen if anything goes wrong, what he'll do and what his big boss will do.

I don't care about his threats. This isn't Singapore. It's London, so if the shit hits the fan, I'm covered. I have the money and the resources. Ready and available for any worst-case scenario.

He fishes for his phone again and thrusts it in my face, swiping through photos and videos of suitcases rammed with cash.

'The money's there. It's yours when you get results,' he says.

Chann's hectic behaviour is at odds with the way any match fixer I'd ever seen would act. My mind is made up. There are too many warning signs. Too many red flags. I'll not work with Chann or Krishna or their people. They're either clueless or reckless. Or both.

'Give me my money back!' He's almost shouting.

Fucking hell. Keep your voice down. Out of the corner of my eye I see an immaculately dressed blonde woman float into the restaurant. Her startling presence throws me. I can't concentrate on Chann. Perfect hair, fancy make-up, high heels. She looks more suited to the fine dining establishments of Mayfair than a run-down curry house on a rainy Tuesday night in Kingston.

Every other table is available, but she picks one directly opposite ours and sits down with a waft of expensive perfume.

A few minutes later, the door opens, cold air rushes into the restaurant and a man walks in. He strides across the floor, looks directly at Chann and me and sits down at the same table as the Mayfair blonde. Their body language is unsettling. Their conversation isn't relaxed or natural. My heart sinks. What the fuuuuu . . . this is no venue for a romantic date.

The more animated Chann gets, the twitchier I get, the more attention *we* get from the mystery couple. Chann's acting like he's high on drugs. His eyes are getting bigger and bigger.

I text Benji under the table: 'How long's left? Let's go.'

The half-time break has come and gone. The teams must be back on the pitch by now.

Chann cranks up the pressure: 'I want my money back. This game's not fixed.'

'Look, this is how business works,' I say.

Chann won't let up; he doesn't care about anything but his money. He grabs his phone from the table and opens an in-play betting app then waves the screen at me, pointing at the live score updates, clearly agitated. Dagenham & Redbridge have equalised. It's 1-1. All bets are off.

Fuck. My heart's pounding. Benji and Krishna appear at the door. I don't even hear what Chann is saying any more.

I stand up and pull my coat from the back of the chair, grab my bag with the money and make for a swift exit. The blonde woman glances over.

Shit.

I bolt for the door and whisper to Benji, 'Something weird's going on.'

Chann shouts after me, 'Hey, hey, where are you going?' I leave him to pay for the drinks and poppadoms.

We're back out into the South London night and speed-walk down Kingston Road. It's five minutes to the car. My assurances that the game would finish 1-0 are worth nothing. If Chann or Krishna got round to putting on a bet, then they've lost their money.

I can see the car 100 yards away. So close, but it might as well be on the other side of the earth. 'Give me the keys, Ben. I'm gonna drive.' Fuck the ban.

I point the key fob at the Mercedes and it lights up like a spaceship. A sixth sense tells me to get to it as fast as possible, a nasty premonition that something bad is about to happen, that my life is going to change forever. But no matter how quickly I try to walk, I can't get to the car. I'm wading in mud, splashing through potholes full of water, kicking up stones from the ground. My brain tells me to move but my legs won't respond.

Suddenly I hear shouts and screams reverberating up the dark, narrow alleyway. A group of people start running towards us through the darkness. Casual dress. Are they football fans? Is the game over?

'Ben, what the fuck's going on?'

The whole scene plays out in slow motion and fades to black and white. I'm frozen to the spot. Arms reach out to grab me. I experience flashbacks in glorious technicolour. A montage of every moment of the match-fixing escapades I've been caught up in over these past few years rush in rapid succession through my mind: all the penalties given away, all the goals conceded, the yellow and red cards given.

Am I hallucinating? Scenes project in vibrant colours on to the alleyway walls all around me, lighting up the dark autumn sky: my first meeting with the match fixers, Tan sitting on a bed with his back to us in a room at the May Fair Hotel, watching the big TV, chain-smoking cigarettes, Dom the French, Hunken, the money at the Dalston stash house, piled as high as my waist, stuffing wads of cash into a sports holdall, running around London dishing it out like a Mafia bagman . . . I'm transported back to the beginning of it all, everything, right up until this moment.

'Stop! Stop! Stop!'

I'm a rabbit caught in the headlights of an oncoming juggernaut. Suddenly, we're surrounded by about twenty people.

I turn to poor Benji. His eyes are popping out of his head. He's mouthing to me: What. The. Fuck. Is. Going. On?

Ben is a warrior. He would run through a brick wall for me. But this isn't something anyone can fix.

A female voice says: 'Have you got anything on you that you shouldn't have?'

I blurt out: 'Yep, I got some cash in my bag.'

All I can think about is the *real* money. I see a million pounds vanishing right in front of my face. I curse myself. Why did I come to this stupid game? Why did I meet these two clowns? That idiot Delroy. Boats, fuck. I told you to be careful about that meeting. I'm feeling hard done by. Boats, what have you done, man? You've put me in deep shit.

Quite literally. I'm standing stock still, stuck in the mud in a car park in the pissing rain.

'Moses Swaibu – you're under arrest for conspiracy to defraud the betting trade.'

I have no idea what they mean. For a split second I take some comfort from the terminology. 'Defrauding the betting trade'? I've never placed a bet in my life. Maybe they think I've done something I haven't, something they'd never be able to prove?

Fleeting optimism is instantly replaced with harsh realism. This is about Chann and Krishna and the money in my bag. I was warned from the start by the first syndicate I'd worked for: 'If you ever get arrested, you'll never see us or the money again.' The syndicate made me rich. I was hoping they'd make me richer still. That's never going to happen now.

I visualise the piles of cash stacked high in a giant safe in the back room of the Chinese restaurant. Diners oblivious to the fact that they were sitting a few yards from millions of illegally obtained pounds. A small portion of the millions stored there is mine. I could call ahead any time, swing by the restaurant and with-draw – from my cut – any amount I wanted. The system worked well. I avoided the risk of my bank asking difficult questions about how I'd come into a sudden fortune. Being paid like this, it seemed unlikely my illegal activities would ever come to the attention of the authorities.

Now I'm damaged goods. Persona non grata. All ties with the Big Boss, Tan, severed forever. I can't chance exposing a link to him without risking violent retribution. I can't say or do anything that will lead the police to his network.

It's game over. I've been caught with my pants down. I'm going to jail.

I squint my eyes in the gloom to see who's talking to me. It's the Mayfair blonde. And there's her 'date'. She takes handcuffs from her pocket, but not regular ones – white plastic zip-tie fasteners. They look like something you could buy in a garden centre. Before I know it, they're cutting into my wrists.

'My girlfriend's at home. Can I call her?'

'No, wait till you get to the station.'

'What station are we going to?'

'Birmingham.'

Just as I bend my head down to step into the car, I hear Chann's unmistakable voice from behind. He winks at me and flashes me a look like a serial killer, then goes back to smiling and goading the officers with cocky insults as they lead him to another car in cuffs.

This is London. Fuck. Why are we going to Birmingham?

The last time I saw that mountain of cash in the Dalston Chinese was only two days ago. Why didn't I take out more on that visit? All I can see in my mind's eye is the *money*! Money I know I'll never see again.

The final text message Tan sent me rings in my ears: 'Swaibu, greedy man no see clearly.'

CHAPTER 2

FOOTBALL SAVED MY LIFE

I feel like I was born into survival mode. This isn't me talking in hindsight. This is just me closing my eyes and thinking, *How did life really begin for me?* I'm twelve years old. Or I'm thirteen, or fourteen or fifteen. It doesn't matter. I remember one night in winter, any night in winter. The cold air cuts through my flimsy Nike school jacket. I desperately need to come indoors. I knock on the front door so lightly out of fear my stepmother, Anne, will answer it and tell me, not for the first time, 'I can't do anything for you.'

Then she fetches my dinner and puts it on the doorstep, serving it up to me like a fucking dog. It's a regular punishment, this routine of being locked out after missing the curfew. If I'm not home by 4.30pm, my dad, Bashir, will bolt the front door for the night. I'm trapped outside in the big, bad world. The curfew even applies to weekends, unless I'm playing football. Then again, I'm almost always at my mum's – Bella – on Saturdays and Sundays, with no curfew.

My stepmother acts out this cruel farce countless times over the years when my dad is away. We have blazing arguments until she cries. Who does this to a twelve-year-old? Part of me feels sorry for her. As I grow older I realise she is also being mentally abused. It's all hidden behind her alcoholism.

She spends untold lonely, drunken nights at home. Cases of Blossom Hill white wine fill the storage cupboard. What a mess. By comparison, our drug addict neighbours always appear to be clean and tidy. On several occasions when I'm shivering on the doorstep, the couple next door let me in and I sleep in a room with a bed and wonder what all the needles and other drug paraphernalia lying around the floor are for. I realise you can never tell who the addict is, even when they're right in front of your eyes.

As I sit there on the doorstep, I can't help but wonder if this is it. Is this all I'm meant for? A life dictated by the whims of a man who believes in nothing but discipline. A future that feels as ensnared as the cold, desolate space I'm sitting in?

When your emotions are stripped from you, it feels like you're falling from the sky without a landing pad. I was so young and happy, full of joy and energy. Imagine that innocent spirit being stolen away. This early in my young life I can't work out or begin to understand what abuse is.

I can't fathom why this is happening. What did I do to make someone kill me this softly? This is my own father, but he isn't alone.

Anne witnesses everything over the years. A big part of Bashir's anger comes from her make-believe scenarios, covering her drunken tracks. I'm barely into my teens and I come home from school and find her pissed and lying naked on the floor, holding a glass of wine in her hand. I was still a young boy, a virgin. My life is survival and football. I've never seen a naked woman, never mind this woman, my dad's wife, living in my house. I know it's wrong but who do I tell?

All I can do to fight back is speak my mind when Bashir isn't around. I swear at her and call her a fucking weirdo. I go to school and ask some of the mandem, 'Yo, do any of your parents get naked for no reason and drink in your house?' My question is met with laughter, and I never ask again.

If I tell the teachers, they'll ring my house straight away and leave messages, as they do any time I'm disruptive, without knowing the root causes of my behaviour. My dad answers the phone and tells them everything is fine, he'll deal with it. Sometimes I don't feel like talking to the teachers at all. I can't put on a fake smile. Rather than ask me what's up, they speak to my dad on the phone. 'Moses is really quiet today. Is everything OK?' The abuser is gonna say, 'Yeah.'

When I get home my dad says, 'Why are you not talking in school?'

In my head, I'm thinking, *What do you mean why am I not talking in school? I just got beat black and blue. What do you want me to do – go in there and be happy?*

Then I start to rebel at school and take the punishment at home. I adopt an attitude of resignation: 'I'm gonna get beat anyway.' I'm increasingly rude to the teachers. They'll say something, anything, and I'll snap: 'Shut up, man!' Then they ring my old man and I go home and I get the same abuse. I'm thinking, *Fuck school!*

* * *

Anne threatens me. She tells my dad I'm swearing at her and abusing her when he gets off a late shift. He repeatedly does what he does best – more punishment and abuse. The scariest part for me is the psychological games. Most of the time I'm on my own and they make me think I'm the problem, make me question my sanity. Normally, I don't hear most of the stuff she says. But on a drunken day, she hits me with both barrels:

'Your dad hates you. You fucking cunt. He despises you. He thinks you're a black sheep.'

It escalates quickly into a violent, abusive shouting match. I go to bed. I'm woken up at midnight by this huge, hulking man. He's also drunk. She's crying. He asks her what's wrong. She says, 'Ah, he's at it again.' He drags me out of bed to go through the same cycle again . . . and again . . . and again . . .

Despite the long, cold nights sleeping in the door well, or riding London buses into the small hours, or crashing out on the couch of my neighbours who were taking drugs, I still have to make it to school on time, my eyes burning from lack of sleep, my tummy rumbling with hunger. My body aches, and my head is full of anger and confusion. It's extremely tough with the amount of pain I endure to have to wake up early, go to school and feign normality every day. In class I'm unresponsive, sullen to the teachers, robot-like with friends.

My dad continues to lock me out for many years, forcing me to roam the streets of South London. I become more and more wrapped up in my own head. A resentment and fire grows inside me. The only place I can release this pent-up feeling of anger and pain is on a football pitch. I begin to play football as if my life depends on it.

* * *

It's 5 March 2005. I'm fifteen years old. Me and my Thornton Rangers youth club teammate, Joel Beya, are about to sneak into Selhurst Park to watch Crystal Palace play Manchester United in the Premier League. It's a full house but we don't need a ticket. Our connection, Bev St Ange, is a dinner lady at Palace's training ground. I've been on a six-week trial at the club and Bev and Keisha always keep us Academy trainees well fed, treat us like their own sons. Bev's son, Ricky, is working as a steward at the Holmesdale Road Stand. He opens a side door and we slip inside. The stadium is bouncing and we have a bird's-eye view of the pitch from the nose-bleed seats at the top of the steep, double-tier stand.

It's exhilarating to be at my first live football match and to see the likes of Roy Keane, Paul Scholes, Rio Ferdinand, Ryan Giggs and Ruud van Nistelrooy in the flesh. Two teenage substitutes, Cristiano Ronaldo and Wayne Rooney, tear it up under the floodlights. Little do I know that I'll be on that same pitch a few years later. Palace have a man sent off – Vassilis Lakis – and our keeper, Gábor Király, pulls off a string of wonder saves. We keep Alex Ferguson's superstars at bay to earn a 0-0 draw and dent United's title hopes. Since it's a late Sunday afternoon kick-off, I don't even attempt to beat the curfew.

When we leave the stadium it's already dark. As per usual, my food is wrapped up in cling film ready for my arrival. A dog's dinner. I drop my bag on the doorstep and sit down, still buzzing from being at the big game – full of joy and happiness.

Suddenly the front door opens and my dad is there, towering over me, a giant ex-Ugandan soldier. He says to me, blankly, 'Come in.' I'm confused. It's unusual for him to be home at this time. He's a bus driver and works shifts. We go into the hallway and he turns on the light. His eyes are red, like they're bleeding, but this is his rage. His words emerge slowly from his mouth; the broken English, the distinctive stammer.

He addresses me in his deep African voice: 'Where have you been?'

'Watching Crystal Palace play football.'

He shakes his head. 'Is that in your curriculum?'

I don't understand what he means. I make the mistake of challenging him. I look him dead in the eye and say, 'What?'

I blink once and then his fist connects with the side of my temple. I've never been hit so hard. Loud ringing noises reverberate inside my head. It's his most savage attack yet. I fall to the floor and he grabs me by my trousers and drags me into the bedroom. He kicks me a few times and I fumble for my stepbrother's wooden toy horse, raise it above my head and, suddenly, I black out.

When I regain consciousness, I'm lying alone in the recovery position. I've got a cut above my head. I feel groggy. There's hysterical screaming and shouting from my stepmother. She's out-of-control drunk.

As I slowly come to my senses, my dad appears again and grabs my head and says, 'You're evil!'

Have you ever experienced so much pain that you can't feel anything, no tears, no cries, no shouts, just empty air?

He then hauls me up on to my feet and plants me in a chair. Around this time, my dad and stepmother claim I have evil in my head.

He brings out a pair of electric clippers and begins shaving my head.

'We're going to get this evil out of you.'

He begins to shave my head and I feel completely numb. I can't even cry. Words won't form in my mouth. I sit there in silence. The only sound is the high-pitched buzz of the clippers.

Then he orders me to run a cold bath, strip naked and get in. I climb into the icy water, shivering and shaking, frozen stiff with fear. I can't move.

He commands me to wash the evil out of my body. He's now taken over my body, my mind, my soul. I stare at the toilet, dead-eyed, splashing myself with freezing cold water, minute after minute . . .

'You're an evil child and you must sit there until the devil cleanses you,' he says, and leaves the bathroom.

I sit in the bath for who knows how long – teeth chattering, skinny as a rake, no muscle, just skin and bone. I've never experienced a feeling so close to death.

My father is an angry man, with a volcanic rage. Whenever I'm late home from school it's not just a minor slip-up, to him it's a show of defiance, taken as a challenge to his leadership and ability to parent. A thoughtless slap in the face of the rules he's worked his whole life to enforce.

He's a man forged in a violent world, who demands respect, discipline and order. Being an ex-soldier from Uganda, he's strict and unwavering. A bus driver by day, a drill sergeant by night, his rules are unbreakable. And when I break them, there's always swift and severe punishment.

Bashir's temper is legendary and doctoral at the same time. The beatings are so frequent that I can anticipate the build-up, the crackling tension as he tries to articulate what he's trying to explain to me. Often, I give him a blank look, which invites his trademark haymaker. I try to duck but his fist always catches a part of my head.

I lose count of the number of times I'm on the receiving end of a backhand or a harsh word. It's always underlined with his belief that everything he does, every punch, every word, is for my own good. A strict Muslim, his understanding of authority wasn't shaped by love, it was shaped by survival, by control. By the same harshness he'd learned growing up in Uganda. He fled the country with my mother in the 1980s to escape the barbarity in the aftermath of the Idi Amin military dictatorship of the 1970s. He sought refuge in the UK, a world that still didn't fully accept him.

I have two siblings. Ayub, my older brother, is always the quiet one of the two of us, measured and calm. Sarah, my older sister, a bright light in the family, always full of life and laughter. But none of us can escape the burden of our father's rules. I get more abuse than Ayub because I'm more vocal. I'm hard-headed. My brother thinks before he speaks.

If not for my brother and sister, I might not have lived past sixteen or could be serving a thirty-year life prison sentence. I can't bring myself to tell my mum the truth. I hope the pain will go away. I see her at the weekends, play football, and mask what's really happening.

Ayub finds me in the bath. I'll never forget the way he looks at me. 'Moses, get up.'

I go through to the bedroom wearing a towel, still shaking, curl up on the bed and wrap myself in my duvet like a cocoon. My mind is empty. I'm not Moses any more.

It's the one and only time Anne shows a shred of pity for me, in all the years that she witnesses or participates in the abuse.

She comes in, sits on the edge of my bed and puts her hand on my back. Her attempt to offer comfort. I've got the quilt pulled up over my head. She says, 'Sorry.' It means nothing to me. I say, 'Get your fucking hands off me!'

That night is the turning point. Ayub says, 'Moses, we're going back to live with Mum – we're getting out.' In that moment, he gives us both the courage to leave, to never return. We gain so much strength in one evening. I sit with my brother and we plot to pack our things the next morning. Ayub really saved my life. He doesn't even know how much this is true.

The last time I speak to my dad is the day I leave. I stand in front of him with my brother behind me.

'We're gone, we're leaving.'

I look directly at him, 'If you were to die, I wouldn't care.'

He responds strongly, 'I never want to see you again. Get the fuck out of this house. Never come back.'

Silence. He opens the door and says we should have packed our things long ago.

Me and Ayub, no word of a lie, walk to South Croydon station and get on a train to London Bridge. We walk round the corner to my mum's and knock on her door. I don't even tell her what's happened. I just say, 'Mum, I want to come back.'

'No problem,' she says, steps aside and welcomes us into safety.

* * *

I first kick a ball in my primary school playground, and from that moment, it's clear football is where I belong. I don't fit into many aspects of my life. It's an emotional roller-coaster ride that I can't get off. Things are different on the football field.

31

It doesn't matter where I come from, who my father is, or the toxic vice-like grip he has on my home life. On that pitch, I'm free. I have the ability to express myself and dream of a better future, a feeling of being safe once and for all.

In my early days, I'm scouted by Andy Brogan, a local coach who has a knack for spotting raw talent. He takes me under his wing and starts up youth teams with other dads of the kids from my primary school. His teams – the first one is Mayfield Wanderers, then Thornton Rangers and finally Croydon Athletic – become my escape, my sanctuary.

Andy is my lifetime guardian angel. He's the father I never had and the uncle who guides me. The wisdom, strength and unity I see in his family opens my eyes to a different kind of home life. One I'd never had. I grow up in Andy's house with his sons, Sean and Nicholas, who go to my school, and his youngest daughter Matilda. His wife Shona is the mother of all us boys.

The minute we walk into Andy's house it feels like something we've never experienced. Most of the team came from some form of broken home or parents who are separated, so when Shona makes us breakfast and cups of tea and gives us biscuits and oranges, we all have a deeper connection.

The Brogans live in Selhurst, right next to the famous BRIT School of performing and creative arts. We train at Whitehorse Road Recreation Ground throughout the season. The grass is so long and full of potholes. Ironically the dodgy surface helps to make our legs stronger. One time I fall in a pile of dog shit and everyone laughs. Shona takes me across to the house and cleans me up and sends me back outside to train. These times together create a deep bond. Andy even buys a seven-seater people carrier to pick us up – me, Oliver and Joel Beya, and my friends

Ryan and Jordan – and drive us to our games at AFC Croydon's Mayfield Stadium in Thornton Heath.

Andy is a father figure, not only to me but to the whole team. While I'm steadily being buried in abuse, for some reason Bashir only listens to Andy. He has an easy charm and self-belief in who I am becoming.

When Andy collects me on my own, he always says:

'Moses, make sure you're good at school and with your dad so I can keep this team going. I'll struggle without you.' Part of my heart fills with guilt. I love Andy so much but I can't bring myself to tell him what I'm going through. I always repay him by giving my all on the pitch.

If you ask Andy he'll probably say that Moses was one of the laziest trainees he's ever seen. Truth be told I'm knackered. There are days I might not have eaten depending on the time I get home. Mentally, I'm drained, but I try my hardest for Andy's team and always perform. My dad tells him he won't pay for my annual football registration fees as he's had enough. Andy, being Andy, tells Bashir he'll pay my bill for the upcoming season.

* * *

I have a vivid memory of watching *Match of the Day* for the first time and then seeing Ayub run outside with the ball to play with the other kids. It's a five- or ten-minute walk to the park in Thornton Heath. This is when I realise that I'm better working in groups or playing outside with my friends.

Going to see my big brother play football is a breath of fresh air. He's the best player in the team. He scores all the goals and they're always in cup finals. He is my earliest role model and I always think, *Damn, man, I want to be like my big bro.*

There's only a two-year age gap between us so we're close growing up. Ayub shows me guidance and love through football and this is where our relationship is really tight.

But we also have an intense rivalry – he is so good at football and teases me that I can't play to the point that I end up going to bed crying. I can't articulate my feelings and emotions but his taunts make me really angry.

We are fiercely competitive, even when playing against each other on the PlayStation – *ISS Pro Evolution Soccer* and *FIFA World Cup 98*. He's my biggest enemy when it comes to anything to do with games.

Ayub is someone who always has a level head. I rarely see him get angry and if he is annoyed or upset, something or someone must have really dug deep to trigger him.

My big brother is an amazing role model and human being. I don't know what I'd have done if he hadn't been in my life in those early days. We've been through everything together: from domestic violence to street fights and getting in trouble with older boys to dealing with school bullies. He's always been there and looks out for me to this day. I imagine that we're like Will Smith and Martin Lawrence's characters in *Bad Boys*, constantly having each other's backs.

My dedication also comes from seeing my mum work every day to put food on the table. I never know if she's worried. She doesn't show it, but I recognise life must be tough for her, doing her best to raise two young boys, as we become teenagers and start getting into scrapes.

Football gives me the ultimate freedom. It's an indescribable feeling. All the pressures of life disappear – for ninety minutes I can take a breath of fresh air and be myself. I want to impress my dad on the pitch and when he notices I've played well, I think, *Yeah, man, that's my dad.*

At one stage in my life I look up to him and respect him. When he takes me and my brother to play football we form a good unit, a dad and his two young boys. He comes to watch Ayub and me play football but as we get older and the problems begin, he stops coming. He never gives us any words of encouragement and from the age of thirteen, me and Ayub are left to our own devices. Hanging about on the streets at that time, anything could have happened to us.

I feel a weight on my shoulders to prove to myself I can succeed without having anybody there for me. No father figure. No positive adult male role model. That's where my drive and dedication really comes from.

* * *

Other parents drive their children to football. They might see me alone on my journey. I go from grassroots to high school, from high school to Croydon Borough from Croydon Borough to Surrey, and from Surrey to the district. I have so many opportunities to play football and I also have kickabouts with friends in the streets. On the way to games, I see my friends' parents or guardians drive past and 90 per cent of the time they stop their car, roll down the window and say, 'Hey, Moses, do you want to jump in?' I tell white lies. 'No, it's OK, thanks; my dad or my mum just dropped me off.' I don't know whether they notice something's up. I'm that kid they feel sorry for, but it helps toughen me up.

One time, I have a game for the district at Crystal Palace Park. One of my friends, Tony Cuff, is also playing. His dad has a soft spot for me. He has a good community heart and taxis young players to and from games. I'd been in trouble at school so my dad grounded me for six weeks. Tony says to me, 'Moses, we've got this district game.' It's a semi-final and I know I can't play.

Then Tony's dad shows up at my house and says, 'Moses, are you ready?' My dad doesn't want to lose face in front of adults and allows me to go. To the outside world, my dad is the nicest guy but behind the scenes he's a monster. I think to myself, *Why are you like that?*

I must have been crying and Tony's dad could tell I hadn't slept. He says, 'Moses, are you OK?' And he tries to speak to me. It's the one moment I come close to confessing to someone what is really going on in my life, but I manage to block it out. I get man of the match and our district go through to the cup final.

* * *

We lived in Nunhead, South East London, on a street called Linden Grove, right next to the cemetery.

I'm a happy child. But the family are always struggling. My mum and dad aren't together. I quickly realise this because I'm always with my mum. The time I spend with my dad is limited. My mum and dad go through court or some legal system and I don't see them for a while. Me and my sister are put in homes. My early years are spent being passed around different people.

I have the strange impression that my older sister, Sarah, is my mum because I spend so much time with my siblings. Sarah and Ayub were born in Uganda while I was born in Islington, North London.

We move house a lot, flitting from one area of London to another, from Islington to various parts of South London, Nunhead and Bermondsey.

On our Bermondsey block, groups of children are always playing on the streets. I feel the essence of community and family. I'm so happy to be allowed to play outside with the local kids from as young as five, six and seven years old. Someone always has a ball. I don't even know what football is, but I soon know instinctively that I like running around and kicking a ball.

Both my parents have a very strong Ugandan identity. They come from Jinja, a town in southern Uganda, on the shore of Lake Victoria, one of the sources of the River Nile. My mum's traditional home cooking – fried fish and fried chicken – is what builds that essence of our Ugandan-ness. When Auntie Gladys or Auntie Florence phone, I always have to speak to them. My mum still passes the phone to me now when they ring her up and suddenly I feel like a little kid again.

We spend a lot of time at parties organised by the Ugandan Society, dancing, playing music and eating traditional food.

African parents don't really talk about their past, or how they left their native country, so we had only little information from my mum and dad about their journey from Uganda to the UK as refugees

My mum's a Christian and my dad is a Muslim, so religion is a prominent topic in our house.

Despite everything, we have good values instilled in us, how we're meant to act in other people's houses and have polite manners and do the right things.

* * *

I attend Tower Bridge Primary School which is a stone's throw away from where I live.

Then from around six or seven, I live with my dad in Thornton Heath and go to the local West Thornton Primary School. It's here where I first meet Benji Kudjodji – a friend, a teammate, a second brother. On the pitch, we're equals, and the game becomes our language. We don't need words to communicate; the ball tells the story. We move as one.

I remember once being fed pumpkin and I couldn't eat it because I'm intolerant so I vomit it up. My dad doesn't know I'm allergic to pumpkin so every time I get parts of the Quran wrong he tells me to eat it back up. Then he hits me or slaps me around the head for getting it wrong. This is the early years of my dad abusing me.

* * *

The times I'm locked out of my dad's house is between the ages of twelve to sixteen. Part of the reason why I'm in a near-homeless situation is that my mum lives in London Bridge so it's hard for me at that young age to travel to her place from my Croydon school when I'm cast out. It's four o'clock in the afternoon; Mum's at work. I can't ring her because I haven't got a phone. I don't want to get on a train and go all that way only to have to come all the way back.

I reach the stage from Year 7 onwards when I say to myself, *'I'm going to be late anyway, let me just hang out with my friends. Fuck the curfew.'*

On days when I do come back on time, I don't come out of my room. It's like I'm in prison. No one speaks to me or says, 'Your dinner's ready.' I only know there's food there because

I hear the TV and it's 7.30pm. The living room door is locked. Their bedroom door is locked. It's just me and Ayub playing the PlayStation.

* * *

Going on a family holiday abroad is never an option, but when things are good with my dad we go to Butlin's in Skegness. That's one of the best holidays I ever have because I'm free and happy. We meet different kids from different backgrounds and get to leave the city and go to the coast.

My dad meets Anne on this holiday. I'll never forget it. She's from Hull. I think to myself, *'What was Hull like in the eighties or nineties when she was growing up?'* Not long after he met her, we take a trip to Hull and visit her family home. I'd never heard an old person be racist – but her parents are like, 'Where did you get these black kids from?'

Anne says, 'No, you can't say that.' It paints a picture for me of the era she grew up in. And this is someone who's never lived in London – probably never been in such a multicultural city. She's definitely never been around a broken and damaged child like me. So how does she adapt to this new environment? She's confrontational when she sees the abuse my dad inflicts on me. But much worse than that, she turns a blind eye to it.

The difficulties with my dad really begin when he introduces us to Anne. His behaviour changes. She is the catalyst in our ecosystem. He becomes violent. He comes home from work late and when our household chores and tasks aren't done, he blows his top. There is never a reason or an explanation.

It's the first time I see my dad with another woman. He tries to fit into the norms of her society, her background, her habits.

He becomes violent and aggressive. Anne drinks a lot. She is an alcoholic.

* * *

I join Archbishop Lanfranc Secondary School in Thornton Heath going into Year 6. It's a school of hard knocks – a competitive environment, inside and out of the school gates.

Lanfranc is a school where pupils either go down the good path or the bad path. It's hard to navigate a middle ground. I remember being distant in the classroom, never paying attention to the lessons, because of what was happening at home. Things aren't always easy at school but football gives me a reason to believe. So many days I'm just trying to get through the hours without feeling like I'm drowning in my own life.

Thankfully, Lanfranc excels in sport and I'm a star athlete. I win everything. I represent the school, the borough, the district and the county. At every level, both in football and athletics, 100 metres and 200 metres sprints, I become a champion, win medals and awards. Most importantly, it's fun. I captain the school football team and run the anchor leg in the relay team. I'm so driven I have to learn how to let other people lead as well.

Football gives me a purpose. It gives me meaning. And no matter how bad things get at home, no matter how many times I find myself locked out, the game is always there. Football always saves me. When I'm on the field, I'm not just Moses, the kid from Croydon; I'm Moses the footballer, the one with the talent, the one who can make the last-ditch tackle or man-mark the best striker out of the game. Football gives me confidence in a world that wants to strip it away from me.

I never have a girlfriend. I don't kiss a girl until I leave school. I know I like them, but I'm too shy to approach the ones I fancy, simply because of what I'm going through at home. There is one special girl I really like. Crystal is the best-looking girl in the school. Everybody fancies her. She's my dream girlfriend. Many years later after I leave school, we end up getting together.

I'm more wary of girls in my school because a lot of them are in gangs. They want to fight or get in your face. And because they're in gangs, with us boys on the streets every day, they become my friends.

The teachers are not so bad and we mostly get along. They're just dealing with difficult, unruly adolescents who they can't relate to. The ones who dislike me are the maths teachers and the African ones. They tell me I'm going to end up working in McDonald's if I don't know maths. The Africans try to strike fear into me because of our shared cultural background. They practise the same style of discipline as my dad. The subjects that interest me most are history, geography, art, cooking and anything creative.

My PE teacher, Mr Atkinson, understands where I'm coming from and, more importantly, he is able to channel the pent-up energy within the troubled kids and empower them to release that energy in a positive way.

I fail every exam with the worst possible marks. My GCSE results are a joke. I stare out of the class window at the grass football pitches and daydream. Even in Year 7, I know I don't want to go into further education. I only want to play football.

* * *

I get into trouble for talking back to teachers. They always say, 'Moses, you want the last word?' It's difficult trying to talk to a bunch of adults who are not listening to you, especially when they think you're in the wrong.

It is very rare that you can express yourself honestly or that a teacher actually speaks to you one-to-one. I'm perceived as the perpetrator rather than the victim of a lot of stuff. I have so many fights that people stop fighting me. I also defuse a lot of fights because people know I like fighting so much. I have my close-knit group of friends, my little gang.

I'm feared in school. People know they can't run jokes. The week after my dad shaves my head, my face says it all. Anyone who tries to tease me is met with rage and violence. I tell my best friend Oliver what happened and he puts his head down and says, 'Sorry.' His right arm graces my shoulder. One girl laughs at my haircut in design tech. I take my Sharpie and smash it on the wooden table.

* * *

My stepmother continues to torture me in a way that I'm not aware of at the time. It isn't physical, it's more psychological. Abuse can be very controlling, emotional and conniving. When she's drunk she's not even in control of her body let alone her mind.

If I come home when my dad isn't in and she can't enforce what he enforces, I stand up for myself. When I see a bottle of Blossom Hill wine I think, *Oh shit, she's drunk.* I'm a pre-teen and I'm having a conversation with a grown woman who is completely wasted. But I'm not scared of her.

Anne and my dad have a kid, Joshua. I'm thirteen, fourteen

when my stepbrother is born. There's absolutely no bond between us. The abuse towards me changes to, 'You can't be around this baby because of how you are – you're evil.'

My dad opens my bedroom door and puts Joshua in the room. I don't want to be around a child, let alone a baby. Go away! To this day, I have no relationship with Joshua. Zero. I can guarantee you 100 per cent that Joshua will have asked questions about me and that his parents have never told him the truth.

* * *

As a kid growing up, my favourite players to watch are Ian Wright and Thierry Henry, but to be honest, I love every single Arsenal player. Arsène Wenger's famous side of 2003/04, The Invincibles, who won the Premier League title unbeaten – Dennis Bergkamp, Sol Campbell, Patrick Vieira, Freddie Ljungberg, Robert Pires, Ashley Cole. What a team!

We watch *Gazzetta Football Italia* on Channel 4. The Italian Serie A league is big in the 1990s. Another one of my favourite players, simply because of his purple Fiorentina kit, is the Argentinian striker Gabriel Batistuta. Fiorentina are playing in the Champions League, and this guy scores headers for fun.

A big footballing idol is the Arsenal midfielder, Patrick Vieira. He's long and gangly but super strong. His style of play is powerful, tenacious and aggressive. Every single time he's on the pitch he's involved in a fight. Usually with Manchester United's Roy Keane. But when Vieira is in possession of the ball he moves with a languid physical grace. He reminds me a lot of myself even though I'm nowhere near his level of technical ability. I try to emulate the big Frenchman in the streets or in the football cages of South London.

FIXED

I grow up on 1990s and early 2000s football stars: the original Ronaldo (R9), Zinedine Zidane, Pavel Nedvĕd, Alessandro Del Piero, Lilian Thuram, Marcel Desailly, and as much as we hate Tottenham, Ledley King. These guys . . . I'm like, damn, man, these are men. They're big, they're strong. I idolise them.

* * *

On a freezing cold December afternoon, 2003, on the playing fields of Harvey Grammar School in Folkestone, a football talent scout spots me playing for Surrey Schools against Kent Schools. I'm carrying an injury but I get a cold spray that makes your legs go stiff. I shake it off and put in a top performance. The coach, Ian Webb, comes up to me after the game and says, 'Moses, Crystal Palace want you to come for a trial!'

CHAPTER 3

STREET LIFE

My friends go on to become prominent figures in gangs, then start to get their comeuppance on the streets. You learn fast that the streets don't play fair, but they teach you things no classroom or football pitch ever can. Other friends are either playing football, trying to make it in music or just trying to be somebody.

My friend, Kieran 'Konz' Wilson, gives me the name 'Venge'. Who will this character or persona go on to become? Dangerous, violent, influential and a leader?

I'm quiet but I also have a ruthless streak. When we have issues or street fights, my friends always say 'there's Venge' as I'm a good fighter.

I carry that name and people give me respect. I inherit other people's problems, such as my friend Oliver's. He is my right-hand man in everything, in football and in life. At times he's the eyes in the back of my head.

It's no surprise when Oli gets into street fights and with me being a year older than him, I'm his first point of contact.

He lives in West Croydon, right by the bus station. He makes me feel invincible. We share a common goal and drive to become professional football players. As I turn fifteen, I begin to sense a shift in my mentality. Konz doesn't say much but he's ready for anything. We all have our issues, whether at home, school or on the streets.

Konz comes into school one day and tells me he has a situation with someone I know from a different school. Since we're young and careless we decide it's a smart idea to head to West Croydon bus station and address the situation head-on. This is where anyone who is anyone meets and chills and hangs out. There will be kids from four or five different schools coming to watch the fight.

On the 264 bus from Mitcham, me, Oli and Konz go upstairs and sit at the back of the bus. Konz leans over and fishes a towel from his schoolbag, unwraps it and shows us a firearm. It's a heavy, metal, BB gun with the clip removed. I don't know where he got it from. I'm shocked.

'It's not loaded,' he says. 'Here, hold it.' I turn it round in my hands. It's solid, heavy and looks like a real gun. He wants to use it to scare these boys who are putting pressure on him.

We get to West Croydon bus station and walk straight into an ambush. Konz pulls the gun out so quickly it flies out of his hands, the clips fall on the ground, and everyone screams, 'GUN!!!' and scatter in every direction. Then two kids jump us from behind. We're quickly outnumbered and there's a massive scuffle. I don't even know who's kicking or punching who. I just know I have to get out of there. I wrestle myself free of the ruckus and run and all three of us manage to escape. Then we notice Konz has been cut across his face with a blade.

* * *

Croydon is where everything starts for me. The foundation of who I become. The streets have a raw energy that pulses through you whether you're ready for it or not. My football kit acts like a get-out-of-jail-free card. I can go anywhere in London with my training gear on and no one will bother me: no gangs, no youths. Without it? Whole different story. There are no camera phones or social media. When something goes down, you hear about it directly from the streets, straight and raw.

The early 2000s is bright, loud, chaotic. The world is changing. But Croydon stays the same. Same streets, same faces. West Croydon bus station is the heartbeat of Croydon, always alive and buzzing. A melting pot of people from all walks of life, all cultures. I can smell the food from the Caribbean takeaway or picture in my mind the local African aunties buying fish and meat to stock their freezers.

Buses come in and out, a nonstop hum of engines. It's both a final destination and a starting point. I can disappear into the hubbub. Everyone hangs out there, kids from every school, every borough. I'm just another face in the crowd. I spend hours riding buses and trains, sometimes with a plan, sometimes just drifting randomly. Oliver lives nearby so I grab him on the way to school. The buses are my escape. I catch the 468, hop aboard and watch the city blur past, lost in the rhythm of the wheels rolling along the tarmac. It isn't about where I'm going; it's about the journey, the freedom. In a weird way, I feel like the streets are mine.

Street football, cage football is life. I don't really get into it until I move back to Southwark, fleeing my dad's abuse. The cage games are wild. No refs, no rules, makeshift goals, just kids kicking a ball about on a concrete pitch. And the stakes are always high. Every match feels like a final. When the ball is at my feet, everything else fades away. No one cares who you are outside the cages. All that matters is if you can play. And in those moments, I feel like someone.

* * *

No one has any money. The only people that are getting money are my friends who are selling drugs or older people.

Nike TNs are popular and if you have an Avirex leather bomber jacket you're rich. The Nike tracksuit with an American sign is cool too. Fashion isn't really what it is today. You have to remember I'm coming from the streets – I don't really buy anything. I only start buying stuff when I sign for Crystal Palace and the first thing I buy with my wages is a pair of TNs and a Nike tracksuit. I blow the whole £300 buying those two items.

My friends are heavily into music. A few years later, Konan forms the hip-hop duo, Krept and Konan, and they become successful. Konan is the youngest son of Delroy Wilson, a 1970s ska, rocksteady and reggae singer from Jamaica. I've seen Konan's entire musical journey, and I knew he was going to be somebody one day and vice versa. But Konan was deep in the streets, one of the main faces and names among our peers. I join my first gang PTK – Pups to Kill, the youngers of DTK (Dogs to Kill) – and Melfort Park in Thornton Heath becomes our stomping ground. The older we get, the more active they become, and more gangs are formed, and they start to have problems with other people in different areas.

* * *

Running around on the streets, violence is prominent because people are trying to prove themselves. In those early teenage years, a lot of my friends from the neighbourhood, especially Croydon, are going to prison, sometimes long-term sentences – five years, ten years. This person's going to jail for murder, this person for armed robbery.

Nobody wants to back down in a confrontation, especially when you've got a bunch of ten, fifteen, twenty, thirty kids from different areas that haven't got the best family environment. Growing up in this atmosphere is a double-edged sword. I see the best and worst of both worlds. I know what is happening and I try to avoid it.

I already know that there's no way on this planet I'm going to get to Crystal Palace or to a place in my life where I'm living out my dream if I'm getting into trouble on the streets. I'm not going to allow anything to hold me back.

We don't talk about things like mental health or domestic abuse or self-harm. By the time I get into football I instinctively know the rules: what you should and shouldn't do and, honestly, if you want to stay in the game you stick to them.

* * *

My two best friends are Oliver King-Onzila and Kieran McKennis, but that's in school. Outside of school I run around in different groups. I guess people call them gangs. I travel to play football and compete in athletics events against different schools. Me and my football and athletics teammates are so good that people already know who we are. To them, Moses is cool.

I start hanging out with kids from these five or six different schools along with my own, Archbishop Lanfranc – Haling

Manor, St Mary's, Stanley Tech, Ashburton, Edenham. I inherit people's problems, and a lot of my friends are getting into violent fights. Knife crime is on the rise in the early noughties.

I have a few close calls. One incident stands out in my mind. Me and Oliver get into a fight with a group of kids at West Croydon bus station. I'm going home on my own and they pull out knives on me. I make a run for it, zigzag in between cars and manage to hop on a train and escape. But I know I have to be careful going to and from school. The following day Oliver has another fight with an older group of guys – young men, who have already left school.

Oliver is in Year 8, and I'm in Year 9 – so we're thirteen/fourteen years old. Oliver's having a fight with one of the older boy's brothers on the travellers' site next to the school. They jump in and beat Oliver with a baseball bat and a dog chain. Someone rushes into the school and grabs me: 'You have to help Oli!' A friend runs with me to see what I'm going to do. I tell him, 'Stop! Stay away from this. I don't want no one to see it.'

About fifty kids look on helplessly as Oliver gets whipped like a slave. I run into the middle of the scrum, and they stop. One of them looks up and says: 'What are you doing?' I'm willing to take the beating with Oliver. In that moment a coldness enters me, but the rage is tamed. I know worst-case scenario what I'm able to do because my friends are *at* worst-case scenario.

I always put myself in the firing line. Because I'm in the year above Oliver, we leave school at different times. Plus, everybody's getting detention, including me. I have a few incidents where these same older boys approach me as I'm leaving school, pull out a knife, pull out a bat, just trying to scare me.

The following day in woodworking class, I sharpen a chisel

at the end like a knife. I absent-mindedly stuff it in my school bag, even though I probably won't use it, just in case something stupid happens.

After detention one day, I'm walking out of the school gates and I see one of the bullies. Archbishop Lanfranc sits on Mitcham Road. If you turn right out of the school gates on to this long, straight road it goes to Mitcham, turn left and you're heading towards Purley Way. Usually, teachers stand around the gates accompanied by a community police officer, but this time I leave school late, around four, so there's no one there.

The guy approaches me and we're just talking. He digs his hand in his pocket and pulls out a knife, more like a sword – it's too late for me to reach for my chisel. He thrusts the knife at me. I turn around and the blade slashes the back of my bag. We get into a tussle, but I manage to wriggle free and run home.

This is all caught on CCTV camera. The next day the police come to the school and ask me questions and I say I don't know this person.

I tell my brother Ayub – who's in Year 11 – what happened. We find out this guy lives directly across from the school, so we go and do some damage. I know there's gonna be retaliation.

The day after I'm almost stabbed, the same older boys come to Lanfranc, unaware of what's about to hit them. What they don't realise is that I know a lot of people. I meet all sorts while I'm riding the night buses. And because I'm this young loveable pup and people like being around me, I can say, 'Look, man, I'm in trouble . . .' and they'll help me. 'No problem, where's your school?'

One of Ayub's friends, Jermaine, comes to the school with a gang of fifteen street kids. He was kicked out of Lanfranc a few years before for violent behaviour and sent to a youth detention centre. He lives in Coulsdon and I live in South Croydon so sometimes when I'm locked out, I can stay at his house. The only thing is he is knee deep in street life so he's rarely home.

Jermaine is the first person I ever know who owns a car, at fifteen, a Fiat Punto. He's the first person who I go to with my own street problems. He is the first person that shows me how to make money. He has a certain amount of notoriety in the area.

If I'm honest, being around him scares me. He's gaining more influence in the streets, and I know I'll follow. I see street fights, knife attacks, retaliation, drugs being sold and stolen.

Jermaine asks me to pick out the olders who've troubled us. Behind Archbishop Lanfranc is a travellers' site where some of the kids from our school live. I'm filled with so much rage.

J looks at me and tells me to do my 'ting'. I head-butt the boy who tried to stab me and break his nose. J grabs the other bully and pulls him behind a car. We kick his ass to Timbuktu and back. It's a frenzy: everybody is kicking them and smashing things on their heads. They could've easily lost their lives that day. Nobody calls a halt. It's the worst level of street violence I've ever seen.

Then the older boy's mum comes running out of their house across the road, screaming her son's name. We scarper and jump on a bus and leave the two boys bleeding on the ground.

I'm pumped up with adrenaline. I don't even realise until I'm on the 289 bus from Thornton Heath Pond to West Croydon that I'm covered in blood. I get the train to London Bridge all the way back to Bermondsey to my Mum's. She opens the door and starts crying when she sees my blood-soaked shoes.

The police take me to Norwood police station. The bullies

survive but end up in hospital – one with broken arms and a fractured eye socket.

I'm about to be kicked out of school, a month before school ends, had it not been for Kieran's mum. She provides me with an alibi, tells the police I was with them at the same time as the fight. She saves me. Otherwise, I would have been expelled and arrested. The older kid, whose ass we kick, who tried to stab me outside school, luckily drops the charges. I pass him outside my school but this time he looks the other way.

That's the last time I see those bullies. It's a wake-up call for me. The rage that I carried around for five years left me that day. Rather than a release it's more like an emptiness. The bully got a dose of his own medicine, but I don't feel how I thought I'd feel. I know the olders from the streets look at me fighting and say, 'Yeah, man, you need to be my younger.' They try to recruit me into that street life. Try to put their hands around me. I'm like, 'Bro, I got football, man.' Literally the week after all this happens, I join Crystal Palace Academy.

CHAPTER 4

PALACE ACADEMY

I don't apply for any colleges or further education. I'm banking on football as my plan A, B, C and D.

Joining Crystal Palace FC is a roller-coaster ride. After being spotted starring for Surrey Schools, I go on trial for six weeks at the end of Year 11. I've just turned sixteen years old.

Palace's secretary is a lady called Tracey Earle. She's like an Academy mother to everyone. I open Tracey's letter and it says, sorry, we can't offer you a scholarship, but thanks for attending the trials.

That summer I run and run and run like I'm Mo Farah. In my mind, football is life or death. What else am I going to do now? A few weeks pass. I wake up one morning and open the usual letters. One has the Palace logo and, to my surprise, handwritten with Tracey's signature is me being asked to attend pre-season training, 2005/06.

I go in and train with the signed players at Trinity School's playing fields. We triallists don't have Palace training gear. The old kit man, Brian, with his shock of white hair and big belly, says to me, 'You're number 41, me ol' mucker!' I've never smiled so widely in my life. I feel like I'm putting on a suit of armour, ready for battle.

I'm star-struck to be warming up with the first team. I run round with Neil Shipperley and Tom Soares. When we stretch, I hold on to Clinton Morrison's shoulders, swinging my skinny legs. I forget I'm no longer just a fan; I'm part of the club now. 'Yo, Clinton, can I get your autograph?' He's like, 'Come here,' and puts his arm around me. I'm so happy. I still have the same old boots from my Croydon Athletic youth team days, my replica Ronaldinho red and white Nike Tiempo R10s.

Micky Hazard is our under-16s coach, and we train on the AstroTurf at the National Sports Centre in Crystal Palace. He loads one team full of Academy players, the likes of my mate, Benji, John Bostock and Victor Moses and even includes himself. Micky Hazard played in the famous Tottenham Hotspur FA Cup-winning sides of the early 1980s alongside Glenn Hoddle and Ossie Ardiles. His left foot in those sessions is like a magic wand.

It seems cruel and unfair to make fresh-faced triallists chase established players around the pitch. I come home thinking, *Damn, my lungs hurt.* The fitness is next level plus we never get a sniff of the ball. How do you even get close?

My first proper Academy game is against Millwall. It's a shock to the system. I can't believe how fast and technical everyone is. It's the hardest game I've ever been involved in. I don't know what I'm doing. Then we play Tottenham Hotspur away and I'm at right back, an unfamiliar position for me. I later find out I was up against one of the best wingers in the country. For the entire game my head spins in every direction.

He twists and turns me inside out, does step-overs. He's quicker and faster and better than me. Benji tells me, 'It's OK, don't worry, it happens sometimes.' I already know I'm out of my depth.

I go to bed after the game and don't wake up until the following afternoon. It's the best lesson I learn during my early Palace days: no player is going to make me feel like that again.

* * *

Crystal Palace is a unique club in terms of its location: smack bang in the heart of the 'concrete jungle' where they can cherry-pick the best players from a hotbed of South London talent and bring them through their Academy. By season 2018/19, more than 10 per cent of English players in the Premier League were born in South London. It's an incredible statistic.

It's not like being at Stamford Bridge, Chelsea FC's home stadium, where you're surrounded by multi-million-pound town-houses and apartments.

The Palace Academy team manager, Gary Issott, and Bob Dowie, the sporting director, nurtured an incredible array of talent that were sold on to big clubs for tens of millions and cemented Palace's reputation as one of the best football Academies in England.

I sign a two-year scholarship with the Palace Academy. It's a dream come true. Every morning, I travel thirty minutes on the train from London Bridge to New Beckenham. I bump into other Academy players on their way to training. Victor Moses, who went on to win the Premier League title with Chelsea, the FA Cup, two Europa Leagues and the Africa Cup of

Nations for Nigeria; Nathaniel Clyne played in a Champions League final for Liverpool against Real Madrid; the young Johnny Bostock was wanted by Barcelona after he made his Crystal Palace first-team debut aged fifteen. We walk to training together, compete against each other, and then travel home to different parts of South London: Catford, Peckham, Brixton, Southwark – the concrete jungle.

You have to prove yourself every day against the cream of the crop. The competition is fierce, but if you have it in you, you can rise above the rest. I didn't know it at the time, but in this city these streets were shaping me for something bigger.

Every moment you're in that club you're learning. You learn more off the pitch than you do on it because your character is constantly being tested. You're beaten down, in a good way, on how you should conduct yourself and who you should be. I feel so proud very single day I put on the club tracksuit. I'm so excited I often arrive an hour before training and Brian says the same thing: 'Morning, me ol' mucker!'

Apprentices have to wash boots, and guess who my first team player is? Captain and club legend, Dougie Freedman. I accidentally spill water in Dougie's boots. We're sitting in the canteen and he comes over to my table and says in his thick Scottish accent, 'Wee man, no water, eh?' I think, '*Shit , the club captain isn't happy.*' It never happens again.

Every morning after breakfast, me and Benji go and work on our game. I need to improve my weak heading. And my left foot is for standing on. Plus, my fitness levels are below par. Six weeks in, I'm up to the Academy standard.

With every game for the under-18s, I get better and better. The players see this and I gain their respect. Then Gary

Issott, our Academy manager, gives me the ultimate accolade, the captain's armband. Me and Nathaniel Clyne are a defensive fortress. I benefit from training one-to-one with Victor Moses and Benji. In training, I see Victor do things with the ball I've never seen before.

We used to look at Victor in Palace training and think, *Fuck my life! This guy is different. This guy's a weapon.* When he gets the ball, everybody's calm because we know what's happening next. I've seen it so often in training that if he's in a certain position on the pitch and he shoots, it's a goal.

Victor is a serial winner. He is an unbelievable talent. Football to him is easy, even when he makes his Palace first team debut at sixteen.

I was captain of this team and as much as these guys were superstars, in my eyes, it shows my progress in such a short period of time. The strong mindset of these boys had rubbed off on me. I'm thinking there's no way I can come from that youth team and not be someone in my life.

Victor helps me so much. Me and Nathaniel are the best defenders in the Academy. He's solid; I'm lightning quick. A perfect combination.

* * *

We play Southampton reserves and it's obvious to everyone that a skinny Welsh lad called Gareth Bale is a future worldie. At half-time Gary Issott says, 'That kid is a top player. Someday he'll play for a Barcelona or a Real Madrid.'

A young Theo Walcott is also at Southampton with Bale. The pace of those two is incredible. Bale, Walcott and Adam Lallana are in a fantastic Southampton team who beat us 2-0.

Facing off against the likes of Bale is a surreal moment. Seeing a player like him up close, you can feel his presence, the raw speed, the natural ability. You're thinking, *This is something different, man.* He is almost unplayable, but I manage to hold my own.

* * *

The FA Youth Cup is our equivalent of the Champions League.

Our 2006/07 cup run gives us the feeling that we can conquer the world. The intensity, the pressure, a belief that we could take on anyone.

It's all guns blazing at training; everyone was on point at that time. One of my other best mates from the area was Michael Kamara. He's now Crystal Palace's under-14s coach.

When Michael joins us from Southampton, we're very close – like I am with Victor and Benji – but Michael also played in my position. We're best friends, and rivals. Only one of us can get that professional contract.

It's the fourth round of the FA Youth Cup. We're at home to Plymouth Argyle on an icy January night. It goes into extra time, and we scored. Michael ran the whole length of the pitch and celebrated. I stayed back. This game's not over. I didn't realise at the time how important that decision was. They equalised immediately after we scored, and it was Michael's fault. Thankfully, we win the game 4-2 because of Victor and our mavericks. On this big cup night, the first team manager, Peter Taylor, and some star players, come and watch us play.

The next day we're having lunch, and Taylor walks over, pats me on the back and says, 'Well done. I like you, Moses.'

Then he says, 'Who's the centre back who celebrated?' And he looks straight at Michael.

'Don't ever let me see you do that again!' That's when I know I have the edge over my teammate, my best mate, my defensive partner. The more I felt I had the edge, the more fire it gave me.

* * *

Next up is the fifth round of the FA Youth Cup and we face the biggest day of our young Academy careers: Crystal Palace v Manchester United. Our team is solid; we have a talented group. United have a young Danny Welbeck who was out-standing at that age. We have Victor who is already playing for England Under-17s.

I'm directly up against Febian Brandy, one of the best strikers in our age group.

One thing I knew about Manchester United, it was a psychological battle. We used to wear tracksuits to games. These guys turned up in suits.

I'm thinking, *Damn, the last Man Utd game I saw was that team with Cristiano Ronaldo, Roy Keane and Ruud van Nistelrooy at Selhurst Park.*

I had the ball in the net early on, but it was ruled out for offside. Then United took the lead when Welbeck set up Sam Newson to crack a low shot home from eighteen yards.

We kept it tight until the later stages, but I blame myself for Manchester United's clincher. The ball's been played over the top and Febian's peeled off my shoulder.

We're literally neck and neck running towards the box but our keeper, Martin Pearson, comes running off his line, fumbles Febian's attempt on goal, and we collide, allowing Febian to stroke the ball into an empty net. Final score: 2-0 to the Red Devils.

Manchester United are a brilliant team, full of future stars, but we go toe-to-toe with them. We fall short in the end, but walking off the pitch after that defeat, I knew we'd made our mark. We were a team to be reckoned with.

* * *

Boats is also from Croydon but two years younger than me when he joins the Crystal Palace Academy. We never really train together because we're in different age groups, but we instantly click and become friends.

Boats is one of the smallest players in the Academy for any age group. Everyone loves him because he's a sweet, quiet kid. I notice a lot of similarities between him and me. He is excellent on the ball, but his big problem is being unable to put on weight. Then he has a mad growth spurt and turns into a physical athlete. He is good enough to have been a Crystal Palace player. An overlapping wing back. He was like a modern-day Cafu. Strong, Ghanaian blood – nothing gets past him.

* * *

It's the end of the season, May 2007.

Gary Issott tells me: 'Go get a suit.'

'Why do I need a suit?'

'You're going to the Player of the Year awards ceremony.'

'Gary, where the hell do I get a suit from?'

I buy a grey suit from Zara for £60 with my scholarship money. I know nothing about tailoring, but I do my best to look good. My mum gets time off work as my plus one. The event is held in a marquee on the pitch at Selhurst Park and attended by more than 700 people including the full first-team squad and management.

I'm excited to be sitting at the same table as Victor and Johnny Bostock. 'Vic, mate, I can't wait to see you collect your award!'

I had no idea they were going to call out my name not once but twice. Especially when I'm around two of the best players not only at Palace but in the whole country. The last thing I think is that I will win anything. Just being there is more than enough.

First, I win 'Scholar of the Year'. I'm still trying to get my head round it. Then they announce the award for Vice-President's Young Player of the Year. Again, Moses Swaibu. I'm like, woah! This is mad! Victor and Johnny are nominated in both categories. What's going on? I go up and collect the awards and I don't know what to do or say. They take my photo and I sit back down at our table. Johnny and Victor are delighted for me. Everyone's happy.

Within two years I've gone from living in the worst type of conditions to coming into this family, which we call Crystal Palace, and seeing my dreams play out in real time.

The chairman of Crystal Palace, Simon Jordan, tells my mum: 'We have really big plans for your son.'

I've still got the pictures from that night and if you look at my face it's saying: 'I honestly cannot believe this.' It was surreal.

The applause that night. The pride in seeing my mum smiling. I'd made it. But in that moment, I don't let it go to my head. I know this is only the beginning. I'd been here two years, but the recognition? It was validation, and it was sweet.

* * *

I'm eighteen and I've never left the UK. I've never been on an aeroplane. My passport is fresh off the printing machine.

I have a meeting with first-team manager Peter Taylor the morning after the awards night and he says that I'm a big part of Palace's future and that he's taking me on the pre-season tour to Sweden. He sees me as a long-term replacement for Leon Cort and wants me to model my game on him. The first team. The big league. It's happening faster than I could process.

I play three of the four games on the pre-season tour, perform well and make my mark.

That milestone summer I'm in the *Croydon Advertiser*. In a 'Dressing Room Banter' Q&A feature in the newspaper, Palace winger Paul Ifill nominates me as having the best taste in music. The lads let me put on a few tunes. I feel properly integrated into the first-team squad. I have my spot in the changing room. Everything is going well.

Back from Sweden I make my Selhurst Park debut in a friendly against Everton – a good Everton side featuring Mikel Arteta and Andy Johnson – in front of a home crowd of 20,000. I come on for the last ten minutes, replacing José Fonte. José is an amazing support to me – like a big brother.

That ten minutes feels like an hour. It's a cliché to say but imagine you've worked so hard for something, something you're so passionate about. It almost brought tears to my eyes running out for the team I love, for the team I used to sneak into games to watch.

* * *

In October 2007, Neil Warnock is appointed as Crystal Palace's new manager, taking over from Peter Taylor. Warnock had a different intensity. He had a reputation for getting the best out of his players, and he sees something in me.

He pulls me into his office and says: 'I hear you're a decent centre back. How do you feel about being on the bench at Watford tomorrow?' I can't even get the words out of my mouth.

He says, 'Are you ready?'

'I'm ready!'

He gives me a DVD with videos of Watford centre forward, Marlon King. I take it home and watch it until four o'clock in the morning. I know everything about King: his strengths, weaknesses, where he shoots, where he makes his runs. Key takeaway: don't get caught up in a physical battle – he's probably the strongest striker in the league.

Me and Johnny Bostock are on the substitutes' bench. I don't get the nod from Warnock, but Johnny makes his first-team debut as a fifteen-year-old substitute playing for twenty minutes to replace a Palace legend, Ben Watson.

A fearless Johnny runs on to the pitch and takes the game by the scruff of the neck. It's incredible to witness. The Selhurst Park crowd respond with loud cheers every time he touches the ball. They can see he's a special talent.

Johnny is like a left-footed version of Ronaldinho. Even though we lose 2-0, all the first-team players pat him on the shoulder, give him a thumbs up. I look at Johnny in the changing room and I'm thinking, 'Wow, this kid's fifteen years old!' I'm eighteen. He isn't at all fazed – not by the crowd or the occasion or his opponents. He came on, instantly demanded the ball and played like a seasoned pro.

It was a highlight of my career to watch Johnny Bostock, one of my Academy teammates, make history as Crystal Palace's youngest ever first-team debutant.

* * *

I'm sent on loan to Weymouth in February 2008. At the turn of year I already know that Neil Warnock wants me to go to another club and improve my game. I have a weak left foot and I need to time my headers better.

I'm low on confidence. I sense that I'm losing my edge, losing my touch. I'm too lightweight for a central defender – no way I'll get anywhere near the Crystal Palace first team weighing 70kg. It doesn't work out at Weymouth and, with my initial contract coming to an end, I'm released by Palace. After an unsuccessful trial at League Two Gillingham, I sign a non-contract deal with Bromley in the Conference South in time for the start of the 2008/09 season. It's an attempt to find my feet in the senior game. I'm dropping down several divisions after rubbing shoulders with Premier League-quality players at Crystal Palace, but I'm still only nineteen years old and I aim to prove I belong in a first-team squad.

* * *

In February 2008, my best friend Oliver's older brother Herve suffers a freak heart attack playing for Ringmer FC in the Sussex County League. Tragically, he collapses on the pitch and dies. He's only twenty-seven years old. Oli is distraught. I basically grew up in Oliver's house with his family and I see the effect it has on them.

The last time I see Oliver is when we go out in East London

to a place called Purple E3. We have a fun time, laughing and joking. We chat about football. He's at Barnet Academy, hoping to turn pro. It feels good to take his mind off Herve's tragic death.

Fast-forward to September 2008. I'm in bed fast asleep when the phone starts ringing non-stop. There are fifteen or twenty missed calls from friends I haven't spoken to for a long time.

'Why are they ringing me?'

I answer a call from my friend Joel Beya and he's like, 'Oliver's gone.'

I'm half asleep, woozy. I hear the words but I don't comprehend them or react until I wake up the next morning and see the long list of unread messages.

On 13 September 2008, my best friend Oliver passed away. He'd been repeatedly stabbed outside a bar in Croydon.

The news stops me in my tracks. I immediately feel cold. Oh God, no, not Oli! Oliver was more than a friend; he was family. It's the first death I've ever experienced. I cry every day. I'm broken.

Oliver's death looms large over me and I can't stop thinking about it. Even though I'm playing football, I'm going through the motions. I can't talk to anyone. I'd only signed for Bromley eleven days before Oliver's murder.

We had a tight-knit group from Andy's youth teams, and these were the people around Oliver. When someone dies in those circumstances, you tend to ask what people were doing while he was getting attacked. Why was he even in that position?

Me knowing Oliver, who was a hothead, he would have confronted provocation head-on. I was always like, 'Oli, man, before we do anything, let's think about it.' Oliver's attitude was that he didn't really listen to anyone unless he respected them.

The saddest thing about these murders and deaths is that everyone always starts as friends. Oli and his killer, Tristan Burke, knew each other but fell out when Oli's young brother Christopher started dating Burke's ex-girlfriend.

When Oliver was killed, a few of my childhood friends were there. All of us could have been anything. We're just looking for opportunities.

Oli was well on his way to running the streets and having his own gang of youths. He was loyal to the end and between the three of us — me, Oli and Kieran — we put in the work. I made sure everyone in school knew and found out we got revenge for Oliver, which then spread around Croydon .

Thanks to football, I escaped Croydon after those violent episodes but Oli and Kieran, whose street name is Konz, stayed. If I'd remained in Croydon without Crystal Palace, Andy or my football family, I could have ended up in jail or dead.

There are around 300 people at Oliver's funeral. Oli's oldest brother, Face Squeeze, came to the funeral in handcuffs and with an armed police escort. He didn't cry, I just saw the pain in his eyes. I've never known his real name, only his street name. Throughout our childhood he was in jail. He was a notorious street kingpin with close connections to Brixton.

At Oliver's funeral, I look at his body lying in the open casket and I literally watch the life drain out of him. He is a peculiar shade of grey. He isn't even black. It's a horrifying image. My head is all over the place.

I turn to my brother, Ayub, look him in the eyes and bow my head. I'm numb with grief. Football papered over the cracks in my life, but I suffer like I've never suffered before.

I don't want to see or speak to anyone from my childhood.

They remind me of Oliver, the times together we all shared. I can't look anyone in the eye. I don't want to turn my hurt and anger into hatred or a burning resentment for what could have happened or been avoided that night.

The opportunity to leave London is the only thing on my mind. I have to move away, be on my own and focus. Nobody can say or do anything to help me. But the game being the game, I am still fit, hungry and eager to flush the pain from my system. I need to play football. It is my sanctuary.

CHAPTER 5

THE LINCOLN IMP

When Peter Jackson signs me for League Two side Lincoln City on a short-term contract in January 2009, a condition of the deal is that the club pay for my accommodation. My childhood friend Stephen is living in Spridlington, a tiny, one-horse village in the Lincolnshire countryside. I find a penthouse apartment in the town centre and invite my old pal from the streets of Southwark to come and share it with me.

Pat is a student at the University of Lincoln. He's studying for a degree in Business and Management. He also happens to be the biggest drug dealer in the city.

P ends up staying in Lincoln after graduating to expand his drug empire. Spridlington is a thirty-minute bus ride north of Lincoln. His house is on a three-acre farm with a four-bedroom detached house in the middle of nowhere. It's the perfect place to stay off the radar.

I'm still reeling from Oliver's death, and it's hard leaving Bromley because I don't tell the manager, Mark Goldberg, anything about Lincoln. I signed for Bromley on a non-contract basis, and I'm clueless about the rules around the seven-day window or even that I had to tell Bromley anything. But Lincoln say there might be an issue if they sign me, so I phone Mark and explain that it's an opportunity for me to get back into the Football League. He wishes me luck even though he's clearly pissed off.

Me and my friend, Marcus, had compiled a list of every single club in the Football League and started ringing them up telling them about this great player called 'Moses Swaibu', who's a free agent, looking for a new club. We sent them my stats and sold myself to them. 'Can he come in for a trial, play in a reserve game? He's willing to pay his own expenses!'

The only reply came back from Lincoln City: 'We've organised a trial game against Port Vale reserves. These are the details – come up.'

* * *

Mid-January 2009, I jump on a train from London King's Cross to Newark-on-Trent and change trains for Lincoln. It's a culture shock. It's freezing cold and the town is in the middle of nowhere. What's football like up here?

As soon as I walk into the changing room I'm brimming with confidence. I have it in my mind that no one in this position can be better than me. I don't need to raise my level. I go out against Port Vale reserves and play like I've been in the team for the whole season.

Peter Jackson takes an instant liking to me and I make my full Lincoln City debut in a 1-1 away draw at Morecambe on 10 February 2009.

It's funny because I only play by accident. Lincoln have a veteran centre back, Frank Sinclair, who'd played top-flight football for Chelsea and Leicester City. Frank used to come to training drunk. He was reaching the end of his career.

Jackson shouts at Frank: 'You're not fucking training today; you're drunk again!' The Gaffer thinks I'm not ready, but when this happens, he throws me in at the deep end. I only make my debut because Frank was wasted. It's a sliding-doors moment. The Gaffer tells me later that he had intended to release me before the Morecambe game. He's feeling the heat from the club's directors and needs to save his slender budget for someone more experienced. Freaky good luck for me. Not for Frank. The following month he's sent out on loan to Wycombe Wanderers, never to return.

On the pitch at Morecambe's tight-knit Christie Park on a bitterly cold winter night in the small seaside town, everything seems to move faster. At this lower level of football, a League Two fixture, the ball is pinged back and forward, back and forward. It's relentless. Every time the opposition launches an attack you have to challenge for headers. When the ball is played in behind the defence, you must make sure you're there first. I can't say I'm out of my depth; I manage to hold my own, but it's exhausting.

I train hard every day, first in, last out, and I'm voted man of the match for the next ten games in a row. I continue with the same principles that were instilled in me at Crystal Palace.

Not even in a rude way, I'd think, *you northern lads haven't lived the life I've lived and none of you lot are better than me anyway.* They are technically average. I went from being with Premier League-standard players at Palace to getting released to now playing with and against people that are not even as good as the Bromley players. These Lincoln players are professionals in the Football League – it doesn't make any sense for them to be so mediocre. No word of a lie, when I went into those games, I used to think football was easy.

* * *

By the end of April, I've impressed the Gaffer enough for him to offer me my first professional contract, which is a two-and-a-half-year deal, and even though I join Lincoln City halfway through the season, I'm named the Young Player of the Year.

I'm still a shy kid. As much as I have this front, this aggressive bravado, I am quite overwhelmed with this little city, living away from the familiar surroundings of London for the first time.

Luckily, local people warm to me and the fans love me. I was number 5 and wore that shirt like armour. When the crowd chanted my name, I leapt higher, ran faster, tackled harder. With every header I won, the chants that followed them made me feel like a gladiator. I loved evening games at home, with 5,000 fans packed into the Sincil Bank stadium. Although it's only League Two, the crackling atmosphere at those night matches under the floodlights made it feel like our Champions League.

Jackson tells me there's interest in me from Aston Villa, a top-six club in the Premier League, and Birmingham City, who are about to get promoted from the Championship up to England's top flight. I hear the speculation that Premier League teams are keeping tabs on me, but when I look into Peter Jackson's eyes he gives me the confidence to continue.

I sign the contract on £500 a week with an increase of £250 every ten games.

The Gaffer mentions various bonuses factored into the deal which mean I can potentially take home a grand plus a week. I'm just hearing numbers I haven't heard before. I'm thinking, *Look, I just want to play football.*

I remember having intense conversations with the Gaffer where he locks eyes with me and almost looks into my soul. Every time he does that, it makes me play better. I realise there is something fundamental, something elemental about these interactions. I'm missing my dad. It feels like shit.

I've never had a man in my life that I love and respect. In football terms, this big bear of a man, Peter Jackson, offers me these things. Every manager who puts their arm around me and tries to understand who I am, where I've come from, I feel that I should repay the encouragement they show me.

I leave the Gaffer's office with £ signs in my eyes, but the biggest bonus for me is the club paying my apartment for the duration of my contract. No rent. No bills. No worries.

* * *

I rent a three-bedroom duplex in Friars Mews, a brand-new twenty-apartment gated development in the heart of Lincoln town centre. I call Stephen.

'Yo, bro. Why don't you come and live with me? The club are paying for it anyway.'

He gets the master bedroom with the en-suite bathroom and walk-in wardrobe and brings his girlfriend to live with us. We're all one big happy family. The only rule I have is that Stephen's drug empire stays in Spridlington. He keeps everything illegal outside of my house, but I'm still hanging out with him. Lincoln is a small city, so when we're out and about, people ask questions like, 'Oh, who's that guy?' Or 'Who's Moses, he's always around?'

To the outside world, it might seem naive of me – a professional footballer living with a known drug dealer – but in reality this is my normal world. I don't pick or choose who I grew up with or who protected me before I kicked a ball. I'm a product of my environment. During the most chaotic part of my early career, I played my best football. Even when my local profile increases as Lincoln City's club captain, what nineteen-year-old high on life sets boundaries?

I'm flying both on and off the pitch, full of youthful confidence. Without Stephen's help, where would I have stayed in Lincoln when I was up on a two-week trial? The club didn't pay me expenses or put me up. Stephen did. Where I'm from you don't turn your back on people and loyalty means a lot.

One of the first times me and Stephen are out socialising together, we go to a university party which ends in violence. Pat is six or seven years older than me. He gets into an argument that results in a fight. Suddenly we're running full pelt down Lincoln High Street, legging it, with ten angry local lads in pursuit. I wake up the next morning back at the house and make my way to training like nothing happened.

The feud Pat starts at that party runs throughout my time at Lincoln. Stephen is the talk of the town among those on the streets. As his drug operation grows, so does his reputation. It never once fazes me at any time apart from what happened next. The first red flag.

One day after training the Gaffer says, 'Moses. We've got a triallist coming from Manchester United. His name's Perry. Can he stay with you?'

'Yeah, cool. No problem.' Perry comes to my apartment and Stephen walks into the living room with a bag of weed in full view. Perry's face turns white. Stephen has no idea who Perry is, but he sees me rolling my eyes at him and he makes a swift exit.

The next day, Perry tells Peter Jackson he didn't feel safe. And this is when I'm in my peak form, I'm flying. The Gaffer rings me up and says, 'Moses, let me ask you a question . . .' I say: 'That didn't happen. He's seeing things.' Perry doesn't get signed. It's an early warning, one that will come back and bite me later.

Stephen isn't exactly discreet about his side hustle. He pretty much has Lincoln in the palm of his hand. I walk out of my gated development and see people milling around the corner. But because I'm not involved, I think it's got nothing to do with my football. In fact, I'm oblivious to it all and playing the best football of my life.

Both of us are generating more and more money. There are people coming up from London to visit us, including his brothers, and they're also selling drugs. All my neighbours are white. Most of the city is white. In the 2011 census, 95.6 per cent of Lincoln's population of around 100,000 identified as white; a mere 0.8 per cent looked like Stephen and me and our London friends.

On my first night in the city I go to the local Co-op for some groceries, and walking back I get racially abused for the first time in my life. A car drives by and a bunch of white guys roll down the window and scream, 'Nigger!' at the top of their voices. Welcome to Lincoln. Moving from the vibrant, bustling streets of multicultural London to this small, medieval-style city, it's as if the world has slowed down and we've gone back in time. Tea is dinner up here. Town is the city. The shops usually shut around 4pm. Nobody is on the roads after six. The place is deserted.

The best thing about living in a sleepy town is that all I do is go to training, come home, watch football, play PlayStation, get up the next morning and do the same thing, every single day. It's the first time I've lived in such a small place with no high rises, council estates or kids hanging about on the streets after midnight. Even if I want to, it's hard to go out and enjoy myself in Lincoln. But gradually I begin to see the underbelly of Lincoln's nightlife, the hidden places, the strip clubs, the nightclubs. After dark, this little town turns into a seedy playground.

Street fights turn more violent, followed by more youngers coming up from London to be students at the university, knowing Lincoln is a place to make money. There are so many times we go out on the town after a home game and I see new faces.

The closest teammate I have is Jamie Clarke, who signs for us from Rotherham United in the summer of 2009. He understands me and I'm aware of his own troubles with street life in his home town of Huddersfield. He is a top striker, like a Jermain Defoe-style poacher. Quick, hungry, one of those strikers who loves scoring goals.

We hit it off like a house on fire. We share similar interests, like the same music. When I get to know him better, I realise that the London life I left behind is similar to the one he is surrounded by in Huddersfield. I tell him that the lifestyle his family and their associates are living isn't really something he should be a part of.

He's fine when he's playing football because it takes his mind off his turbulent life off the pitch. He loathes going home.

I invite him to stay in my spare bedroom. But the deeper his brother sinks into crime and that life, the worse it gets. Stephen loves Jamie living with us but it is a recipe for disaster.

* * *

Things start to go wrong when Peter Jackson is sacked after a mixed bag of results at the beginning of the 2009/10 season. We lose three of our first five league games and get knocked out of two cups – the League Cup and the Johnstone's Paint Trophy – all within the first month.

I have a good summer, running circuits between the bridges along the Thames and playing cage football in South London. Coming into the start of the new season we hit a bad run of form, and I notice the Gaffer's demeanour change. I remember going into those first games – especially away at hostile places like Accrington Stanley and Bradford City on their huge pitches – thinking, *Fucking hell, this is shit.*

After I play badly in the first game of the season, a 1-0 home win versus Barnet, the Gaffer says to me: 'Did I make a mistake signing you? That's what it feels like.' I'm stunned. 'How did you go from being our best player to our worst?' I say nothing. I understand the pressure he's under from the club to improve results. I let it go.

On 22 August 2009, we capitulate meekly 2-0 at home to Burton Albion in the league and the supporters turn on the Gaffer. A chorus of boos ring round Sincil Bank at the final whistle. The last straw is losing our next league game 3-0 away to top-of-the-table Dagenham & Redbridge.

Jackson and his assistant Iffy are gone before our next match. Ifem 'Iffy' Onuora is special. I've never met a black guy before who speaks with a thick Glaswegian accent. He's the first black manager I play under. And because there's a lack of representation in management of people who look like me, he feels like a guardian.

When they both leave, it's the first time since Peter Taylor left Palace that I feel completely disarmed.

You can't take anything for granted in football and you can't get too close to people. At any given moment they can pull the rug from under your feet. Peter Jackson gave me the opportunity to get back into the Football League. He told me not to go to the Premier League when big clubs were sniffing around because I wasn't ready.

Any time a manager leaves a club I'm at, it almost feels like your mum or your dad has left and aren't coming home. When I sat down and thought about it, managers leaving made me feel like how I did when my dad abandoned us. And the more I think about it, the more that feeling of neglect and being a worst-case scenario has been completely normalised in my life.

Jackson was the glue that held the team together and even though we were going through a rocky patch, we had a strong core of decent players. Once that's broken up and someone comes in and changes things too quickly, it can put you on the back foot.

* * *

At the end of September 2009, Chris Sutton is appointed as successor to Jackson. Sutton is a no-nonsense straight talker who has a simmering raw energy about him. As a player he won the Premier League title with Blackburn Rovers, forming a lethal strike partnership with Alan Shearer. At Glasgow Celtic he won multiple trophies and played in a European final, losing to José Mourinho's Porto. Sutton and his assistant, Ian Pearce, who was the rock in that same Blackburn title-winning side's defence alongside Colin Hendry, immediately improve the quality of the team.

Not long after Sutton becomes the new Gaffer, Jamie Clarke's family home is the target of a drive-by shooting by local gangsters. His brothers are notorious on the streets of Huddersfield, involved in local gang activity. The next day, Jamie comes into training. I meet him in the car park. We sit in his blue VW Golf GTi. He takes out a newspaper and lays it on my lap. The front-page headline reads something like: 'Footballer's House Shot Up'. With Jamie being a youngster, full of testosterone and aggression and anger, he has two options: to retaliate or focus on football.

'Moses, I'm about to do something crazy. Bro, you're the captain. I'm not really in the Gaffer's plans. Speak to him for me, please!'

Now I'm like, bro – how the hell do I tell Chris Sutton, the legend, that my friend is about to go and do a shooting?!

I leave Jamie sitting in his car and I go and knock on the Gaffer's office door.

'Gaffer, can I talk to you?'

'Yeah, what's up, Moses? Sit down.'

'I think Jamie needs help. He has to stay in Lincoln.'

'Moses, I'll see you later.'

If I told the Gaffer what is really happening, Jamie might have been sacked. I don't want to jeopardise my relationship with Jamie. I return to the car and he's in tears.

He reaches below my seat to take out a towel from a plastic

bag and unwraps the towel to reveal a semi-automatic sub-machine gun pistol. I can't believe what I'm seeing. My heart jumps out of my chest. I turn the music down and we lean back in our seats.

'Bro, I'm gonna do a madness!'

'Jamie! Don't do it, bro! Why the fuck have you got that in your car? Don't do it. Don't do it!'

'Yeah, yeah, yeah, yeah . . .'

Even though he doesn't do it, he leaves Lincoln that day and drives home to Huddersfield.

A few months later, Jamie leaves the club and the city for good. Street life catches up with him years later and he serves a lengthy prison sentence for kidnap and torture. When I hear the news, it crosses my mind: if Chris Sutton had spoken to him maybe things would have turned out differently. All Jamie wanted was a home in Lincoln and to be away from the chaos in Huddersfield. I know this 100 per cent: if Jamie Clarke had been protected by the football community, he would not have gone down the path that he went down.

* * *

That November, Jamie Clarke has one last hurrah at Lincoln City. We're playing AFC Telford away in the first round of the FA Cup. The worst teams to draw in the early rounds of the FA Cup are non-league or lower division sides because they've got nothing to lose and often they'll play the game of their lives. It's that time of the season when they can make a name for themselves and upset a big team, get through to the next round.

Unfortunately for Telford, Jamie is flying. He's the star of the show. He sets up the opening goal for Sergio Torres and then puts us back in front after Telford score a shock equaliser at the start of the second half. We survive a few shaky moments but Aaron Brown wraps up a 3-1 victory for us with a late breakaway goal.

On the team bus on the way back from Telford to Lincoln, Sutton's assistant, Ian Pearce, takes me aside and says, 'Moses, can I have a quick word?' I know when bad news is coming by the way people say my name.

'Moses, I don't know what's going on, but this is serious; I've got something to tell you . . .'

'OK, yeah, what's that?'

'The chairman has had a tip-off that the police are raiding your apartment on Monday.' This is Saturday.

'Listen, I'm only going to tell you this once. I know it's not you, but the people around you; you need to get rid of them. And whatever you may or may not have in your house, you need to get rid of it and tell whoever it is *they* need to do it.'

The words hit me like a punch to the gut. Of course, I know that Stephen is selling drugs. But this is different. This is real. The club know.

'Right. Thanks, Ian.'

Even though Stephen didn't keep drugs at Friars Mews, he definitely had them in Spridlington.

I call him straight away. 'Bro, you haven't left stuff in the flat have you? If there's anything in your room – get rid of it.'

He's gone and cleaned up the house. The police arrive on Monday morning and don't find anything, but this is the start of Lincoln police harassing me.

Following the raid, the club give the police my phone number. An officer rings me up and says:

'Moses, we're not saying you're implicated, but we have this individual, Stephen, who we know is selling drugs out of Lincoln, and we have evidence. Would you please come in for a voluntary interview?'

'I haven't got a solicitor. I ain't got nothing to hide, but why would I be coming in for a voluntary interview?'

Then he says, 'Well, I suggest you do, unless you're funding his drug operation.' Silence from my end of the line. My nervous pause makes me realise this is serious.

I hang up the phone. Refusing to speak to the police has a negative impact on me both on and off the pitch.

Up until that point, Ian and Chris protected me a lot. I never had any issues with them, in training or games, even when we lost. I was almost like the Gaffer's pet. He was very fond of me.

I call Ian Pearce straight away. 'These guys are harassing me.'

By then I've been stopped by the police a few times in my car. No reason given.

'Don't worry, we're going to deal with it.'

CHAPTER 6

DELROY AND THE RUSSIAN

When Delroy Facey starts acting funny, Jamie is the one who tells me what's going on. They're both from Huddersfield. 'Del owes money to the wrong people.' That's how I find out about everything else.

Delroy is a well-travelled striker, a Grenada international, who played for Bolton Wanderers in the Premier League and had a successful career with a bunch of mostly lower-league clubs before he first came to us on a two-month loan from Notts County in November 2009. I know who he is before I even meet him. He's solid. His handshake almost crushes my hand.

When Del comes into the club I'm struck by the ease with which he seems to handle pressure and people. He has a quiet magnetism, the kind you expect from a seasoned pro who knows the score both on and off the field.

His loan spell ends in January 2010, but he signs a proper one-year-contract in July. I get to know him better when we sit in the middle of the team coach on away day trips. Delroy sits quietly, observing. He's a people watcher.

I call him 'Big Bro' out of respect for his age. He's nearly ten years older than me but I've never been shy talking to adults. Over time I notice he's doing little things that he won't mention to me or Jamie and the London boys: he'll go up to a youth player, always approaching them in and around the training ground car park and be like, 'Hey, lend me some money. I'll give it back to you.' But he's not going to. The youth team at Lincoln has a Centre of Excellence, but they don't get paid – their mums give them money for travel expenses or whatever.

When I start to clock these little things, I think, why's he doing this? He's been a Premier League player and these young players are too scared to ask for their money back that he isn't going to pay.

You'd think in our changing room Del would be the first person to try and keep Jamie off the streets, but he doesn't speak to him.

* * *

For my twenty-first birthday – 9 May 2010 – I go on holiday to Miami with Jermaine, a childhood friend. It's my first time in America and I'm like, 'Shit, man, this place is so big.'

J has always been a big part of who I am. He was very well known in the streets of South East London. He was the guy I called when the older bullies tried to stab Oli at school. Jermaine was basically my muscle. Miami is a silver lining. We've both turned our lives around and fly halfway across the world for the first time together.

In Miami, the nights are alive with music, vibes and the

best-looking girls you can imagine – Spanish, Mexican, Brazilian, I can't believe what I'm seeing. I feel like I'm in the middle of *Scarface*.

I meet a young Latino girl at the famous LIV Nightclub at the Fontainebleau Hotel on Miami Beach. Her name is Areli and she's from Chicago. She has that Latino spark, a kind of fiery energy. I'm smitten. She's different from anyone I've ever met. Damn, the way I fall in love is wild and free, while she is unapologetically herself. I'm not with Crystal any more because we lose contact when I leave school.

My twenty-first birthday boy's trip turns into an annoying holiday romance for both Jermaine and Areli's friend. But we don't care. I'm staying at the Ritz-Carlton with a sea-view room. We eat, sleep and talk for five days straight. I forget I have a real life back in the UK. My head is fully gone. We sleep outside together by the pool, watching the sunrise and sunset.

I've never felt more alive, never felt like someone truly understands me the way she does. My life up until twenty-one is survival and football. Nothing or nobody stands in my way. Even at Lincoln, the girls I see are all students, and we exist in separate worlds.

I use my mobile phone contract when I'm in America but am ignorant about roaming charges and I rack up a £3,000 phone bill. I get hit with a County Court Judgement (CCJ) for not paying it. This comes back to haunt me when I need credit to buy my next car. This is when Michael 'Boats' Boateng comes back into the picture and my world changes forever.

Back in the humdrum world of English football, I'm like, 'Damn, man, is this love or is this lust?' I'm confused, but I just want to spend time with Areli. I speak to her literally every day for a whole year. Lincoln is cold and grey. But what was Miami? It was all temporary, wasn't it?

* * *

The car drama starts the previous November, coinciding with my apartment getting raided by the police in Lincoln and Delroy arriving there on loan. We have a few days off, so I drive down to London.

It starts small, a blip on the radar, a misunderstanding. At least, that's what I try to tell myself as the police come knocking in the early hours of the morning at my mum's flat in London. I'm arrested and spend the whole afternoon at Peckham police station. I'm accused of handling stolen goods and the theft of a white Audi A3.

Apparently, I'm 'involved' in a scheme to collect a car, purchased with stolen credit card details.

I'm picked out of a police identity parade of twenty people and the victim of the crime pinpoints me in court as the getaway driver. My brother Ayub's friend, Junior, is also in the ID parade. You can't make this up.

'It was pitch black; he drove down our drive at high speed. I couldn't see him properly, but I know it's him,' the victim states in court. Not only am I not there and know nothing about it; I can't drive. I failed my driving test four times. My driving instructor comes to court and testifies how bad I was in my lessons. There is no way on earth I could have driven that car.

But they charge me and I have to go on trial at Guildford Crown Court. It drags on for six long weeks, the whole of the summer of 2010. I miss all of pre-season training travelling to and from Guildford every day from my mum's.

I sit in court, listening to the accusations, the whispers, the weight of it all pressing down on me. I keep waiting for someone to step up and explain the mistake, to point out that I'm not the one they're looking for. Luckily for me, my mobile phone provider tracks that my phone was at home on that day. Plus, I have an alibi – a girl I'm seeing is with me at the exact same time the car was purchased using the stolen card details.

Then Junior owns up to it. It was him who bought the car over the phone using stolen credit card details. He went to pick it up from the house of the family dealership and drove off wearing my old Bromley FC tracksuit top that I gave him once the season had finished. The daughter picks me out of the ID parade instead of Junior.

She specifically says the driver is wearing a football tracksuit but doesn't know which team. I'm obviously playing for Lincoln, not Bromley. But Moses Swaibu is a football player. Bob's your uncle, there we have it. He must be our man.

A case of mistaken identity, they say. Junior has somehow got himself tangled up in this mess. I get busted, then released. Junior ends up in jail.

Ian Pearce, Lincoln's assistant manager, comes to court to give evidence and show his support. Considering he's only been at the club a short time, he takes a liking to me and treats me like a son. After I'm acquitted, he drives me back to Lincoln and we pass the journey talking about his life and mine, his experiences with Blackburn Rovers in the Premier League and his time at West Ham United and Fulham. Ian instinctively gets my journey and knows where I'm coming from.

Six weeks on trial for a crime I didn't commit. I never once think, 'I'm going to prison.' But the reality is, if I hadn't had the safety net of support from Lincoln City, if I'd been found guilty, my career would have been over.

* * *

Chris Sutton identifies problems at Lincoln City, but he can't find the solutions. His standards are too high for a League Two side like Lincoln. He signs better players, improves the squad, but we're too naive for this division. Not streetwise enough.

Sutton brings his young son to training, walks his dog and lets Ian take the sessions. That's how frustrated he is with the team.

Sometimes he joins in the training games and even though his knees are knackered, he's still the best striker on the pitch. You can see why he's played at the top level. He loves winning. He can't handle going into a losing situation. He doesn't have the temperament.

Despite winning the Premier League as a player, I realise that in football, no matter who you are or where you played, as a manager, the moment you lose respect among the players, you're done.

He beats us down in a way that some of us can take. He's good with the young players, but the senior ones are like, 'You're a fucking idiot.'

Sutton's high expectations and standards can be demoralising. If we lose on a Saturday, the following Tuesday he organises an in-house friendly against Aston Villa, due to connections from playing there at the end of his career.

Villa are in the Premier League, so they field youngsters and fringe players against our first team. We're low on confidence; we've been shot down. I don't know whether the Gaffer sees it as a tactic to boost team morale, but it has the opposite effect. They toy with us and beat us easily every single time. It's humiliating.

* * *

Accrington Stanley is a hostile away venue at the best of times. If you know football at that level, the Crown Ground is one of the worst places to go and play. Everything's shit, with all due respect. Shit stadium and the fans give you hell. They're from Lancashire and all the Lankies are right in your face.

When we travel there on 17 September after a topsy-turvy run of early season form, I sense something is wrong with the Gaffer. His demeanour and attitude towards the team have changed. I'd go as far as to say that he addresses us with a certain level of disgust.

The Accrington coaching staff take the living piss out of him on the bench. They slag off his career and Chris not being picked again for England after falling out with Glenn Hoddle. 'Sutton, you're fucking shit!' On a truly miserable Friday night, we get thrashed 3-0, Scott Kerr is sent off for a wild tackle and I'm an unused sub, watching the horror show unfold from the bench.

A 1-0 defeat at Stevenage is followed by a drab 0-0 draw at home to Burton Albion which proves to be the final straw. The result leaves us twentieth in the League Two table with just eight points from nine games. When the Gaffer took the reins exactly a year before, Lincoln City were twentieth in the table . . .

Next morning, I get a phone call from Ian.

'Just to let you know, the Gaffer has packed it in and I'm leaving with him. Things haven't worked out. I love you to bits, Mo. Keep your head down. Stay out of trouble.'

Sutton cites 'personal reasons' for leaving but I reckon the Accrington game broke him. I think the stuffing was knocked out of Chris Sutton that night.

Sutton and Pearce leaving is kind of my last hurrah at Lincoln City because whoever comes in next will be at non-league level.

The first thing a new manager's going to do is try to trim the wage bill. I'm one of the higher earners among the younger players in the squad. I imagine the scenario: 'Let's try and get rid of Moses.'

* * *

I'm like, oh my God. Everything unravels when Steve Tilson arrives on 15 October 2010. As much as things aren't going right on the pitch, my life off the pitch is falling apart.

Our defence has been leaking goals all over the place. One of the first things Tilson says to me is, 'I don't rate you as a player, and it's probably best you call your agent and try to find another club.' I'm not going anywhere.

I say to Tilson, 'Is there anything I can do, Gaffer?'

'Not really. I'll be speaking to you at some point, but until then you'll be training with the youth team.'

How do I go from being Young Player of the Season and attracting interest from Premier League clubs to now not even training with the senior team?

I'm expecting things to get worse, which they sadly do. The new Gaffer has a wholesale squad clear-out – he even gets rid of Scott Kerr, our captain, a club stalwart and a talismanic figure. He destroys the heart of the team. Any side he picks to go out and play, they don't give a fuck.

He gets it terribly wrong. There's a good reason why he's

been a lower-level manager his whole career. He can't deal with personalities and egos.

You have Del, me, the boys from London. Our changing room is like a family, full of fun and banter. But that only works when you're winning.

As we're doing that – win, lose and draw to keep that family – Tilson comes in, hears things from upstairs and he breaks that core. It isn't until I come back to train with the first team that Tilson realises the value I have on the squad as a human being. By then it's too late. He dismantles the squad because he's intimidated by us.

* * *

The chicken and the newspaper change everything. In many ways, this is the biggest turning point in my career to date.

My regular routine before training is to stop off at the Tesco on Wragby Road, buy a 20p *Sun* newspaper and some ingredients for dinner. On that night's menu: chicken fajitas.

I park my car outside on a double yellow line with the hazard lights on and go into the supermarket. I scoot round quickly and scan my shopping at the self-service checkout, pay and leave the store through the automatic doors. The security guard, a black dude, knows me. 'Hey, Moses!' We chat about Lincoln, our prospects for the season ahead. Then he says, 'You haven't paid for the chicken.' 'Yes I have!' 'It didn't scan.' I walk back inside, scan it and pay again with the coins I have. As I'm about to leave, the security guard tells me, 'We've called the police!'

'Uncle, what's going on?!'

I can't believe it. I have to laugh. Tesco is next to the club training ground, round the corner from my house. Plus, I'm a known Lincoln City player, with £40 in my pocket. I have the means to pay. I call my sister Sarah, and she says, stay there, don't leave or they'll try to arrest you.

Police came, no questions asked. 'You're under arrest for theft. Leave your car parked here. You're coming with us.' They handcuff me and tell me to get in the back of the cop car.

The bizarre thing is they take the chicken away in a police evidence bag. But it's not even funny because I know the agenda. It feels like they're trying to run me out of town.

I go through this period thinking, *What the hell? These guys are really trying to take me out.* I'm arrested for stealing a chicken? Then when I go to answer bail I'm arrested again for allegedly stealing the 20p newspaper. They have absolutely no evidence, not even from CCTV cameras at the store, but they claim it happened at the same Tesco.

At training the next day. I go to speak to Steve Tilson and I'm like,

'Gaffer . . .'

'I already know, Moses – get out of my office.'

'Fucking hell!'

'You're training with the youth team today.'

I tell the boys they've dropped the chicken charges but rearrested me for a 20p *Sun* newspaper! Then the *Lincolnshire Echo* print my rearrest – again on the back pages. The headline is: 'Moses Swaibu Steals Chicken'. They've got a photo of me, the Tesco and the chicken.

In the changing room, Delroy says, 'Moses, stand up.' I stand up. 'Did you steal this chicken?' Everyone's laughing.

'No.'

'All right, cool, sit back down.'

Then he says, 'Fuck this! Nobody does any interviews with the *Echo*. No one talks to them.' He gets the entire squad to boycott the *Lincolnshire Echo* – no post-match interviews, nothing. Don't forget we have their sponsorship logo on the front of our strips. It turns into a circus and leaves the chairman and the club with egg on their faces as the players all stand in solidarity with me.

After a month, Tilson comes to me and says, 'You need to tell the players to speak to the *Echo*.'

'I ain't doing that.'

Then I ring the PFA and tell them what's happening. Tilson says I have to leave the club. The end is nigh.

* * *

One of my best mates, Mustapha Carayol, signs for Lincoln from Torquay United. Mus was born in The Gambia but moved to England aged six and grew up on the North Peckham estate.

Me and Mus play five-a-side football together at his local youth centre. Throughout the summers of my time between leaving Crystal Palace and playing for Lincoln City, from 2008 to 2011, I spend pre-season back in London. These are extraordinary times. Mus and I host small-sided games and run clubs, utilising the areas and environments we grew up in across South London.

Every summer we enter competitions in some of the most intense environments, the heartland of London street crime. Our love for football overpowers the dangers all around. The media call them 'concrete jungles', but to us it's our homes. It's what we know. Some friends have passed away either through gang violence, murders or street crime. We are the role models and visionaries of our generation.

The local barber shop in Kennington hosts a seven-a-side football competition with a £1,000 prize up for grabs to the winners. This barber shop is on Camberwell New Road opposite the notorious Brandon Estate. We wait in line to get a haircut, tuning into the regular barber chronicles, listening to the juicy chitchat from the streets, talking about women, who's done what, with who, and more importantly, why everyone else's Premier League team is better than the other's. If you want to know what's happening in the area, you go to the barbers.

Little did the other teams know we are all professionals; me, Mus and Daniel Johnson – another mutual friend from south London who came through the Aston Villa Academy and went on to play for Preston North End – are in our sevens side.

We enter the tournament, get to the final without conceding a goal and win the cash. The final is against a bunch of grown men from Brixton. Gangland dudes. If you know South East London like I do, you know that Brixton and Peckham don't get on.

These OGs are so pissed off when we beat them 5-0, they bully the ref into replaying the final. 'You cheated us! These guys are pros!' We're like, cool, we'll play you again. This time we win 8-0. Now the OGs are going nuts. It's pandemonium. We take the prize money, get the hell out of there fast and treat ourselves at Nando's Camberwell.

One of Mus's friends also plays with us during those summers. He is tipped for a professional football career when he's killed in a drive-by shooting in Peckham in September 2010. He is accidentally caught in the line of fire of the gunman's intended victim. He's eighteen years old. His death is a horrible case of wrong place, wrong time. It hit the whole community. I wasn't aware of the gang warfare in that area as I lived in Bermondsey and Mus was in Peckham. I do know that the shooting divides the borough.

It's the first time I see Mus in such a state. The club allow us to take the week off.

* * *

Now we have two wing wizards at Lincoln City. Mustapha and Albert Jarrett – a Sierra Leone international – are arguably the best wide men in the league. I rarely play at full back, maybe once or twice, and only due to injuries.

Not long after he takes over, Steve Tilson puts me at right back directly up against Mus in a training game and we almost come to blows. Me and Mus are going at it. He glides past me a few times, I kick him. I get the better of him, he grabs my shirt and I'm like, 'What the fuck are you doing?' As the game wears on, a weird animosity builds between us. It's getting tetchy.

It doesn't mean anything that we're best friends. We're on this pitch to compete. No matter who you are, when we cross that line . . . come on – let's have it! It's war. We're both lightning quick, but Mus is technically better than me, so I lose this particular battle.

The rules of the game: the loser has to wash everyone's boots. The Gaffer favours Mus in the training session and decides I'm the worst player. Tilson is trying to get into my head, trying to break me.

The forfeit is that we have to take turns trying to hit the crossbar with the ball. The loser washes the whole squad's boots.

I'm like, 'I ain't fucking doing that.' Mus pings the crossbar with his first strike.

The Gaffer pipes up: 'Everybody give Moses your boots!'

It's the middle of winter and it's freezing cold.

I've got twenty pairs of boots. I'm getting hammered by all the boys. Everyone's bantering me: 'Oooh, Moses, wash my boots for me now!'

'No way, man. I'm not washing no one's boots. I tell you now, I'm not doing it.'

Tilson says: 'If you don't wash the boots, I'll fine you two weeks' wages.'

The boots are caked with icy mud. I'm thinking, *Nah, fuck that. I ain't cleaning no boots.*

We finish training and go for lunch. Me and Delroy and some of the senior first team players sit together in the canteen.

'Moses, go wash my boots.'

'I'm not washing the boots.'

Then the Gaffer walks in, and he's like, 'Moses, have you not washed the boots?'

'I'm not washing them.'

And everyone is like, 'Moses, stop having an ego, go wash the boots! You lost!'

I might've lost but nobody really knows what I'm going through, or how the manager is treating me.

'Listen, I ain't washing no boots. Man, fuck this, I'm going home.'

It's the end of the day; everyone's boots are there.

The Gaffer says, 'If you go home, I'm going to fine you.'

'Go on, fucking fine me, then.'

It's the first time in my whole career I ever swear at a manager or indirectly swear.

I go to the changing room, grab my bag, pull on my hoodie, jump in my car and drive home.

Then the club try to suspend me, but they can't because of employment law. That's when I contacted the PFA.

They are trying to humiliate me. To be honest it happens more often than people think. When you're not wanted, some clubs try to push you out rather than do the honest thing. Mus takes a photo of me sitting down as my teammates throw their boots at me. I've still got that photo.

* * *

After Stephen's drug bust, I leave Friars Mews for an apartment on my own in the new development at Brayford Wharf, Lincoln's version of Canary Wharf.

I got my first car, a brand-new black Mercedes-Benz, fresh out of the showroom. Mus has a white one, identical model. I have to drive all the way up into the NCP car park to get into my building. I'm like, let me just park it on a double yellow. I don't care about parking tickets because it's only a tenner.

I live below the local newspaper offices. My friend picks me up from training, so I leave my car on the yellow lines.

The neighbours notice this and it irritates them. 'Mo, that car's a nuisance; it's always there. Why don't you just drive all the way to the top of the parking lot?'

'I ain't doing that!' But this has a negative effect on me because everything that's happening outside my house, the newspaper reports to the club.

When Stephen gets jailed, me and the boys – Mus, Cian Hughton, Kern Miller and Joe Anderson – move into a four-bedroom house on Gabriel Crescent, directly opposite the club's training ground.

At the height of Stephen's local infamy, before his arrest,

people from London come up to Lincoln to go to the university. They know who I am, and we all go out on the town together. It gets back to the club; Moses has an influence on the city because he's bringing up these people and he's helping Stephen build his drug empire.

I guess this is how it appears to the club. It's what they think is happening. I'm totally oblivious to it.

* * *

New Year's Day, 2011. Not a happy one for me. I've gone from being a fans' favourite and people loving me, to suddenly no one gives a shit any more. Fans and little kids are coming up to me, shouting abuse. We're playing Bradford City at home on the first day of 2011. The fans have made up a chicken song about my Tesco arrest. As funny and jokey as it is, the new song backfires on them – and me. The first few minutes of that game, Bradford swing the ball into our penalty box and the fans start up a chorus of the chicken song.

'Who's that sneaking out of Tesco, who's that sneaking out the door, who's that sneaking out the side . . . it's Swaibu and his mates . . .!'

The song distracts me, and I turn round at the last second and they score. The BBC Sport match report says it all: 'The Imps, who have not played a game in five weeks, were behind after just two minutes when a dreadful mix-up at the back allowed James Hanson to poke home.' I'm the dreadful mix-up. It's me.

It's the worst game I've ever played. I feel sick. A ten-year-old kid comes up to me in the car park with his dad and says to my face, 'Swaibu, you're fucking shit!'

The first team wear suits to home games. I loosen my tie.

I look at this kid, thinking, *Woah, flipping hell, man.* But the kid isn't finished with me, 'Did you really steal a chicken?' His dad pulls his arm: 'Come on, son, let's go.'

Why do I pick out that moment? It's one thing getting abuse from your fans, but I'm being insulted by a child. You know you've reached a new low when a kid is having a go at you.

I hate to admit that he's got a point. Damn, if it had come from anyone else it would have been a different story. But what do you do when a ten-year-old tells you you're shit? It hurts. It's my lowest point in football so far. It can't get worse than this. I can't sink any lower.

The fallout from the game is intense. I'm not allowed to train with the first team and when I do come back to play, I'm on the bench. The manager starts playing mind games with me. He says, 'Moses, you're coming on in the 89th minute.' I refuse to come on.

* * *

When Delroy calls me, I can hear the pressure in his voice. He doesn't say, 'Hey, what are you guys up to?' He's like, 'What are you man on?'

I reply, 'Nothing. Chilling.'

'Come down to my room.'

We're in a Holiday Inn on the outskirts of Northampton, at the side of the motorway. There's an early curfew when footballers stay overnight at a hotel before a match. I tell my roommate where I'm going and he's fine with it. But then Del says, 'No, both of you come down to my room.' We've been summoned by the elder statesman.

Del's hotel room is dimly lit by a mini drop-down light.

He isn't alone. Beside him sits a man introduced as 'The Russian'. Six feet tall with a granite face and an accent that makes anything he says sound like a warning. Between the two of them they project a careful, restrained menace. It's instantly clear that Delroy hasn't ordered us down to discuss tactics for the next day's League Two game against Northampton.

I'm thinking, 'What the hell is going on?' I don't like this feeling because Delroy is someone I look up to. Bro, we're not on the streets here. If I wanted to be a part of that life, I could have done it many years ago.

As soon as I see the duffle bag with €60k in it, I know this is serious. All they do is reaffirm it.

'Yeah, mandem, there's sixty bags there. If we do this tomorrow, it's light work.'

The Russian keeps it short and sweet: 'I need you guys to lose tomorrow.'

Me and two other teammates sit down on the bouncy bed wearing our club tracksuits.

Delroy cuts to the chase, his tone smooth, almost rehearsed: 'Sixty grand cash. You can take it tonight. All we need is a 1-0 at half-time.' It's a premeditated meeting. Delroy feels comfortable around the Russian. It's obviously not the first time they've met.

Delroy asks an open-ended question.

'Who wants to sleep with the money?'

We could have taken twenty grand each and all said, 'Oh, I'll sleep with the money!' Think about what that really is. It's grooming.

But I'm like, bro, why am I going to sleep with money that isn't mine? The chances of one in three are the odds. Someone's going to want to sleep with the money. One teammate takes the bag, sleeps with it, and this is what I'm wondering. Imagine sleeping with that amount of money. What type of dreams do they have that night? I really want to know: when he sleeps with the money, what is he thinking?

If I sleep with that money, I won't feel any different in the morning because I've already made my mind up. I'm not doing it.

Usually, the whole team goes for a walk on match-day morning. But we don't want to let the money out of our sight. It's in our possession and I'm part of that conspiracy. It's getting closer to the game and the money is now in a bag on the team coach. We're driving to Sixfields Stadium on the opposite side of town. The kit man hands us our bags from the trunk of the coach. There's sixty grand in one of the bags. €60,000 stacked neatly in rubber-banded bundles, in a kit bag, in the away team changing room.

Tilson reads out the team sheet and Delroy is the only player who starts the game. My teammates are on the bench. I'm not even in the squad.

We look at each other like, 'Oh God!' One of the teammates is superstitious. We grew up in the same environment but he's someone who's like, 'I don't even need to think about it. I'm not doing that. I know it's wrong.' He ain't doing it. No, absolutely not. I think about it for a minute. I'm like, nah.

They can't put on the fix because before the fix can happen, Delroy needs to notify the Russian that we're all in. They need us three to be on the pitch. And they need a signal. There's no signal. It doesn't matter anyway. We lose the game 2-1. More importantly, it's 0-0 at half-time. The fix is off.

On the way into training the day after the match, we meet

the Russian to return the money. He gets out of his car, Delroy hands him the bag of money. 'Alright cool, next time,' the Russian says. Shrugs his shoulders.

Then we go about life like normal. I don't ask questions about how long Delroy has been involved in this. I don't need to ask questions because I said, 'No.'

* * *

'Lincoln City footballer charged with stealing newspaper'. This is the headline on BBC News on 24 January 2011. The report says I have to appear before Lincoln Magistrates on 18 February, charged with theft. It says I joined the Imps after being released by Crystal Palace in 2008. That I previously won Lincoln City's Young Player of the Year award. Suddenly the good times seem like a distant dream.

It's official. The public naming and shaming is complete. I've been officially charged with stealing a newspaper from Tesco the previous September. This is on the back of the chicken humiliation the month before. It's the beginning of the end.

Everyone has been taking the piss out of me for months – the lads, the fans, the whole town's laughing. The *Lincolnshire Echo*, the club's sponsor, prints a photo of me with the chicken on the back of the paper. Imagine if social media was as prominent back then? I would have instantly gone viral, become a meme.

* * *

The January 2011 transfer window is in full swing. While I'm training with the youth team, Tilson brings in fresh blood, so I get edged further out of the picture. The day after the news story breaks saying I've been charged for the stolen newspaper, we're playing Cheltenham Town away. Tilson says, 'You're going to be on the bench.' I know I'm not going to play. And I'm thinking, 'What an idiot.'

I'm training with the youth team, then I'm being told to travel on the team coach all the way to Cheltenham just to sit on the bench? Bullshit.

On the bus to Cheltenham, I sit next to Delroy. As usual, a man of few words. Then he turns to me, like, 'Yo, bro, remember that thing the other day?'

'Yeah . . .'

'Make sure that's between us.'

'Yeah, man, say no more.'

That's the last I ever hear of it. It goes out of my head. Nothing happened so I have no reason to think about what Delroy said that night. I'm a professional footballer, so my mind is programmed to focus on Tuesday, Saturday, every other day's training; Tuesday, Saturday, Tuesday, Saturday. We don't have time to contemplate the 'what ifs' of the Northampton fix. I just want to win my place back in the team. The days all roll together and we continue.

* * *

My Lincoln contract states that every ten games I play, I get a wage rise. There is a period when I'm stuck on seven games. If I play three more games, my salary goes up. Are they intentionally not playing me to avoid paying the extra money?

There are only two explanations: A) The manager's being a dick, or B) Why start playing me when they have to pay me more money, and they don't rate me?

Tilson turns to me on the bench at Whaddon Road and

says he's going to put me on. I refuse, and he says he's going to fine me again. Somehow, we hang on for a precious 2-1 away win but, as predicted, the seat of my tracksuit didn't leave the bench.

I call Nick Cusack at the Professional Footballers' Association, the PFA, and tell them that the manager's bullying me. They try to help me. The day the transfer window is closing, Tilson says, 'Look, Moses, you need to think about your career, so probably best you leave. We've had enquiries from Forest Green.'

I'm playing in League Two, so I tell him, 'I don't want to go to the Conference.'

'Look, we're going to offer you eight grand to leave.'

I'm like, 'Hell, no.'

Throughout the day, they increase the offer three times, from eight to nine to twelve grand. An hour before the midnight transfer deadline they dangle a final cash carrot: 'We'll give you £16k to leave.' I'm thinking to myself, you know what, I might as well just take this money and go.

I have an hour to work out whether I'm gonna leave or not. I call James Lippett, my new agent, and drive home to Gabriel Crescent.

I ask Mustapha, 'Do I take the money, or continue to take the abuse I'm getting at Lincoln?'

Mus says, 'I can't lie, bro. If I was you, I'd take that money and go get another club.'

I phone the club secretary. 'I can be at the stadium in twenty minutes to sign this off.' My contract is mutually terminated. The money is in my account the next day. That's how much they want me to leave. In football, you normally get paid at the end of the month, but they send me an immediate bank transfer. I think, shit look at all this money in my account! As a twenty-one-year-old, that sixteen grand feels like 160 grand.

I pack my bags in double-quick time and before the clock strikes midnight, I'm on the A1 back to London as the transfer window closes. I hit the London city limits around 3.30am. I have a key to my mum's, open the door, park my car behind the house in the garages and go to bed.

The day after the money clears in my bank account, as if by magic, all criminal charges against me are dropped relating to the chicken and the newspaper.

After I leave, Lincoln's season unravels. On 15 January 2011, Delroy had taken the captain's armband from me in the 2-1 home defeat against one of his many former clubs, Wycombe Wanderers. Lincoln win eight of their next fifteen matches and sit comfortably in fourteenth in the League Two table. Then Delroy dislocates his shoulder on 15 March in a 1-1 away draw at Macclesfield Town. Their main man is out for the rest of the season. Off the pitch, Del is up to all sorts, but on the pitch, he always shows up when they need him most. It's not a coincidence that, in his absence, the team fall to pieces. Lincoln City lose nine of their last ten league games, with a solitary draw, and are relegated from the Football League on the last day of the season.

Steve Tilson orchestrates a mass clear-out of players, including Delroy. Tilson miraculously keeps his job but is sacked that October after Lincoln win only three of their first fourteen games in the Blue Square Bet Premier League and sit one point above the relegation zone. When he gets the bullet, Tilson is preparing for Lincoln's next game, away to Alfreton Town. Remember that name.

What's crazy is that all this happens within the space of a few years. Me and Ayub flee our dad's abuse; I leave school and join Crystal Palace's Academy; win two Player of the Year awards; Oliver's brother Herve dies of a heart attack on a football pitch; I sign for Bromley; Oli is stabbed to death; I move to Lincoln and live with a drug dealer; my apartment gets raided by the police; I'm on trial, wrongly accused of buying a car with stolen credit card details; my brother's friend goes to jail for the aforementioned crime; Mustapha's friend is shot in Peckham, sparking gang warfare; I'm arrested for stealing a chicken . . . and a newspaper; the new Lincoln manager hates me; Del introduces me to match fixing; I get hounded out of town and essentially paid to leave Lincoln City. And now? I don't have a club. Even football, my escape, my lifeline, is letting me down. My career is in a tailspin.

The year drifts by in fragments, a series of unsuccessful trials. One day I'm in Northampton colours, then at AFC Wimbledon (one reserve game, they don't sign me), the next I'm packing my bags for Gillingham (for about a month), followed by Kettering, then my friend Femi gets me a trial at Dagenham & Redbridge (for two months, no dice – 'We ain't got the budget!').

Mark Stimson is the manager at Gillingham when I'm on trial there. When he leaves to take the reins at Kettering, he calls me: 'Look, Moses, we're looking for a centre half.' They'll pay me £350 a week.

I need guaranteed first-team football and the Conference is still a good level.

After my first game at Kettering they go into a transfer embargo and the chairman stops paying everyone. I continue to come in.

There are days I travel from London to meet the manager at Redbridge Roundabout then drive the two hours up to train at Kettering. It's too far to drive home every day. It's the first time I stay in digs, with an elderly couple. I don't like the experience.

It's just as well I don't stick with Kettering. After losing their old Rockingham Road ground in 2011, the club go into administration during the 2011/12 season, finish bottom of the Conference National and are demoted two divisions to the Premier Division of the Southern League.

I have so many first-team games under my belt at Lincoln, mostly as captain, so I'm surprised I can't find another club. Each new locker room makes me feel like I'm slipping further away from who I'm supposed to be. I want to believe each move is a chance to prove myself, but deep down, I feel like a pawn in a game I can't control. Always the outsider. A fleeting figure, trying to leave a mark in dressing rooms that get emptier each time.

Every trial, every stint at a different club gives me the same feeling. I've played almost 100 senior games in the Football League by now and I'm still young – I turn twenty-three in May 2011. But it feels different now. Like I'm being tested, but with no real chance of passing the test.

* * *

Eventually, I land back at Bromley halfway through the 2011/12 season. How long can I do this? Football isn't really going the way I expected it to go. This isn't me quitting. I'm just thinking to myself, *What's next?* Do I see myself going to another team? If I play well at Bromley, it will attract interest from bigger clubs. If I go and play in a higher league, then what happens? Do I have what it takes? It's the first time I really start to doubt myself.

The manager, Mark Goldberg, says, 'Moses, we want you to be captain. I don't want you to leave. We want to get promoted, one day we'll be in the Football League and we want to build a club around the current team.' It isn't a crazy ambition. The players that he signs are decent quality and considering the money they offer me and their budget for that level of the football pyramid, where the teams with the better budgets usually get promoted, it feels promising.

Bromley pay all our wages half cheque, half cash. My brother Ayub acts as my agent and negotiates a £10,000 signing-on fee plus £850 a week basic. Not bad for a part-time footballer in a sixth-tier league.

The half cheque, half cash payment scheme is a way of controlling the players. The cash bit is like giving a kid pocket money. They've got it and can spend it straight away. Players like having cash in their pocket and it's an instant reward for their endeavours. Most of the league is at it, paying their players this way.

I'm young but also a senior player and the club know I have sell-on value. I'm a class apart. The Bromley fans are surprised when I sign and we've got the makings of a decent squad.

We train twice a week and play games on a Saturday, sometimes midweek. Four days of the week you can suit yourself. Some of the older players have jobs but I set my sights on maintaining some form of professional football career. But Goldberg is not a football man, he's a businessman. He famously squandered £40 million on Crystal Palace and took them close to oblivion during an ill-starred ownership in the late 1990s. I end up picking the team with him and the vice-captain.

I'm basically managing the team. I give team talks. Mark trusts me 100 per cent. When one of our players – an honest, whole-hearted professional who I nickname Braveheart – sees me, he instantly knows that I'm the exact type of player he wants around. Training is even better. The standards are high. Because of the players we sign, our training sessions are immaculate.

My first season back at Bromley culminates in us avoiding relegation in a wild game against Truro City on 14 April 2012. We fight back from a goal down to win 2-1 in the worst conditions I've ever played – driving wind and rain, and the pitch is almost flooded. The boys drink beers and we're in high spirits on the way back from the game.

It starts to go wrong after a lot of fallings out with the manager. When things are going our way, everything is good, but the moment we stop getting paid and players aren't treated the way we should be, that's when the wheels come off the Bromley bandwagon.

This is supposed to be familiar ground, a safe place where I can find myself again. But match fixing rears its ugly head, like it's been waiting in the wings for just the right moment.

Me and Crystal reconnect when I go to get my hair cut at the barber shop where she works shortly after my holiday in Miami. We become an established couple. My dream high-school crush is now my girlfriend.

In the summer of 2012, Crystal finds out she's pregnant. I'm thinking, *shit, man, what's going to happen with football? How do I feed my baby?*

I can feel the walls closing in. The silent invitations, the whispering gets louder, sharper. It feels like the shadow game never let go of me. Last time, I said no. I knew that one day, I might be desperate enough to listen.

* * *

No doubt they pick me because they know what I'm about. I'm the club captain. They know I'm a leader. They absolutely knows I'm not going to tell anyone. Players come to me with personal problems all the time. I'm their point of contact between them and the Gaffer. The players are like, 'Moses, the chairman ain't paid me. Can you speak to the Gaffer?' I'm a natural middleman. Unknowingly in training for what's waiting for me around the corner.

This is semi-professional football. There's an essence of amateurishness or a lack of quality. For most players at this level, you only train twice a week and people still have part-time jobs.

In the likelihood that a player snitches or tells on me, I'd say, 'To be honest, Gaffer, such and such has come to me about match fixing, and I've considered it, but I'm not going to do it.'

And the Gaffer would have believed me because Bromley at that time weren't giving anyone else a ten grand signing-on fee and putting them on the money that I was on. There's a hierarchy. But then the whispers turn into actual words. Somehow, I sense it's been coming. We're warming down at training and a call comes in saying, 'Moses, we've got a meeting.'

CHAPTER 7

CIGARETTE-SMOKING MAN

20 August 2012: The May Fair Hotel, London

When we get to the May Fair Hotel, I'm introduced to this guy, who's the direct line to the match fixers.

This other middleman is an older ex-player who goes by the alias 'By'. He's as solid as a rock, immaculately groomed, clearly looks after himself. By is the facilitator; he's the Delroy Facey: 'I know these guys. Let me introduce them to you.'

He's waiting for the text that says, 'Yeah, tell them to come up.' We're in the downstairs bar. We're not Premier League players. Not that we shouldn't be here, but we're obviously *not* Premier League players.

Mayfair is the heart of London's bustling West End, surrounded by casinos and posh restaurants. The hotel lobby reeks of privilege and wealth.

It's like those Italian Mafia films where they take their wives or girlfriends out for a fancy dinner. That famous scene in *Goodfellas* when the doormen of the Copacabana lead Henry Hill and his wife, Karen, through the back door into the kitchen, bustling with Chinese cooks, and all the way to the best table in the house. That's how he impresses her. The May Fair Hotel is that type of place. It's the high life. Except we've come straight from training and are sitting in the upmarket hotel bar in our tracksuits.

We've been summoned. The waitress asks them for their drink order. Will they' get an alcoholic drink or just a Coke? Meanwhile, I'm lounging back with my old-fashioned cocktail in hand, swirling the golf-ball-sized ice cube around the glass. We're not really talking much. Someone says, 'Yo, what's up?'.

But it isn't a 'yo, what's up' conversation because they know what we're walking into. The last time I heard about match fixing it was also at a hotel. The Northampton Holiday Inn and the May Fair are two different extremes. The end game is the same.

The lift glides up through the floors until we reach our destination. It levels out and a muffled *ding* sounds. The doors slide open. We walk down the corridor, our shoes sink into the plush, royal red carpet. It feels like we're on a film set.

We reach the door of the hotel room. This is it, no turning back. I gently rap the door twice and enter. The first thing we see is a small, dark-haired man sitting on a huge bed with his back to us, watching a giant television and chain-smoking cigarettes, one after another, stubbing them out in an ashtray by his side.

This main guy is Tan. He's five feet standing up. He's tapping away on a laptop. He lights another cigarette. I'm thinking, 'Bro, you can't smoke in this hotel!'

Tan speaks to us through a translator, Hunken. I'm instantly impressed by this lean, unassuming young Singaporean man. He's clean-shaven, wears thin-lensed glasses, a well-tailored suit and expensive shoes. Even though he smacks of a teenage business student, he also looks like he belongs in Mayfair.

Hunken stands up, offers each of us his outstretched hand to shake and says in a calm, measured tone, 'Relax. Did you enjoy your drink? Please, sit down.'

Just like in Northampton, I sit on the bed again. This time the bed isn't bouncy – it's a firm, higher quality bed.

Tan addresses Hunken in rapid-fire Chinese and Hunken translates it into English. Tan keeps repeating, 'There's no pressure.'

Then he says, 'If business is successful, we pay you good money. When we pay you good money, everyone gets twenty grand each.'

Fuck off, twenty grand?! I'm only on £850 a week . . . twenty grand!

Tan turns back round to face the TV. Meanwhile, the other middleman, By, is playing it cool. Legs crossed, chewing gum.

He strikes me as someone who doesn't take risks. He gives off a take-it-or-leave-it vibe. After every sip of his drink, he casts his eyes round the room. It feels like we're being observed. He tries to reassure me: 'It's going to be OK, it's simple; you can do it once.' A hundred and one thoughts race through my mind when the conversation ends abruptly.

The Boss nods and Hunken says, 'That's it; thank you for coming. Tomorrow, you're playing. We want you to be losing 2-0 at half-time.' Match fixing isn't always about winning or losing, or the correct score, but goals scored in a game or a half.

They want us to concede twice before half-time. The second half we can play normally.

Hunken reaches into a bag and pulls out a thick, white paper parcel. This is the hook. 'We're all about loyalty and respect, even if you don't want to do anything,' he says.

He hands me the parcel: 'Thank you for coming to the meeting. There's no pressure. Let us know in the morning.'

It's like they're saying, 'Welcome to the family!' This is how the family works.

* * *

I leave the hotel and jump in a car. That's when the excitable chatter begins. I am counting the money. I don't know how much is in the envelopes but this ain't the wages I get at Bromley! It's thick!

Is it illegal to take cash from a stranger? I'm a normal, aspiring, lower-level footballer trying to do the best I can, and here someone has just covered a year's wages in return for doing nothing.

At that exact moment a text message arrives from Crystal, who is heavily pregnant and has sent a list of things we need to buy for the baby.

'Yes or no, I get to keep this money?' This is exactly what happened four years ago at Lincoln. This shit's real.

And they called it pocket money. I'll tell you why it's so significant. Pocket money is what you give children. When you think about what he says, it's subliminally telling us we're kids. You're my kids now. Here's your pocket money. Keep it. You're in the family. Here you are, son. Go and spend it as you wish.

To the likes of Tan and Hunken, what's five grand? Take it. Buy a new car. To them, it's nothing. They're just here to do business. And in this business, if you say you're going to do it, do it. If you don't, no problem.

'Mandem, this happens.'

'Moses, I don't know, man.'

'Bro, who knows what these men are bringing me to the May Fair Hotel for?'

'It's a different level to the Northampton situation. It's a slicker operation.'

The first thing I think to myself is: *Who hands out money like that? Is this illegal?* I say, 'If I take this money now, can I get out of it later?'

'Bro, you can't get arrested.'

'Hey, take it. I could have found that on the floor. You can justify that.'

The game is the next day. I don't have much time to think about this. I have to tell them before the game whether I'm in or out. I tell them, 'I'm in.'

'OK, mandem, look, let's just do it once, innit.'

And I genuinely meant, let's do it once.

* * *

'Dan' Tan Seet Eng, a Singaporean businessman, is unlike anyone I've ever met. His presence fills a room without any need for him to raise his voice or even say much. He's slender, always dressed in simple, understated clothes that somehow look expensive. His eyes tell you everything – they're sharp and calculating.

He isn't the typical loud gangster type you see in movies. He's calm, polite, almost unassuming. No aggression, no intimidation. He uses his composed authority, built on trust and loyalty.

The way he talks about gambling is like that of a philosopher, someone who has been through it all and understands the game better than anyone.

It's this quiet power that is more unsettling than anything else. You can feel his control just being near him, as if everything he wants to happen will happen because he's already figured out how it's going to play out.

Tan has a theatrical way of carrying himself that makes everything feel important. The way he holds his cigarette, the pauses before he speaks, the way he watches you. It all builds up a mystique around him that makes people want to follow his lead. He is a man who loves high stakes and treats every bet and match like a carefully planned and executed masterpiece.

But underneath this composed surface is a razor-sharp mind that is always calculating, always strategising, always thinking ahead of the curve. I soak everything up like a sponge, just as I did in football. When I start talking about how the game works, he listens closely, like he's learning from me too.

Tan understands football, not as a sport, but as a game of influence and leverage. Sometimes it feels like he's been watching me the whole time, from the moment I break into Crystal Palace's first team. We formulate twisted plans and laugh together, showing Tan we understand what he's about. When I say 'we', I mean his right-hand man, Hunken, the underboss.

He knows exactly where teams are weak, how to get inside a player's head, and use that to control them. This isn't some small-time operation. They are organised in ways I'll only later understand. They want control and ownership of clubs in the UK, with me on board, and they know how to achieve it.

I am the guy he turns to because I am the one who helps him to make it happen. I am the 'black friend' he's never had. I am the 'blackie' in his operation, the one straight out of *Narcos* or the life of Pablo Escobar. My recommendations almost always pay off, and when they do he sends messages in broken English on Skype with meaningful emojis. Skull means he's really mad and when I reply with an angry orange face he says, 'him fuk me.'

He knows how to play on people's pride, their insecurities, and their hunger for money or status. He doesn't need to make threats. He makes people understand that he can either make them or break them. That's where I go wrong. I see how the inner workings of his operation are set up, but I start realising I'm not being paid what I'm worth.

In a way, Tan represents temptation itself. He is the promise of easy money, of breaking the rules, of living the kind of life most people can only dream about. He quickly understands the English game and the league and he wants to raise the stakes and take control.

What is match fixing? What is the definition? Who goes to prison for this, especially in the UK?

Tan operates in a moral grey zone, and he seems to draw others into it simply by existing. Working for Tan means accepting that you leave a part of yourself behind. And yet, even knowing this, people can't resist him. Player after player falls under his spell until half the league are in his pocket.

Being in his orbit feels thrilling but dangerous. There is always a sense that his calm exterior is hiding a darker intensity, something quietly ruthless that will surface if anyone tries to oppose him. He is as precise in his manipulation of people as he is in his orchestration of games. And he knows that once you've worked with him, he has a hold over you. He gets into your mind, makes you crave the thrill of pulling off something forbidden, and makes you believe that, under his guidance, nothing can go wrong.

In Tan's world, we aren't just fixing matches; we are surrendering to a vision of power so seductive it is nearly impossible to turn away from, even as it consumes us.

CHAPTER 8

THE FIX IS IN!

Fix One

The scoreboard flashes above me. For the spectators, it's just another match. But to me, it is the start of something bigger.

Far away, in dark, smoky rooms and hidden venues, the real people are watching. The bookmakers in Asia have already changed the odds, moving money and placing bets. The money is traveling down phone lines, through the ether, from one side of the globe to the other. I can feel it, just like I can feel the grass under my feet.

If the fix comes in, it's invisible to the crowd, but if you know what to look for, you can see it. Every stray pass, every poorly kicked shot, every goalscoring opportunity squandered, every defensive blunder. I can sense the tension in my teammates' feet. It is all part of the plan. I'm a single cog in a much larger machine.

I try to picture the guys on the other end of the phone lines, keeping close tabs as the action unfolds from afar, making sure they get the result they want. I'm not the first in this racket, and I won't be the last. But tonight, it's my turn.

As the games go on, I feel more connected to every part of the network. Every bookmaker, every handler, every fixer. All of them connected. Money moves from hand to hand, through secret accounts, and eventually into wallets. I witness it happening, sometimes asking Hunken how it all works.

The final whistle blows and I feel a chill. The night air is cold, but the tension doesn't stop. I know the next step is coming. This is just the beginning. In this game, the money never stops. The people in charge never stop. And now that I'm in, they won't stop watching me.

That night, I sell my integrity for a blank cheque.

* * *

This is when I first meet Dom the French. He's the syndicate's middleman. After the game, I'm introduced to the French. He's suave, sophisticated and looks like a playboy rap star. A former goalkeeper who played international football. I don't know in advance that he's at the game. But I guess it makes sense. He's here to watch the players, make sure we're doing our job. They're not going to give you five grand each, place their bets and then you don't do it.

The pitch is like a bowling green. You can smell the freshly mown grass. It makes you eager to get out there and play.

My first fix feels like I'm running away from something; something so wrong it feels right. A mixture of good and evil. It's the most creative process you can imagine. My whole life in football came with unknowingly not predicting scorelines. Everything seems too easy, up until the moment I arrive at the ground. Now I'm nervous, anxious. I feel a burning sense of pressure. What if something goes wrong? As we warm up, the sea breeze blows in my face. We're in the most picturesque of settings; a perfect summer evening for playing football. For fixing football.

Chris, my childhood friend, is on the opposition's team sheet. He's a powerful, left-footed striker, someone I had many battles with when we were younger. The ground has a scoreboard right above the goal. Talk about setting the scene for the perfect fix. I reconfirm I'm all in, 100 per cent.

We go back to the changing room to prepare for kick-off. The Gaffer reads out the team sheet. Good news, I'm all starting. The closer it gets to kick-off, the more ruthlessly certain I feel about the decision I've made. I already have a mind map of the pitch. I watch Chris lace up his boots and launch a few perfect practice shots at goal. The first thing I'll to do is mark him tighter than ever. When I played school football, Chris was one of the best strikers in my age group. He's built like a UFC fighter, strong as an ox. He loves pinning his defenders, rolling them, using his brute upper body strength. His only problem is that he's all left foot.

The stands are packed, the crowd singing and cheering, as football fans do. They don't know what's really happening. They don't know they're part of a set-up. I look around and feel sick. This isn't just a game any more. It's the start of something that goes right across the world, to places I can't even imagine. The plan is simple. Just do what I have to do, don't try to show off. The real game, the shadow game, the one the crowd don't see, is going on behind the scenes of the theatre. I'm a just an actor, about to take to the stage.

We kick off. I command the line. Every centre back who's played at a middling standard of football knows what positions to adopt to mark their striker. Mine is always down the channel side. Get in the channel early, protect the space. I quickly suss out that if I go too tight to Chris it will play into his hands. I'm always the last line of defence. My central defensive partner, Liam Harwood, is slow and hates playing a high line. Every game without fail I have to shout at him to step up. Our right back doesn't listen to instructions, but he's brilliant streaming up the wing on the overlap. I know his lack of discipline will give them an advantage because he has a habit of delaying his recovery runs. My left back has a wealth of experience but also loves bombing forward and hates defending. As a sweeper I can encourage our full backs to play higher while I control a high line and instruct our central and holding midfielder to sit back in recovery positions.

Chris couldn't have played a worse opening half-hour. I let him roll me three times in a row on his good side and each time he misses the goal by a country mile. He has pace and power but no composure or finesse in front of goal. Every time he blows another chance, I look up at the scoreboard.

Our forwards are playing out of their skin. We get the ball and launch a quick counter-attack. There is a potshot at goal. It hits the post. If that ball goes in it's all over. There'll be no match fixing. The whole thing grinds to a shuddering halt. It stops before it's even started.

Then there is a play to go one-on-one with the keeper and they flick the ball just over the bar. They're doing things in the game I don't even see them doing in training. I feel a rush of adrenaline. My neck is on the line, I need the money.

The best way I can describe it is that it's like a bank robbery. You need a getaway driver, and you need people to go into the bank. You need someone working behind the scenes. When you watch these movies, they have logistics. But then the getaway driver might have parked on the opposite side of the road, rather than outside the bank. You lose time, right? Or he stalls the car. Everyone panics.

What I quickly realise, the moment we kick off, the instinct as footballers kicks in. I'm a defender – I can backtrack, I can jockey, I can dive in. I have more actions and opportunities to do something that's going to manipulate the outcome of the result. This fix is easier because we have to concede. We don't need to score.

Our goalkeeper makes a great double save – the first from a direct free kick and an even better one minutes later when he somehow blocks a fierce volley from Chris at point-blank range. I'm developing a tic; every time they miss the goal I glance up at the scoreboard. The game is deadlocked at 0-0. Five minutes to play until half-time.

Luckily our high defending pays off. A deep cross into our box eludes the keeper. Someone attempts to hoof the ball clear but instead manages to bundle over a forward with a clumsy challenge. A sharp blast of the ref's whistle. Penalty!

I can't believe what I'm experiencing. That's when I realise a fix can happen by accident, without any need for manipulation. A striker converts the spot kick. One nil. But we need another goal before half-time. I'm looking at the stadium clock thinking, fuck, this isn't coming.

The last five minutes of the half are bedlam. As the clock slowly ticks towards the break, time becomes elastic. My heart beats faster and faster. Our forwards play their hearts out. Chris continues to miss sitters. On the stroke of half-time, with the ref checking his watch and with the last kick of the half, they launch a cross into our box. Our winger traps the ball on his chest but it rebounds up on to his outstretched arm and he falls over and grabs on to the ball. What the fuck is he thinking? An inexplicable move. It's a 'Hand of God' moment! But this is no divine intervention. It's sheer, clumsy panic. Another penalty! This time it's Chris who blasts the spot kick into the net. I look at the scoreboard: 2-0. The whistle blows for half-time. Holy shit, the fix is in!

I storm into the away changing room and scream. Everyone is confused. The Gaffer has one hand on his head as he gives the team talk. I pretend I'm furious. Early into the second half, back playing normally again, the opposition bag a third to seal victory, but we finish the game the better team. Our player fluffs a chance for a late consolation goal from the penalty spot and the final score is 3-0.

As I walk off the pitch, I don't know what to feel. I know we've hit the jackpot but once I understand how these actions can or can't affect a game, I notice human nature always takes over, no matter who you are. To successfully fix a football match, you need to be a stone-cold, ruthless, take-no-prisoners type of individual.

Finally, what blows my mind is the insane coincidence that my childhood friend, Chris, is the one who, unwittingly, scores the penalty that brings the fix in.

* * *

My phone pings. It's a text message: 'Call this guy.'

A man speaking English with a thick French accent answers: 'Moses, you drive back with me. I'm going to book us a hotel in London.'

Dom the French climbs into my Mercedes and we set off on the two-and-a-half-hour journey back to London in the pitch black. I'm buzzing with excitement that the fix came in. I pulled it off. But the French is acting the complete opposite.

'Bro, without you this wouldn't have happened,' he says. 'You wouldn't be sitting here so happy. Your guys didn't come through with the goods. If the boss was here, bro, trust me . . . he will pay but will never do business again.

'Let me be honest with you, man. That lot could have fucked up this bet. You need to keep the money.'

His straight-talking manner calms me down. It makes me think: maybe he's got a point?

The French continues, 'Bro, Moses, 100 g's. C'mon, bro, you know what you have to do, don't you? If I was you, I'd be taking the whole thing. They got their pocket money but, bro, do they think they're going to the Premier League or World Cup attacking and trying to score the way they did?'

It's a lot to take in, I barely have time to gather my thoughts and comprehend what he's suggesting.

'Where is the money?' I ask.

'The money's coming tomorrow.'

'That's not what we agreed. Tan and Hunken said we get paid as soon as the game's done.'

But we don't leave the ground until 10pm. By the time we get back to London, it'll be past midnight.

The French says, 'Bro, everything's closed. The market's not open.'

I'm thinking, *What the hell is he talking about? They're trying to rip us off.*

'Trust me, it's coming tomorrow,' he says, reading my mind.

He explains to me that we have to wait twenty-four hours for the money to be 'washed through the casinos'. Then it's paid out via the syndicate's restaurants.

'I've booked a hotel in Knightsbridge. If you don't believe me, stay with me.'

I didn't trust him. There's no way now the fix has happened that I'll let him out of my sight.

We hit the M25 motorway and he asks me to play some French gangster rap. I turn to look at him and he puts out his fist for me to bump. He's got a huge grin on his face that lights up the whole car. His beard is trimmed super smooth and he's elegantly dressed.

'Moses, if you help me, I'll help you.'

'What do you mean?'

'These guys did not do their job. They shouldn't be paid. I'll let you decide whether they're going to be paid or not tomorrow when I go and get the money. But trust me, the money's coming.'

'Bro, you're right, I'm keeping that shit! It's get down or lay down.' The French smiles at me and calls me 'a real g'.

'This is how this shit's done, Moses. You're either in or you're out. Bro, no hotstepping. I can feel one day you might run this shit and be me. I started off like you, all innocent and shit, loving football. But this game is dirty, bro; there's no love here so you shouldn't care.'

As we approach Knightsbridge, the French says, 'Moses, let's go get this fucking money; we aren't sleeping tonight, bro!'

* * *

We can't check into the May Fair Hotel, so Dom gets the boss to book another room in Knightsbridge.

The hotel we stay in is opposite Harrods, the famous luxury department store.

Twenty-four-hour room service. Dom is constantly on his phone with Hunken. It's obvious that the others hate this cocky French guy. I don't care; he's helping me get the money.

I can't sleep, not with everything that's at stake. Last night is replaying in my head. A fixed match, money changing hands and my part in it. I'm locked in. There's no going back now. The money's coming today. I look at the others in the room. They're nervous. Now we all know it's real. We've crossed the Rubicon. We pulled off a heist and no one was caught. Not one of us is even a suspect.

The next morning, the Boss sends the French instructions to book the May Fair Hotel. Again, we start camping. An hour turns into two hours, two hours turns into three. It's almost midday. Finally, Dom gets a text: 'The money's on its way.'

'Moses, first collection point is in Canning Town.'

I know the area well because it's two Tube stops from where I live. We're waiting in Canning Town McDonald's for the green light to pick up the cash. I've got my white Mercedes sitting outside in the car park. Strange because I was thinking we'll go to the drive-through.

I'm with this dapper French guy and I'm in a Bromley tracksuit. We stick out like a sore thumb. There's a bunch of youths skulking around, doing this and that, poking their heads in. I say to Dom, 'Bro, we've got to go.'

We get into the car. He gets a text: 'Come to Canning Town underground station'. We drive to the Tube station and a skinny little Chinese guy who looks like he's about sixteen years old walks towards the car with plastic Sainsbury's shopping bags.

He says one word – ('French?') – and hands over the bags. They're full to the brim with cash to the point where it's spilling out, so I push it back in. Then I yank my seat back and stuff the bags into the footwell. Off we go, back to the May Fair.

The French asks to connect his phone to Bluetooth so he can listen to some music. More French gangster rap. Two minutes into the drive. Bang. His ringtone blasts through my car stereo speakers, interrupting the music. It's the Bosses – Hunken and Tan. Broken English in a Chinese accent.

Hunken says: 'Hello, Dom. Game went well.'

'Very well.'

'You've collected the money?'

'Yes.'

'Player OK? They paid?'

I interject, 'No, I'm in the car. This is Moses Swaibu.'

Hunken says, 'What happened?'

The French mumbles swear words under his breath: 'Vazi, Vazi, Vazi, Vazi, Vazi, what the fuck, bro?' Maybe he doesn't like me talking to the bosses?

Dom mumbles something to Hunken in French. Hunken says, 'What do you mean?'

I butt in, 'We're heading back to the hotel.'

'Dom, give Swaibu my number . . .'

Now I've got direct contact to these guys. Hunken knows I'm built differently and may cause problems, so he quickly reaches out to befriend me.

As we're driving back, I'm thinking Dom's right.

Why should I pay the players for something when I've taken the biggest risk?

* * *

Back in our room at the May Fair Hotel, we empty the shopping bags on to the bed and count the money. There's £150k. I put 100 grand in a duffel bag. The French takes a 50k slice.

Me and Dom go to walk out of the room.

It's around 5pm. There's a bureau de change opposite Harrods. The French changes £30,000 into euros.

'Bro, I want to go shopping!'

We walk to Selfridges where I've arranged to meet the Ferrari Boys.

My older brother, Ayub, had a larger-than-life group of friends from the streets when I was growing up. From early 2012 onwards, I start hanging out with them and we rent a variety of supercars from Dave's car rental at Tower Bridge and race each other around London – we rent Lamborghinis, McLarens, Ferraris, each one more insane than the last.

I name us 'the Ferrari Boys' because John, the biggest personality in the group, says, 'I'm gonna get the Ferrari.'

I tell J, 'I'm gonna get it first!'

He beats me to it. He takes the Ferrari for a month. Tells no one. Out of the blue, he picks me up in this spectacular, jet black 458 Italia Spider.

We race up and down Bermondsey, cruise around Surrey Quay, play a real-life game of *Need for Speed* under the Thames, through the Rotherhithe Tunnel and back. Fun times.

Dom the French asks me, 'Do you want to come party in France?'

'No, I'm good.'

At Selfridges, the French says to one of the Ferrari Boys, 'Let me buy your hoodie.'

My friend replies, 'It only cost fifty quid.'

'I'll give you a grand right now.'

He stares back in utter bewilderment.

After the French leaves, everyone has one question: 'Who the fuck's that guy, man?'

I'm like, 'Just some guy, bro. Just some dude.'

* * *

I make over £100k in the first fix. They want me to fix more games. This is where the planning and precision takes over. The fact is that more happens off the pitch than on the pitch. My job is not to launder money but to become a distributor. I do what Dom the French does.

I am the operations director. Here's how it happens. Here's how it comes. This is how we distribute. This is what you need to know tactically. I know how they put on the bets. I sit down within that period with Hunken and Tan to understand the business.

When it's time to execute, I know that the best odds I can get is time lapse. If more matches are fixed, the market and the margin goes down because what you want to do is put on big liquidity to facilitate market movement.

For example, if they put a million pounds on a game, they're not going to put on a million pounds again because of the market movement and there are too many inconsistencies that may flag irregular betting patterns. Whereas if you leave a delay, you can afford to pay a team a lesser amount because of the structure of how people are paid.

My ruthlessness came from that first fix.

I thought worst-case scenario, I fix that game, or I don't fix that game. If I don't fix that game, they're never going to use me again. That was a fact, because I said I was going to do it. I didn't. But then they'll go and fix for other teams, which I later found out. How would I have felt if I didn't make any money, but everyone else is and I can't get in on it? Or, if I can't get in on it.

My cold-blooded streak emerges from wanting to maximise the opportunity in that first game. Adopting this merciless approach is a turning point for me in football and match fixing. When I get home and I think about it, I see myself as the captain of the operation.

What follows is a long period where no games are fixed. So, I'm playing normal. I'm going to play as usual. Except the downside is that I have too much time to think. First time in Northampton, first temptation to fix, I said no. Second time in London, I briefly pondered and signed up to the fix.

While I process it all, I'm trying to make excuses to justify why I want to do it. I spend a lot of time in my head until the next fix comes around. It's a four-month wait until fix number two. I never doubt that I can pull it off again. I use those months to work out how to thrive financially without fixing. How do I get paid by not match fixing? I physically can't fix every game. I'm trying to work out how to operate on my own.

That first game makes me realise you don't need four or five players; you only need one. If I can pinpoint the games I can do versus the games I can't, I can almost guarantee 100 per cent odds. In hindsight, that period of time I have to think works out better for me because I'm able to control a lot more off the pitch. The syndicate instruct me to do more things off the pitch than on it. I quickly discover I'm good at working out a strategy on how to learn the business.

My conclusion: my main ambitions going forward lie off the pitch, not on the pitch.

* * *

In the space of twenty-four hours, I go from thinking about it, agreeing to do it, implementing the plan, then stepping up to the plate as a new middleman.

I look back and I ask myself if the other players had fulfilled their roles in the fix and got an equal amount, and Dom the French hadn't tried to rip off the boss, and I'd never connected my Bluetooth to his phone, what would have been the outcome? Would I have made another decision and not continued the fix because I would have never known the deal? I only began to understand the answers to these questions later.

If we only fixed that one game, I would never have known other teams are fixing and instead gone into games and played normally.

* * *

Fix Two

This game is big. Those who know about the fixing always want choices. For me it's simple: you can't have one foot in and one foot out.

I focus on so many details around the fixing of games, especially when my natural instinct is to follow the money. My target is to earn half a million pounds in the first few months of the new year. This fixture is the biggest risk I'm taking to date.

I'm injured and not even in the squad. No matter, the Boss has my loyalty and trust. He asks me if I'd be interested in winning a game. At first I'm confused, then I realise later he's started to employ players from other teams.

I give him the names of five players. I tell him that they're happy to do the business on our side. But I don't tell this to the five players. The Boss wants our opponents to lose the game and for me to make sure there is a three-goal aggregate: 2-0 at half-time and 1-0 in the second half before seventy minutes. I can't work out why he would want such a score? Then he says he's betting big money on this game and it will be worth £100,000 for our players.

Little does the Boss know, the players are never made aware of the fix. I don't mention a word to them about the potential £25,000 each.

No need for face-to-face meetings. This is my area of expertise. Tan already trusts me to get on with the job. The business is growing bigger, at a rapid rate, which means more risk. All I have to do is confirm the players are in. The opposition players also don't go to a meeting. I don't know their names or who is involved until kick-off.

I drive to the away stadium that afternoon. It's cold, wet and windy; a typical non-league fixture in England in late December.

I take my seat in the stand next to Hunken and give him the heads-up. Straight from the kick-off I notice the opposing team are defending too deep, right on top of their goalkeeper, inviting pressure from us.

I can't work out if their whole back line is in on the fix or only a few? We go route one and take an early lead. Our player latches on to a long punt from our goalkeeper to make it 1-0. The opposition's defence is all over the place, mistake after mistake, skating about like Bambi on ice.

Then Braveheart squanders a gift to double the lead. Our left back whips in a low cross and one of their defenders dives across the box like he's been shot out of a cannon to stop the ball with his hand. There's fixing games but this is a circus. Braveheart's weak penalty is saved. It's still 1-0. We need another before half-time to keep the fix on track.

The home side's players don't even attempt to track our runners. The entire starting eleven must have been at the May Fair Hotel last night. It's a shambles. Anyone watching would think the players haven't slept after a night out on the booze.

One of our players runs forty yards without a challenge in sight and pings a pass to our young winger, who rarely takes a shot at goal.

He goes on a mazy dribble, lashes a speculative shot from outside the box and it flies in. I'm sitting there thinking, 'Surely their keeper must be involved?' It's like watching the perfect fix play out in front of my eyes.

I have a picture in my head of the Boss and Hunken sitting in a back room, like a Chinese remake of *Wolf of Wall Street*, throwing money in the air, laughing and chain-smoking.

So 2-0 at half-time. The fix is on.

We have a talented teenage striker on loan from Championship side. He's on fire today. We launch another attack, same pattern of play. We win the ball at the back, and nobody in the home team breaks any lines to catch up or track back as the ball goes into midfield. This young striker hangs out on the right, goes one-on-one with their left back, who makes no attempt to tackle him, and unleashes a screamer into the top corner of the net to make it three.

The final whistle blows. The fix is in. Game, set and match. If you tried to emulate this exact result again and again, it wouldn't happen.

Full time 3-0. Another £100,000 in the bank.

An emoji arrives from the Boss:

👍... followed by the details of the meeting point to collect the money.

This game makes me realise I need to start doing this on my own, following the same formula.

* * *

It's December. Christmas is rapidly approaching. The club stop paying us for almost two months. Crystal is six months pregnant. The Gaffer has already fined me several times for missing training to go with her to medical appointments. I've just bagged £200k fixing two football matches. I don't need the money.

Sure, I was motivated by the lure of the match-fixing money. But I use the lack of wages and the imminent arrival of my baby daughter to justify to myself why I decide to match-fix. If I do this, it's because we're not getting paid. The other side of it is, even though we aren't getting paid, eventually I'll get paid. I just don't know when. I'm trying to concoct an excuse to account for my actions.

Here's how it works. From pre-season, no non-league club pays you. I sign in pre-season, and I get a cheque for ten grand. I also signed for £850 basic. All I had was the ten grand cheque, deposited in my bank. The following payments of £850 will come when the season starts.

However, as my contract is different from everyone else, the club either holds back my payments or they decide not to pay me. Leading into Fix Three, I'm thinking about the fact that we're not being paid, even though I've got the cheque, but that isn't what we agreed or shook hands and signed on. I can either go to this meeting and get five grand or I can go to the meeting and match-fix and get three years' worth of money.

Or I don't match-fix and wait until we get paid, but then they're going to come back and ask me if I really want to fix games. I don't want to overthink this decision. But I've already taken the pocket money.

It's getting on top of me; there's a lot to deal with. Halfway through that season, I tell the Gaffer I need a break.

I send a text to him on Boxing Day:

'Gaffer, it's Moses, are we training in the evening 2moro? I have a consultation with the midwife at 10.45.'

He doesn't reply.

The 29th is the fix. After that, we're at home on New Year's Day – a 'normal' game. I don't want to play in this 'normal' game.

I text the Gaffer again on New Year's Eve:

'Will it be ok if I take 2mrw off as I have a few family problems and I'm currently not in london?'

This time he replies.

'Ok but you have to accept a fine. Happy new year mate.'

I'm like, fuck it. All right, cool. Let me just continue. This is when I'm thinking, forget football. I'm doing this instead. Before I'd only fixed two games and now I contemplate doing more. But I've got money now. I don't want to play football – I'm doing a lot more off the pitch than I was on it – 80 per cent of my fixing is done after the manager's text.

It's what tips me over the edge in terms of deciding I don't need this shit. When our wages stop, I ease my conscience by thinking if the club aren't even paying us, then why should I be concerned about fixing their games?

Football is not worth more than my unborn daughter. I use that to vindicate even more the decision I made in the beginning, which is: I'm glad I went and did that because look at the way I've been treated.

Even though it's wrong, this is my reasoning for continuing. The Gaffer doesn't care about my family and my daughter because at the end of the day, football isn't football any more. These people will use you until the point where you're just another disposable player. And this is very common in non-league football, even to this day.

Let me be clear, this doesn't mean I'm saying, 'Yo, people, go and match-fix,' because by no means should you do that. But just realise that when you drop down to that level, not everything is rosy.

After I get the manager's texts, I feel anger rise in me. I need time off. Hunken asks me to recruit other players. He wants to know whether I'm interested. With the text from the Gaffer fresh in my mind, I reply, 'I'm in.'

CHAPTER 9

MOSES IN THE MIDDLE

Dom the French disappears in a puff of smoke. The French has committed a match-fixing sin. The day we're paid for the first fix, he took £30,000 and some of the money that was earmarked for the players. His persistence in trying to convince me to take the whole pot led to him not being transparent about his motives. The real value of the game was £150,000.

By has already paid for setting up the meeting. After Dom and I go to the bureau de change in Knightsbridge and then shopping in Selfridges, he tells me he won't be back.

'Moses, man. I'm out. It's my last fixed game.'

The week after that first fix, Hunken summons me to a meeting. 'I can't get hold of Dom.'

I'm like, 'Oh, shit. That's what he was doing!'

'Swaibu, you're going to take over.'

I knew Dom went off to party in France, but I didn't know he was going to run off with the money.

The Boss puts a bounty on his head. Throughout the season

he asks me if I've heard from him or know anything about his whereabouts. It turns out the French has previous. He also walked away with £50k from an earlier fix. He didn't pay the players and took £30k for his middleman part.

Hunken hands me the responsibility of directly handling their money in London. I need to come clean and tell him what happened. He asks if the players got paid. Luckily for me Hunken has information from Dom that none of the other players did the right thing on the night. When I tell him I kept over £100k, he said it's fine. This was his sign of loyalty and truth.

How could I ever imagine that after one game I'd be given so much responsibility? I got the respect of the bosses straight away. They're thinking, *Wait a minute, this guy's good.* Dom the French vanishes and they don't have a UK agent. They lost someone in their organisation because he got greedy.

My first fix was Dom's last rodeo. Maybe he looked at this as his big chance to hit the jackpot. It was a weird situation – this guy, who I knew for less than twenty-four hours, does a runner, coinciding with my first gig, and then I take over from him. Another sliding-doors moment.

The vacant middleman role is up for grabs, and I step in. I'm trying to be a hero. It feels like something I have to do. I watch Hunken build his thing, slow and steady. He knows who to trust, who to bend, who to break. I build a solid relationship with him. He runs the show but I'm his right-hand man.

At first, it's just a job – money in, money out. The cash flows, and I make sure it goes where it's supposed to. Late nights in parking lots, quick exchanges, always on the move. I'm everywhere, making sure the operation runs smoothly. I'm the one who gets it done.

One cash drop-off stands out in my memory. It's a Saturday evening. There's a regular family driving along the motorway in a mid-range car. Mum and Dad are in the front, and there are two kids under the age of seven in the back and a baby seat in the middle. They ain't going to attract the attention of the police. Why would they?

They're heading for London via Newcastle or Manchester or some other city in the north of England. They'll be making a number of stop-offs along the way. Everywhere they stop they pick up money, lots of it. It's money that's going to be washed through casinos and restaurants owned by my match-fixing syndicate.

Money which is going to be paid out to all those players who are going to throw games for me. As big as this match-fixing operation might seem, it's a small part of something bigger. Contrary to belief, match fixing is not a victimless crime. It's the same as anything connected to a complex international criminal organisation. It feeds into the other endeavours they control, from drug peddling to prostitution, human trafficking and political corruption.

And it's all part of a larger flow of the illegal movement of money, and the illegal manipulation and movement of cryptocurrencies. Follow the money.

That Saturday evening I've been waiting for the drop-off longer than usual. I message Hunken:

'Where are they?'

Hunken never asks for my postcode but one thing is guaranteed: the moment the fix comes in and money has been received through the platform, the Boss goes out of his way to make sure the payment lands on time.

Not once is there a delay, apart from tonight. I know a courier is coming from Manchester but I have no idea it will be a man and his family.

I meet the car on Tower Bridge, one of London's most iconic tourist attractions. The Shard looms large behind us. It's a cinematic scene with a humdrum cast. The dad gets out, opens the boot and takes out a nondescript holdall. I know there's £25k inside. He doesn't make eye contact, hands me the bag and shuts the boot. No words are spoken. I catch the eyes of the kids who smile back at me.

Why would the Boss send these people to meet me? Then I realise, it's all part of a bigger and wider web. This ordinary-looking family handle the money and they'll never get stopped or searched. They're dressed like actors and it's the perfect play.

The dad gives me a thumbs up, hops back into his car and drives off, disappearing into the tourist traffic, the traditional red buses and black cabs of central London.

My Bosses are always eager to pay out on a successful fix. Unlike my club's erratic payment process, I always know the match-fixing money's coming, usually within twenty-four hours. It's guaranteed. Sometimes, if it's less than £25k, the money arrives on the same day.

If there's ever a hitch, they might chuck in an extra grand or £500. Just for the inconvenience.

Weeks pass. The game keeps going. The stakes get higher. Two more matches are ours, and no one notices. No one questions it. A 3-0 away win that shouldn't have happened. But I control it all. And then I realise what I'm really doing. This isn't just fixing games. We're building something bigger. I know the risks, but I'm in too deep now.

* * *

In the long gap between my first and second fixes, I don't really need to rig a game. That was the easiest part. I made a lot of money from the first fix and they recruited me to take over from Dom the French.

On top of that, there's the margins. If I'm working more off the pitch, I'm not going to make 100 grand, but I can book a hotel, five grand. They return my deposit, two grand. I meet a player, three grand. I need to bring them together, four grand. If there's a successful fix, I'll get eight grand. I'm getting bits and bobs of cash all the way along. Every action has a payment attached to it. I have my wages, if you want to call it that, but then I also share the liquidity of the syndicate's investments.

On average I'm pulling in around £10k a month just doing odd jobs: driving around, booking rooms, speaking to players, making sure I'm also doing my homework. I ask a lot of questions: 'Look, Boss. Why can't we put on a bet tonight?' He says, 'No, there's no live game. Let's wait until we do it for this team.' He has an aggregate of players that he knows directly and more importantly people that are involved in the fix. What I quickly realise is that he is recruiting other people like Moses Swaibu.

When the Boss speaks to me on Skype, he'll say, 'OK, so what have you done today? How can we get to this player?' I'll ask him to give me more time and he'll say, 'Fine, but make sure by this date you have done X, Y and Z.'

At an anonymous Chinese restaurant in Dalston, the cash is stacked and bundled and stored in a back room. I can go in there any time of the day or night and say, I want to take out

100 grand of my money. I don't want that money at home. I basically use the Chinese takeaway as a savings bank.

* * *

Here's how the distribution money tree goes down.

Every fixed match has a window of twenty-four hours, so whether a match is fixed on a Tuesday or a Saturday – it can be afternoon or evening – they know there's a significant time difference between Europe and China and that the markets are delayed.

A prime example: if a match is fixed on a Saturday, 3pm kick-off, you will receive the cash on Monday. The cash must be laundered through their businesses. Any game worth over £100,000 in payouts to players goes via the casino. Anything under £100,000 is washed locally via takeaways and restaurants across London. In the beginning I don't quite understand. The money always arrives in GB sterling currency, but they place spread bets in multiple monetary regions. Therefore, they need the time delay to secure any guarantees. I'm only made aware of this when I ask Hunken more and more questions.

The syndicate also needs to carefully control the movement of funds. Players earning tens of thousands will raise suspicions. When I collect the money, Hunken always tells me to pay the players every twenty-four hours so I can understand the system. There will also be times when the markets are not always good. For example, due to the delay midweek they won't get big returns because there isn't a big enough open market and players are always paid less.

After a while it's easy to get the hang of. Nobody handling or giving me the money ever makes eye contact. The money can't stay still, it always has to keep moving. Once you handle a few drops and get a consistent flow, it's like going to the gym. Drop your bag in your locker, come out, get changed and go to training. That's the mentality I maintain to keep myself sane. I buy an electric money counter which helps a lot. I always go over a count three or four times and use up thousands of rubber bands bundling up the cash.

Central London is the best distribution area where I can easily blend in. Dave, our car rental guy, always lets me take the white, supercharged Range Rover. Plus, I have an Aston Martin Cygnet 1.33 Edition city car as a day-to-day runaround. Every time I drive the Range Rover into the city, I make sure I wear my Bromley tracksuit to avoid attracting unwanted attention. I keep my gym clothes in a sports bag in the boot and the money in a similar-looking holdall. If I was stopped, I can say I'm coming back from training or a game or going to a meeting. It never happens.

I build up a mini mountain of cash in Dalston. Every note I make is tucked away at the back of that Chinese takeaway. The Aston Martin smart car is subtle. I park it on a side street and make a specific order to the woman at the counter. When they bring me my bags of food it's really cash. She never once makes eye contact.

When I'm collecting my own money – usually around closing time – I go into the back of the Chinese. I open a locked door that looks like a toilet or a storage cupboard. The money is stacked up to my torso and I'm 6ft 3in. I bundle it up with rubber bands and seal it with cling film. It makes me paranoid. Did my neighbour see me coming home? Despite the paranoia, I like the work. I'm making fast money – forty-five and ninety minutes. It's addictive and even more addictive is the power that comes from the responsibility.

Late night in London's East End is the most dangerous time for my cash runs. I don't know the area well. But everything runs like clockwork.

Distribution, or distro, is the most interesting part of the job. Every time I get the money – £100k, £200k, £300k – I believe it's a test. I know it because the Boss goes quiet, as does Hunken.

The Boss loves an emoji. His favourite is ☆ or a thumbs up 👍 followed by, 'Players happy?' I always reply 👍 yes ☆ followed by his last reply. He spells my name wrong. 'Swabo! Remember greedy man no see properly!'

Every time I meet a player or a group of players when they have the money in their hands, I can see New Year's Eve fireworks lighting up their eyes. I once had that same look.

Hunken books a hotel room, usually at the May Fair, and sets up a video call on his laptop with the Boss, so he can see and speak to the players. The players are enthusiastic to do more. I stand next to Hunken as they sit listening to the Chinese voice on the other end of the line, on the other side of the world, like they've received a call from God, sending them on another Holy mission. The players have heard of me but never met me in person. The ones who know I'm part of the criminal syndicate call me Jon Gotti.

Dalston and Mayfair feel like Gotham City to me. London is a special place when it's lit up at night. This is plain sailing, a total breeze. Nothing goes wrong once. That's when you're at your most vulnerable. You dive deeper, take more risks. One night I take home half a million pounds just to see what it feels like.

* * *

The Four Ps is my know-your-player format. Any approach or agreement I make and someone says, yes, they're in or it's a maybe, I ask myself if I can tick these four boxes in my head. Then we have the perfect fix.

Persistence: it's sexy and sophisticated, not an annoyance. In any given season there are so many variables, with players' injuries, suspensions, inconsistent form or being out of favour with the manager. This is what leads me towards acquiring a goalkeeper in the end. The last line of defence is the hardest person to get to fix anything on the pitch. He's the Golden Goose of the whole fix.

Purity: I measure how pure a player is. Don't get me wrong, the players love football, hence the reason they play, but most players at that level all have a price. How much do they cost? If I give a player £500 pocket money, will he say yes or no if he's on £250 a week at his club? Versus a player on £500 a week being given £2,500 just to attend a meeting. Who's going to say no to that? For only having to sit down and listen to a plan they can always opt out of?

Persuasion: this is my all-time favourite. Here comes the villain in any given movie. Nothing's ever enough; the lure of the bright lights, of holidays and fast cars. More money and the buzz of knowing how important you are to the whole operation. Every footballer loves a good night out or an expensive drink. Mayfair is a hotbed of wealth and privileged good times. Fine dining, expensive champagne, beautiful women and swanky nightclubs. The right-hand man, Hunken, seals every deal. He is young, elegant, smart and has the perfect glasses. How can you say no to someone so sure? His voice is soft and he smells like he bathes in Harrods.

Perfection: as the big boss will always say, 'Good business!' in his broken Chinese-English. It is the master plan played out like an opera performance. Perfection is our standing ovation. When the money comes in, the emoji he uses on Telegram is a simple thumbs up 👍 in yellow. Every box is ticked, ready for the next game and the next fix.

* * *

I want to be Hunken. And I'll tell you why. I love the way he dresses. I love his style. I love his calmness.

When I say love, I'm attracted to it. Not in a sexual way, but it's like, damn, man, I want to be him. I want to be that guy. There's the flash guy, the John Gottis or the Pablo Escobars of the criminal world. Then there's this villain. He's the brains. He's the Cali Cartel. He's the machine. He never raises his voice, never lowers it. He always speaks in one measured tone. Total control.

He can be standing in front of you and the last thing you'll think is he's part of an international organised crime group. I see the Boss in a lot of these iconic villains. He may be only five foot two, he smokes, he shouts, he curses, he threatens. If the boss ever stepped aside or got taken out, Hunken's the real driving force.

I spent the most time with Hunken, I watch him in action and I learn from him. I see him speaking to people in that warm, relaxing tone. The voice of reassurance.

You can listen to Hunken before you go to bed and his voice would put you to sleep.

It's Beauty and the Beast. Hunken's the beauty, the Boss is

the beast. Ultimately the Beast and the Beauty are just flipping burgers, playing with this ball of fire. They're two sides of the same coin. It's the two sides of the human psyche, the Jekyll and Hyde in everyone.

* * *

In 2012, the only betting-related activity I'm familiar with is friends losing money on roulette machines. The Boss has created his own gambling platform. I'm always curious why we were paid so much for the first fix. I ask Hunken. He explains that the Eastbourne Borough–Bromley game is the first match the syndicate fixed in England, so the market was high. The market was high enough for a predicted scoreline, one where they had an illegal market with thousands of people across Asia staking odds.

The more influence the Boss obtains in the Conference South – by now he has half the teams in the league in his pocket – it brings down the odds for us and increases the revenue for him. I'm aware of this and I want more money. I've gone from £100k+ down to £15/25k per game. The maths, my specialist subject, doesn't add up. To put this into perspective, for every game that's fixed, let's say they make £1 million and they pay us between £15k and £25k. I'm taking the biggest risk but only getting 2.5 per cent. Then Hunken explains the costs to me. There is a percentage for everything: the mules, the distro, the bank accounts, the exchange rate, even down to the staff at the restaurants. 'Moses, don't be greedy,' he says. 'Your time is coming, Swaibo.' But I'm not buying any of it. I do some simple mental arithmetic. These guys have ten teams. One team is worth £1 million. Surely ten teams are £10 million?

Then I begin to realise I'm wrong. Everything is based on the odds and the aggregate. If a player gets booked or sent off, the payout is £7–10k, which is so much easier. If your team concedes at a specific time, that's £5–10k. Once the bets are spread on a handicap, the money starts to make sense.

Just like everyone else, I have the idea that match fixing means to lose or throw a game. In fact, it means the opposite. Match manipulation and fixing are the same thing. There are more red cards and bookings and scorelines on specific minutes that year than there are matches being fixed. The media and football gatekeepers talk in a complex, ignorant way that conditions your mind into thinking they're correct 99.9 per cent of the time. In reality, it's all part of one big family tree. To fix a game and manipulate a game is the same thing.

Some players spend half a season out suspended at key moments, missing the odd game and training session to give the team due to fix that Tuesday or Saturday an advantage. All that team needs to do is score or concede at specific times. I'm just scratching the surface of the puzzle. I spend days online seeing if anyone has figured this stuff out and I can't find a thing. All I see is how much is being spent trying to cure the thing – hundreds of millions of pounds on a global scale. What makes things even more complex is that nobody is ever arrested or gets lengthy jail time.

Sometimes I meet Hunken and he says, 'Moses, watch the magic happen.' All you need is the Wi-Fi password at the May Fair Hotel.

He's always in contact with people on the ground watching the game and a platform that has thousands of users and numbers on display like the stock exchange. I've never in my life seen so many numbers and zeros. An ever-changing digital display of Chinese symbols and numbers, the odds on the market moving up and down in red and green lights. It's like those dummy trading accounts when you convert the currencies and the demo account tells you that you have £100 million. But this is all happening in front of my eyes.

When the results come in, we head down to the hotel bar then on to the Palm Beach Casino on Berkeley Street. Hunken not once breaks out of character. He tells me he would never gamble. 'I see what it does to humans,' he says. But his boss is his boss, so we must follow the rules. That's his culture. Me and Hunken become close. Every day he offers me more support and mentors me about the business. He says that the Boss is a nice guy when he's winning but a monster when he loses.

One time they ask me to book an apartment – well before the days of Airbnb. I get £2k for every booking I make. The rooms per night range from £300–500, with a £500 deposit. They get bored holding meetings at the May Fair Hotel. On this occasion, I end up losing the £500 deposit. I book a non-smoking room forgetting about the Boss's dirty 100-a-day habit. The hotel emails me with pictures of the damages to the room. The Boss has been putting cigarettes out on the floor. It looks like he's been shooting at the floor with a gun; there are literally 100 black marks. It's the first time I see Hunken laugh. His laugh is awkward. I can tell he's not used to humour. He lowers his head and cackles a few times, then snorts like a pig. It's strange but funny at the same time.

* * *

To me, Hunken is the real MVP. The maverick. The Incredible Hunk. If you ever need anything or want someone who understands the business, Hunken is your man.

Working with Hunken fills me with confidence. Despite only being in his early twenties, he's the underboss of one of the biggest criminal networks in the world. He's studying mathematics and politics at university. He has a baby face and glasses. Everything he does is smooth. When he speaks, you listen. The Boss relies on him in ways that surprise me. Hunken is the face of the business and the Boss is the ultimate Godfather. Dan the Don.

I always voice my concerns to Hunken. On days when the Boss doesn't take my advice, places bets on teams and the fix doesn't work out the way he expects, he always requests to speak to me. He sends me irate messages on Telegram with abusive emojis. Hunken simply says, 'Boss is angry, give him a day or a week. He'll calm down!' I let it pass.

He says, 'Swabo, you want more money? I need you to find the players that fucked me!'

What he doesn't realise is that this is above my pay grade. After my first £100k I ask him how I can do that again. The Boss tells Hunken to speak with me. He tells me, 'Moses, you'll become a millionaire one day. Boss wants you to expand. He really likes you. At the end of the year, he will plan a trip for all of us, if the fixes are successful.'

Throughout the year of match fixing, Hunken not only helps me understand the business, a part of me also thinks he's being trained to take over. The Boss is getting older and angrier. Things are going wrong weekly rather than monthly. Players stop caring and fix games in a shambolic fashion, potentially jeopardising the whole operation.

As for Hunken, he remains calm at all times.

CHAPTER 10

HOW TO FIX A FOOTBALL MATCH

After I get the New Year's Eve text from the Gaffer, I decide to take the fixing to a new level. I play my aces, enlist another player and expand the capacity. I take on more responsibility. Plus, I tell Michael 'Boats' Boateng for the first time the truth about match fixing and the control I have within it.

The state of play is always for me to organise. Planning games becomes like a cup final, the detail that goes into the multiplicity of outcomes. Everything in a fixed game has to make sense. For all the computers and technology, data and cameras in the world, this stage had to play out with the precision of a classical orchestra.

If we lose, it has to be credible. If we win, it has to be thrilling. If we draw, it has to be convincing. I consider every eventuality and everything that can go wrong.

Imagine if this level of detail is replicated across the whole business? First, we have a meeting, but before the meeting every person involved is playing their own game, with key performance indicators, some big, some small. You're judging the elements and events of risk as they happen. We're playing a different game. The game we play is football magic. Nobody but us knows the outcome.

The next six fixed games are chaotic, gung-ho, kamikaze football.

* * *

Fix Three

When we reach this game, I've become one of the main men in the organisation. The Boss has me seeking out players, learning the business and managing meetings. The business (match fixing) has already been presented to some of the opposition players around the time of our first fix. The Boss wants market share and a complete takeover of the league. I don't meet any of the other side's players prior to the game. Another player takes care of that side of things as he has a mutual friend at our Fix Three opponents.

Boss says if I can bring in five players from each team he'll make it worth my while. Even though our players messed up the first game, this time round I tell them, 'Don't fix the game, just turn up to the meeting and get some pocket money.'

I'll do the business on the pitch as I can control the scoreline. I'll give them some money on the backend when the fix comes in. There's no risk for their involvement. Hunken sets up a Skype call on his laptop. The Boss says, 'Swaibo, tell the players I want one goal, either half.' Our opponents open the scoring in the first half and we equalise in the second. But the game has to end in a draw.

This will be the first fixed draw. It sounds simple, but it's always easier to lose a game. He gives the opposition team their lucky number: £50,000 for the team, £10,000 per man. Before the Boss leaves the call he says, 'Swaibo, make sure it happens.' 'OK!' The call ends. I take my £5,000 pocket money.

The atmosphere is strange. During the game, I keep looking towards Hunken to see where he's sitting. I spot him right in front of our fans.

I know what needs to be done. The guy from the other team looks excited, wide-eyed. We concede just before half-time. It's more subtle, nothing outrageous. It's not directly my fault but I can see that my fellow centre back's positioning is off. I drift towards the back post leaving the penalty area as wide open as a whale's mouth. 1-0. My job for the fix is done.

I switch back to playing normally, commanding the defence, winning my headers. Our players, who fucked up the first fix by attacking too much, are now doing what they should have done in the first fix. They keep possession and see out the half. Hayes stop pressing high and allow us to play keep-ball. The game is worth £100,000 for both teams. If this is successful, my teammates will want in again.

The second half kicks off. An opposing player tells me explicitly on the pitch for us to attack and score quickly so we can all revert to playing normal. We end up scoring with our first attack. 1-1. The fix is in.

For the rest of the game their players barely make any runs. And if they do it's up blind alleys, down dead ends. I know they have the trust of the player that they're paying off. At corners and set pieces they say to me, 'You're the guy that's making a killing innit?'

I nod my head and continue playing. I don't have the same

emotions that I did against Eastbourne. It's quickly become normalised and, worse, easy.

The game finishes 1-1. We all shake hands, and the player says to me, 'See you next time.'

My own players tell me to meet them in the car park. I remind them that without me this doesn't happen and give them each a couple of grand. No complaints this time. That night I meet Hunken to discuss the next game. Boss sends the usual thumbs up emoji. The next morning, I go and collect £100,000, and pocket fifty. I meet the player from that day's opponents in central London, hand him his cut and hop back in my car.

* * *

Fix Four

Have you heard the classic football cliché, 'a game of two halves'? It definitely applies here. We need to draw the first half and win the second. These are the direct instructions I receive from the Boss. Both teams, or at least two players on each team, are aware of these instructions.

Boss begins to slip up. I discover that other teams are being manipulated by the syndicate. No more face-to-face meetings. He's gaining market share but what does this mean for me? I'm making more money off the pitch than I am on it.

Organising and analysing comes at a higher price. Many evenings I sit with the Boss and Hunken explaining to them the current status of the league. Any recommendations I give comes from my insider knowledge. I use my network of players – with their own contacts within the game – to keep me informed of what's happening and how a team are doing, a form guide of sorts. I feed this back to the Boss who values my opinion.

There are times when the odd fix or predicted scoreline doesn't work in his favour. He wants me to sort it out and get information. For doing this I can make anything from £25–50k a month. It doesn't happen often, but when players promise games and don't deliver, I doubly make sure our games do deliver. I have the power to influence even the Boss and advise him if the fix is a good or a bad idea.

As the game approaches, the money is in place. Hunken has his match tickets. The pitch is in shocking condition, like a muddy ice rink. I can tell the other team want this fix to happen quickly. They start off at a high tempo, pressing us back. It's the first fixed game where we are all introduced via Telegram in a group chat. My pseudonym is the mafioso legend Jon Gotti. The players discuss precisely what we'll do and when. In the opening twenty minutes, I try and give them an advantage to score. The ball is played over the top, and I intentionally slip, but the striker misses an easy chance.

Then they do the same again. A route-one long ball, straight down the middle. The ball bounces directly in front of our defence, nobody attempts to head it clear and they take full advantage. 1-0.

Then one of their defenders steps off our attacker at the edge of the box and allows him to equalise: 1-1.

It all plays out pitch perfect. Once the successful fix is delivered on a plate, it will be worth £25,000 for five players – at least to the Boss's knowledge.

The team are buzzing in the changing room at half-time. We're back in top form and make it 2-1 shortly after half-time. Funny thing about this goal is that the scorer doesn't want in on any of the fixes, but that goal could have earned him a £5k bonus.

It's a war of attrition in shocking conditions. Both teams power through the mud, white chalk from the linings of the pitch all over our kit as we throw ourselves into last-ditch slide tackles. Our keeper is playing a blinder to maintain our lead. Right up until the ninetieth minute we still need a win. I'm not privy to their winnings but I can see and hear the urgency from their team and defenders urging them on to score. Suddenly it's 2-2.

Into time added on and we desperately need a winner. They defend deeper and deeper. I can sense something is coming. One of their defenders sticks his foot out and gives away a penalty. You could have seen that coming from outer space. I remember kneeling down thinking if Braveheart takes the penalty, we're going to miss. The game is tied at 2-2. Here it comes, the last kick of the game. He steps up and strikes the ball beautifully with the instep of his right boot and it flashes in off the post. The keeper dives the right way but has absolutely no chance.

2-3. The fix is in. Inadvertently Braveheart saves the day.

* * *

12 March 2013 – Barcelona 4-0 Milan (win 4-2 on aggregate)
UEFA Champions League Round of 16
Camp Nou
Attendance: 96,000
16 March 2013 – Billericay Town 1-2 Welling United
National League N/S
New Lodge
Attendance: 408

Betting experts flag up the fact that more than £1 million is staked on this game – a bigger market than a Champions League match involving Barcelona played in the same week. The vast sums are gambled on the Asian betting exchanges, despite only 408 spectators attending the game.

* * *

The Gaffer calls me: 'We need you to play on Saturday.' I say, 'We're having a baby.'

He replies, 'Yeah, but you can still make it in time for the birth.' It's a three o'clock kick-off. Crystal is getting induced.

I say, 'Gaffer, that doesn't make sense.'

Football is not worth more than my daughter.

My beautiful daughter Taliya Swaibu is born on 30 March 2013. Initially, my relationship with Crystal, my childhood sweetheart, is fantastic. We're so happy and excited to become first-time parents. Taliya's scheduled late arrival means we're already settled into family life. Crystal asks me why I'm considering retirement. I tell her I've lost the will and hunger. She hasn't a clue what I've been up to.

The day Taliya is born, everything stops. For the first time in years, my thoughts are clear. I'm holding this little human baby, feeling her tiny hands, and I realise I'm not living for myself any more. I don't know what kind of world I'm bringing her into, but this isn't the one I want for her. It's the first crack in the wall. The first real doubt.

She's born at the height of my match fixing. It's those months, March and April 2013, when I'm in the middle of my most intense run of fixed games. My relationship with Crystal starts disintegrating because of who I am, my secret line of work.

It reaches a point where I don't care about anything else but getting to the money by any means necessary.

I'm getting colder and harder than ever. I'm using my newborn daughter to justify what I'm doing. After the club stop paying us, I make excuses to fix. The worst thing is that I start believing my own spin and I'm even asking questions of Tan that I shouldn't be asking.

I say to him, 'Boss, I need more money. I want to get paid. I'm all in.'

I've turned into a machine. And deep down I'm thinking, this is wrong. It's like I'm tapping into my dad's attributes of abandonment, self-sabotage, procrastination. But I'm a survivor. I've done this shit on my own. That instinct kicks in again. I don't need anyone. I've got myself. Sink or swim. It's lying repressed within me and it all came bubbling to the surface when I embarked on this criminal escapade.

It's not about money any more. There's only so much you can physically acquire before you think, *What the fuck am I going to do with this?*

But with power, it's a case of how long is a piece of string? That power will mess you up in ways that you can never imagine. I don't think with power there's an in-between. When you consider powerful people in the world, at each major stage in their life they have to make difficult decisions. It's what comes with having power. And in those decisions, you must figure out, are they the right decisions or are they the wrong decisions? Regardless, you have to stand by those choices. You can't be powerful and admit guilt.

* * *

Fix Five

The scene is set. Me and Hunken board a train from London Waterloo for the evening fixture. We sit in a first-class carriage for privacy and have a revealing conversation about his background and upbringing.

'Why do you do this?' I ask him.

'Moses, I was born into this family. This is my life and this is our culture. I'm sure you understand this.'

He repeats the question back to me and I reply, 'When I make my first million, I'm out.'

The naive motivations I once had of being free, surviving, football saving my life and everything else has gone out of the window.

Now I want the same power and control as Hunken. He is slowly starting to become my evil best friend. I'm Pinky and he's Brain, my new right-hand man. We arrive at the ground, I get him his ticket and he sits in the empty stand. That night he is the first spectator in the stadium a few hours before kick-off. He puts his hood up and waves me off like a proud father.

The Boss wants us to lose by a two-goal deficit. By now I'm an experienced fixer, the pressure is off. I have learned and mastered what to do to control the whole team and predict scorelines on my own. Ten minutes before kick-off I receive a Telegram message from The Boss, 'swaibo' followed by a thumbs up emoji.

This usually means the bets are on, everything's in place. We walk out on to the pitch. I shoot a glance towards Hunken in the stand and he nods. I've already told the other players who know about the fix to wave to that section of the crowd. The fixes became much easier. I have the full trust of the syndicate. No more meetings with players sitting on a king-size bed, like attentive school kids, listening to Headmaster Tan on a Skype call.

This is how it works now: I give the Boss my word on the fixed games and outcomes. Nothing ever goes wrong. I tell him we have five players. He guarantees the fees for each fix: £25,000 for standard games, £100,000+ if there are added incentives like exact-timed goals or yellow or red cards.

We start brightly and take the lead straight from the kick-off. The ball is sprayed out wide left and is played into our striker, who takes a pot shot from outside the box with his weaker foot and it flies into the top corner. Seventeen seconds gone: 1-0 to us.

This isn't part of the plan. The Boss's bets hinge on specific aggregates: if we score first, we have to concede enough goals to hit a 3-1 scoreline. Every goal we score means recalculating the fix, adjusting the margins. If we get this wrong, the markets will collapse, and the syndicate could lose millions.

When we score I have to maintain a muted response. If I celebrate, the syndicate will know the match isn't fixed. I'm always last to run and pat everyone on the back.

I play a short pass into Braveheart knowing he hasn't checked his shoulders. I spot the interception happen before I even play the ball. Staines accept the gift and play the ball into the box. A wild effort from their centre forward misses the target.

We hit them on the counter-attack and an opposing defender chops our man in the box. Penalty. I pray that Braveheart misses, which he does. But this game is not going well. What starts off as a simple task quickly turns into mission impossible. None of their players are compromised and we look like we're going to score every time we go forward.

The penalty save alters the entire momentum of the game. I go up for a corner, the ball breaks out wide right. As it's about to go out of play, I attempt a flashy back heel that doesn't come off.

They hit us on the break and our right back passes back to the keeper, the worst player in our team with the ball at his feet. He plays a lazy pass to our centre back who tries a Cruyff turn and loses the ball. I'm still jogging back from my failed back heel – I'm not exactly busting a gut – so there's a huge gap in the middle of our defence. One, two, three passes and they make it 1-1.

Welcome to non-league football. You couldn't make this up if you tried. When that goal hits the back of the net, the first thing I say is, 'That's worth at least a few thousand!' They're right back in the game.

Half-time in the changing room, I blame both our right and centre backs for not clearing their lines. My fake grilling is designed to deflect suspicion away from me. I was halfway up the pitch but nobody wants to challenge why I attempted an ambitious back heel. They could easily argue it was a first phase mistake. As I look round the changing room everyone has their heads down. We lack character and belief. Even Braveheart looks worn out, still reeling from his penalty miss.

I think about the vulnerability of lower-level players, plying their trade near the bottom of the football ladder. The evenings and nights of planning that went into these fixed games became like therapy sessions. Hour upon hour we went into forensic detail about the human mind and the links to betting.

'What does everyone need, Swaibu?'

'Follow the money, boss!'

'Then tell me how these players think, what they eat, what motivates them? What's their Achilles heel? Think beyond the game, Swaibo.' He starts to examine society and asks me why Black people always want to spend money. His favourite catchphrase is, 'Greedy man no see properly. You will learn, Swaibo.' He's like some kind of match-fixing Yoda.

I sit there and listen like I'm in some warped classroom. He's right – with all this money I'm getting, I don't want to be seen or heard in case I raise suspicions. This is the perfect crime, high rewards and low risk. Hunken has a physical tic of adjusting his glasses when the Boss speaks. I'm not sure if it's a signal or him feeling uncomfortable. As Boss says again, 'Hunken is very smart for a reason, Swaibo. Make money, don't spend money.'

I look round the changing room that evening, with the Boss's words echoing in my head and know I must do better in the second half. My team is weak and our opponents can smell blood.

Time begins to run out. I need something to happen ASAP. Thirty minutes left to play. We start defending deeper and deeper. My centre back partner is young and inexperienced. He loves taking the ball and stepping out of defence into midfield. His youthful enthusiasm coughs up possession, they send a low pass-cum-cross into our box, but we're all asleep at the wheel. No one even attempts a tackle.

2-1. One more goal to keep the fix on track.

By now I begin to understand sometimes fixing happens without even having to do anything audacious. It's a bad night for the team in addition to some terrible individual performances.

I get stranded out in the left back position. I try a half-hearted clearance which ricochets off an opposition player who feeds a through ball directly to their striker for a first-time finish. 3-1.

The fix comes in on the eightieth minute. Staines win the game and we head into the changing room. The deafening silence is interrupted by the Gaffer saying, 'Just go home! That was shocking.'

I skip having a shower, meet Hunken at the gate and we take a train back to London. I don't know what to feel. Every fix feels like a mission. I'm a sniper in a war, killing parts of football. My reward is more money, more power, more respect.

But the mission has turned into a ticking time-bomb. It's pandemonium. This is where I start to feel out of control, the downward spiral begins and the pressure intensifies. I know at any moment something can go wrong. But when you're going full throttle, there's no time to stop and you can't look back.

On the train back to London, me and Hunken sit mostly in silence. I'm deep in thought. £300,000 in cash: banked. I'm like a junkie, craving my next fix.

* * *

Fix Six

I become greedy for more. I don't want to share any profits with the cowards. I've got my eyes set on £2 million. I go into games like an army general, block out the external noise and get the job done. Every plan needs me to deliver.

The instruction from the Boss is to concede three goals as quickly as possible then play normally. It's too far for Hunken to travel so for the first time he doesn't watch the match live or report back.

In my pre-match team talk out on the pitch, I tell the squad, 'Look, we're playing away so let's keep it tight in the first half.' I make sure the fans also hear these tactics. I don't want anyone to attack as we've been leaking goals too early in recent matches. The idea is to throw them off the scent. Vocalising this approach makes it easier for me to make mistakes.

The original players who were in on the first fix begin to throw me sour looks. They know I'm taking all the money, but they can't do or say anything about it. I know their dirty little secret and they know my true identity. The mysterious phantom the players nickname 'The Ghost'.

The rumour going round the league is that 'The Ghost' is the main fixer who controls the outcome of games. Nobody bar a select few know who I am and what I'm capable of doing. I become the enigmatic Zorro of the league. The Joker. The masked fixer.

* * *

I decide to bring another player into the shadowy world of 'The Ghost'. He's the first player outside of the ones that were on board for the first fix.

'Bro, I have something to tell you. I just need you in or out. A simple yes or no.'

'Moses, I already know. Why did you keep it from me this long?'

He gets involved because he also isn't being paid, and this is a way for me to leverage my proposition.

He isn't like the others. I buy his heart and soul for £25,000. It's the first time I split the money and pay someone.

I gave him very specific instructions for Fix Six. We needed to concede in the last ten minutes.

The ball bounced into our six-yard box and he cleared it off the line. The reflex reaction of a footballer. But he's not thinking about the fix. That was when I was summoned by the Boss. Now this player has to make amends for his mistake.

I say to him, 'Bro, you've cost me money, so the next time you have to do what he says,' and that's why going into the next game, he did what he did.

CHAPTER 11

TAN'S BABY

The fixing starts getting far more complicated. There's a lot more detail going into it. Plus, there isn't a live betting market on every game.

During that season, they can only put on bets that are equivalent to where the market is at that moment in time. Towards the back end of the season, it's full-on, gung-ho. Everything speeds up, intensifies and is condensed into a period of three months – February, March and April.

Between the first fix and playing normal games, I spend my time figuring out ways I can run the whole operation myself. I don't really know how to do it because we're just one team.

With the next game, Fix Seven, those players were already incentivised by the Boss. I don't know this in advance. He just says, you're playing such and such tomorrow, we're having a meeting. When we arrive at the May Fair Hotel, we meet some players from the other team – opponents coming face to face for the first time pre-match.

It's confirmation – as if it is needed – that I'm caught in a spider's web of corruption and deceit involving multiple clubs and players.

For all I know, I could have been walking in the front lobby doors at the May Fair Hotel to hook up with Tan and Hunken, and another Moses Swaibu is coming out the other side, leaving a meeting. Hunken and the Boss are hosting meetings all the time with many different players. They're the puppeteers, directing the marionettes from a hotel room in the heart of London.

This is when I start to lose control. It's the first time I realise other teams are fixing. Players from different teams come and go, like actors rehearsing their roles in a bizarre theatrical performance. Curtain due to go up on the show at 3pm tomorrow.

It's where it begins to feel strange for me, going into a game knowing full well what the outcome will be, with my teammates oblivious. I know *my* outcome, but I don't always know what the 'The Ghost' in the opposition team has agreed to do at *his* May Fair Hotel meeting.

* * *

Fix Seven

Every game so far has played out like a dream. Now the Boss wants to up the ante, increase the stakes. He wants an even riskier fixture. He confides in me that he wants millions back for this game. By now I have the power of leverage. This will be the first time a game will be fixed twice with the same team. However, something doesn't feel right. My mask is slipping. This is the game when I know I've lost control.

The Friday evening before the game, we meet in the May Fair Hotel. For the first time, two teams come together to discuss the details of the fix. It shows me that the Boss is openly taking over the whole league. Up until this point, everything is subtle.

This is Dan Tan's baby. It's the perfect fix because you have two teams specifically saying, I'm going to get sent off at this exact moment. This is how we're going to do it. When I get sent off, I'm going to head-butt you. Then you're going to push me in the face. I'll foul you at this point and give away a penalty. I'm going to score, so you mark this side. It is meticulously choreographed. We're about to stage a theatrical performance with a cast of actors.

I've never fixed a game like this before. I figured out how to do it myself, but this is the first time that players on the opposing team know I'm involved. Nobody knows or says a word or even considers speaking about games being fixed.

One midweek evening at training, I see a letter from the FA pinned to the noticeboard: 'Be aware of gambling rules and match manipulations.' It's warning teams in the Conference South about their conduct. Suspicious betting patterns are confusing the markets. I'm thinking, *Imagine the FA knew how much of this is going on.* I'm not worried. What can they prove?

I begin to understand more and more the motivation of the players I've recruited. Or, should I say, corrupted. Fixing games becomes part of the culture of the league. Many senior players are at the tail end of their football careers, with day jobs, families to feed, mortgages to pay. Fixing provides them with a better car, a family holiday abroad or disposable cash.

The white players, who mostly work in construction, want one-off games and advance odds so they can stick on a bet. Nobody is a career criminal so you can see mistakes happening before they happen.

I tell the Boss, 'Don't listen to these players. I'm hearing a few are going into the bookies to bet on games.' In the beginning the bookmakers paid out. As we approach the end of the season, more and more players want in. Clubs at the lower level never pay players during the summer. There are also other managers withholding payments and making fake threats about players' wages. I used fixing as an excuse to say a big 'fuck you!' to the league and my manager.

One thing is for sure, I need to bring someone new into my world of smoke and mirrors, someone I can trust not to snitch. I have over half a million pounds in cash in Dalston. If I speak of this, I also need to show and tell. But one thing greed will do is make your mind run at 100mph. That day I make my biggest mistake.

The Boss wants to see new faces. Other teams fucking up means he begins to have trust issues, even with me. His trust and loyalty turns sour. After his cultural lessons on colour and race he stops trusting Black players. The white players are his new truth tellers and his new generals. He specifically says to me, 'Swaibo, if I don't see a new face, no more match fixing or money.'

I have so much money saved I decide to ask him if I can leave the cash at one of the stash restaurants. He says as long as I come to collect it, the money is mine and available at any time.

At the May Fair Hotel pre-fix meeting, a player from the other team brings along his five agreed fixers while I have my one. The Boss offers me a vote of confidence, 'Swaibo, that's OK, I know those players of yours are too scared and they are cowards, but I still trust you!' Our player glances at me like he's about to win the lottery.

If we pull this off, it will be a daring heist. Going into that game feels like we're gonna do a smash and grab. This is blatant, with no interest in who's watching or the potential risks. It's a circus, but it's an incredible buzz to know that it's eminently achievable.

It shows what is possible; that you can manipulate every and any game you want to. If there's a will, there's a way. The power in this is almost godlike. We're using people as pawns in our game.

Hunken dials into Skype on his laptop. The Boss kicks off the meeting saying he needs tomorrow's game to finish 4-0 to our opponents. We must concede three goals in the first fifteen minutes of the first half. This is next to impossible. The £25,000 I'm giving our player has a new incentive. The Boss says, 'For correct score I will give Swaibo £150,000 and the opposition players £50,000.'

I have butterflies in my stomach, swiftly followed by a feeling of being overwhelmed. It's the biggest fix to date.

I scan the room. The players are sitting around like newborn puppies about to have their first meal of the day. Boss asks me to articulate the plan.

Every time they go long, we defend deeper than ever. I'll mark the striker on his right side rather than the left to give him an advantage. Rule number one as a centre back: you always mark channel side. Their player says 'Perfect', flashes a big Hollywood grin and bounces on the bed.

I say that our man on the pitch will do everything he can to give away free kicks, while shouting at the referee. Pressure the ref into making snap decisions. I tell their player that every time he comes short, a big hole will open up behind me for one of their midfielders to exploit. They need to make the same run into that gap again and again.

He bounces up and down on the bed saying, 'Yes!'

With ten minutes on the clock, the ball gets played out wide and our whole defence are in our box. Their best striker of the ball in midfield can't miss an open goal. If he hits the target, our keeper's biggest weakness is he can't handle long-distance shots.

1-0 to the opposition.

I explain my plan standing up with a pen and paper in my hand, sketching instructions out on the bed. Hunken surprises me by fishing into his bag and saying, 'Hey, Swaibu, use this!' He hands me a whiteboard, the same kind we use in football as a tactics board.

When the first goal goes in, I'll step into midfield which will be the trigger for the third man to run in behind our defence. We will hold a high line, gifting them an opportunity to go clean through on goal and a one-on-one with our keeper. My guy will make sure he plays everyone onside.

2-0, eleven minutes played.

A few players say, 'Bro, you're a genius!', 'This plan is so sick!' and 'It's going to happen! 3-0 guaranteed.' The fix is on.

The Boss is chain-smoking fags and rubbing his hands together with glee. Then he starts tossing out bonuses. 'I want to make this special for everyone; this is big money I'm putting on. Who wants to get sent off?'

'I'll give you an extra five grand for a red card.'

He'll also pay for 1) conceding a penalty and 2) if they score the penalty. It's like being on a Saturday night TV quiz show with cash prizes being offered to do crazy stunts. *Game for a Laugh*? Game for a Fix!

He's never given instructions like this before. My fellow fixer leaps up off the bed and says, 'I'll do it.' Boss flicks his cigarette, 'What's your name? You do this business I will hand you an extra £10,000 just for you.'

On thirteen minutes, he brings a Hayes player down in the box. It's a stonewall penalty. They slot it home. 3-0 within the first fifteen minutes. The beautiful fix is alive and kicking. We're 90 per cent home and hosed.

Hunken stands up smiling, also rubbing the palms of his hands together, 'Yep, very good. This is really good.'

Four players, two from each team. First half, second half, red cards.

Our player is meant to get sent off earlier. He tries with a wild tackle, but the referee only shows him a yellow card. He deliberately tries twice to get sent off.

When I walk into the changing room at half-time I look towards Hunken in the crowd and hear fans shouting for the first time, 'It's a fix!' I do my best not to make eye contact with any of them.

The Gaffer asks if everything is OK. One of our best players has gone from man of the match-winning performances to mistiming simple tackles, gifting free kicks.

Back in the changing room, our player keeps his head down. As the team trots back out for the second half, he looks at me, smiles and says, 'I'd better fucking get my money!'

In the hotel room, the Hayes player acts out his red card, 'This is how you get sent off. I'll take you out with a high tackle, you get up, react and push me in the face.' It happens exactly as they rehearse it.

We concede another goal in the second half and it finishes 4-0. The beautiful fix, Dan Tan's Baby, is in. This time when the opposing players shake my hand at full time, they say, 'See you next season!'

The Boss wants to meet our player after the game so we return to the May Fair for another Skype call with Hunken. He's over the moon, praising his efforts in the game, explaining how happy the whole syndicate is back in Singapore. So many people made money. Hunken gives him a glowing report.

The money is ready. I go to the Palm Beach Casino with Hunken, followed by dinner at Nobu. The season is almost over and the Boss wanted to end it with a bang. Tan has just delivered a bouncing baby to the world of match fixing.

* * *

Fix Seven is the point where Tan realises that he can feasibly manipulate the entire league. This is when the building blocks towards that aim are put in place.

But it also gives him an unforeseen headache. The Boss went from being happy to, 'Damn, man, more people involved, more control. We've potentially got another version of Moses in the team.'

Hunken and the Boss take a shine to our player like they did to me after the first fix. He showed real intent by getting sent off. That's what the Boss loves. If you show them, even if it doesn't happen, that you've really tried, that's what they love. The Boss wants his telephone number. Mo, you deal with it. Now he's involved.

Boss wants direct contact with him. Luckily for me, unlike the others, he went beyond the call of duty. He was asked and he delivered. He restored his reputation in mine and the Boss's eyes. The Boss now realised he didn't need to rely on Moses to do everything. He now had other players.

This perfect game is the end of a new beginning. It is the peak. It is the perfect game because you could never have predicted that exact result. It starts to feel like it's all coming to an end. End of the season, end of match fixing.

After Fix Seven comes the offer from the Boss: 'You guys need to come to Singapore. Let's expand this now.' I realise I'm becoming blood brothers with the devil. Selling my soul. I've had enough, but I just want one last hit.

* * *

Fix Eight

In what seems like a previous life, I had driven to collect my first car at Southampton Mercedes. The familiar journey to play the next game is loaded with fond memories. But I have a job to do. Money to make and orders to implement.

I don't want the Boss getting closer to our player. He has half the league working for him, and I sense my time is coming to an end.

We need to keep a clean sheet in the first half and lose the second half 3-0. This game is worth £50,000. Only fifty grand! This is how I begin to view the value of the money we're getting. It looks like a lot but considering the amount of money the Boss makes that year is in the millions, £50k is buttons.

Our player doesn't want to draw any more attention after his kamikaze antics. The risk once again lies on my shoulders. He's already under scrutiny following a weekender away in Ibiza. In the dressing room, some of the lads discuss it behind his back: 'How the hell can he afford that?' I pretend I can't hear.

Hunken hates taxis but also doesn't like travelling around with the muscle. His security people are only ever present at the

May Fair Hotel. He humbly hops on and off trains and takes public transport everywhere. He becomes a recognised face at league games. After the 'cowards', as the Boss describes them, speak to Hunken on Skype, Tan's foul language gets even worse.

'Swaibo, make sure the cowards don't fuck me today!'

This is a weird game. It's heading towards a properly boring 0-0 stalemate. Nothing happens. As long as we concede three goals, I get paid. Me and our player agree if he has direct involvement then he will get half of my winnings.

With fifteen minutes to go, the opposing team finally break the deadlock. I make sure as a left-sided centre back I'm positioned outside the near post almost in a left back position creating an overload at the back post. I know that their biggest strength is set pieces and crosses. The cross comes in from the right, and I blatantly turn away from the ball, making no effort to jump, and their substitute heads it past our keeper from close range.

1-0.

We start to tire, defending deeper, inviting them on to us.

Fixing becomes easy. Late winners are the norm. That's how football goes for a mid-table team.

Corner kick. The ball gets floated into the box, misses the first man, and their six-foot-four centre half taps it into the net. Nobody moves.

2-0.

Four minutes to go. Their last chance of the game and their striker rolls past me into space in the box, shoots, our keeper parries the ball away and our winger goes in for a 50/50. The referee awards a penalty.

The winger isn't even in on the fix. Their sub, Craig McAllister, steps up and completes his ten-minute hat-trick.

3-0. Game, set and match.

Back to London with Hunken in preparation for another £50k.

* * *

Banks are normally closed on a Sunday. But this is no ordinary bank.

After Fix Seven, I drive to the East End of London to collect my money. The Chinese takeaway in Dalston is closed, but, as if I'm some kind of celebrity, they open it especially for me. It's the first time I reach my milestone. Sitting alongside an arsenal of tightly wrapped bundles of banknotes, just over £1 million is staring me straight in the face. I've never seen so much cash in my whole life.

I'm tempted to bag up the whole lot, but it's not that easy. I need to consider two questions:

a) Where do I take that amount of money?

Let's say I take it home. Then there's too much money at home for me to leave alone for twenty-four hours.

b) Even though it is mine, what am I going to buy?

There are only so many cars you can rent. You can't buy a house. You can't pay your rent or your mortgage with cash. You can buy a couple of material goods, but I can't live in an apartment with designer furniture or wear Louis Vuitton clothes, because I have neighbours.

Luckily, I have an underground car park. I go out in the day and I always come home at night. People know I play football. I make sure to avoid attention. But I can't buy anything fancy even if I want to.

On top of that I've got my daughter's mum, Crystal, who

knows nothing. Changing that lifestyle is a whole different thing. When I mean take it home, I'd be taking it home to our house. What happens if the police knock on the door?

I have between £60k and £80k in an actual bank account from wages and savings. I can't put 100, 200 or 300 grand in there because the minute I do that, how do I explain that money? What am I going to say in a worst-case scenario? I'm not stupid. I can't confide in anyone. If I tell people I've got fifty grand, someone's going to tell someone else . . . you have to remember where I'm coming from.

You hear stories of people getting robbed, of being set up. No one knows me close enough to know what I'm doing. The best thing to do is to keep it that way.

I walk everywhere. You see me with a sports bag, carrying a football and wearing a tracksuit. If I move into a penthouse apartment or buy a place outside London it would've been different, because I'm not actually a Premier League footballer.

I go on a few holidays. I have a good time. Mykonos twice and Ibiza with the Ferrari Boys, and Dubai before it all went wrong.

I go to some good parties in London. My friends are rappers, a few VIP concerts but that isn't even because of the match fixing. When I go to nightclubs and hear the music, it gets me thinking, *Damn, man, I've actually got the means to live this life but nah, let me just chill.*

Before the old Chinese lady closes the restaurant door behind her and pulls down the outside shutter, she instructs me to text a specific number when I'm finished.

I stayed for a good hour. The space isn't any bigger than a public toilet. A public toilet crammed full of cash. I feel like

Al Pacino at the end of *Scarface*, but without the drugs and the murders. I've made it to the top.

At the same time I'm feeling this new sensation, I'm not happy. I can't spend the money in the way I thought. Sure, I've had a fun time partying; women, holidays, my cars, the Ferrari Boys are thriving, blowing money right, left and centre, racing each other to Kent and back in supercars.

But these flashbacks of the good times don't make me feel anything. I want more. More money, more power, more opportunities. How can I build my own empire, become my own Big Boss?

I'm growing tired of the command system. Hunken is great, but I want us to build a pipeline into what he calls 'The Golden Mile', which will have us sending players via Europe, sponsoring teams to take over the league above. It's time to conquer the Conference Premier.

CHAPTER 12

MOSES' TEN COMMANDMENTS OF MATCH FIXING

1. Loyalty is a lie.

Keep your eyes closed and your ears open. If you do this practically then you're existing in a world of make-believe. I learned this with the first £100k: never let anyone know how much money you have. Violence speaks in silence. Wise words and lesson numero uno from the boss of all bosses: 'greedy man no see clearly.'

2. Thou shalt not indulge in code switching.

The less you talk the more you make; the more you talk the higher the risk. Cold hearts always win. There's no room for emotion or feelings when the betting algorithm goes live. Code switching is street slang for changing language.

3. Thou shalt not covet the bait.

Pocket money 101: everyone has a price. Players always find the median; never too high, never too low. Everyone has a sweet spot that brings them to the table. The moment the bait hooks you in, reverse-engineer the appeal to their pockets. This means working backwards. We know what they want but can we identify the risks and problems before we do anything? Work back to front, not front to back.

4. Honour the family (players).

Everybody says no in the beginning. Those who haven't played or been in the game don't know where to start. The family are organised, players are punctual, on time. Discipline is all they know, so sell them structure.

5. Thou shalt not take the name of the LORD, the boss of bosses, in vain.

At the head of the crime family is a boss. He likes his ego rubbed and his orders carried out. Speak to him how he wants to be spoken to and never correct him. Learn the language of broken English and temper tantrums.

6. Credit and time.

The Bank of Dalston, your credit and sweat equity – the work you put in before you're paid – is essential. What's your pipeline like? Consistency is alignment: meaning not going off and doing your own thing, in simple terms; stick to the straight and narrow, follow the yellow brick road. This provides stable growth and enterprise to expand. Leverage is your key. An example of sweat equity: if you help me with something for a whole year knowing you believe in what I'm doing, when we start making money you will be paid sweat equity since you were there from the start.

7. Remember the Sabbath day, to keep it Holy.

Sunday is a day of rest. No open markets, no communication, nothing. Never contact anyone on a Sunday. It's a sign of bad luck and loss. Straight out of the match fixer's playbook.

8. Your people are your partners.

It's what you're told to believe, but having things on a hook is a form of dependency. Players form bad habits, especially underpaid, lower division ones, when money is paramount. A simple and easy rule to follow: the family wants law and order. It's the science behind the way you're treated and groomed at the same time. There's a time to talk and a time to listen. Nobody is ever safe. Betting is unpredictable, so the stakes are always high.

9. Thou shalt have no other gods before ME.

Your boss is a godlike figure, but only in his own head. Even when he's no taller than five foot five! His streak for alignment smooths his approach to the business with plenty of growth opportunities. The boss needs to feel power and have the nicest things. At the same time, he plays around with you like a toy or something easily replaced. He's a match-fixing sugar daddy. Everyone comes to him for their fix, which is money, and the things that make you more and more eager to be an acolyte. Other bosses are always on the lookout for the best talents or middle people.

10. Thou shalt not snitch or bear false witness against your syndicate.

Everything goes away! Literally . . .

* The language spoken in the commandments is a mixture of football lingo and words and phrases only those involved will understand.

** This code is difficult for law enforcement to crack. What are we actually talking about? There are no laws or governance or a handbook explaining all this, so, if breached, the rules can be deadly.

CHAPTER 13

BRAVEHEART

I'm human. I love, I laugh, I cry, I scream, I shout, I bleed. I have the same feelings you do. Braveheart brought me to my knees in prayer for forgiveness. The season is ending. Three league games and a cup final to go. I feel more and more pressure.

It's getting harder to breathe, not physically but deeper, like I'm suffocating. The weight of it all is pressing down on me. Six more matches fixed, each one a step further into something I didn't plan on. I keep ticking off boxes, but I feel like I'm disappearing.

Tan's name echoes in my head, a reminder that someone else is pulling the strings. He's untouchable. Everywhere I go, every move I make, he's there, lurking.

I feel more and more pressure going into games, especially when Braveheart just wants to be a leader and captain. He isn't the best player in the world, but he has the heart of a lion. There are times in games where he would make costly mistakes, worth tens of thousands of pounds, but all he wanted to do was play for the love of the game.

I often meet him down The Blue – the central marketplace in Bermondsey – for a quick bite to eat on our way to training and we chat about family and football. He knows who he is, but who am I? I'm a lost boy in a young man's body. I was Braveheart once. I cared and shared the same enthusiasm for the game and all the benefits it brought, not only for me but my family. The more he spoke the harder it became for me to continue living a lie.

Braveheart asks me questions about the Football League and being a professional, saying he'd give his right arm for an opportunity to play at that level. He is a man of God, a good, honest family man. He has respect and loyalty for the club badge. His character shines throughout the period when we aren't being paid. He tells us to still respect the manager and makes references to the couple of hundred he gets a week in wages. He is never afraid to speak his mind as a true leader. But he also isn't stupid.

The same loyalty he has for the football club's manager is the same loyalty I had for the head of a crime family, the Boss of all Bosses. Two completely different worlds: the Gaffer and Tan. Fighting for different causes; one for Football League status, the club's ambitions, and the other fighting for market share and greed. I made my choice and I'm not turning back.

I become the evil stepbrother trying to bring down the family dynasty while Braveheart has to puzzle out what is going on. I am a man on a mission, or at least I thought I was. I have a number in my head and I'm not going to stop until I achieve it – £2.5 million is my target. I'll get there by any means necessary. Nothing or no one will stand in my way.

My financial projects will consist of pre-seeded revenue on expanding into Europe and cornering the whole of the UK.

I have everything in place. Braveheart begins to suss what is going on, but he doesn't rat me out. He never snitches, he remains loyal. Like a true general.

That's why I answer my phone and tell him what he needs to hear. I know I'll never speak to him again, but I don't care. I have to make this money and expand the operation and my influence.

* * *

The final fix, match number nine, is when some of our supporters begin to twig – they're actually doing this. It's also the first time I recognise what the hell I'm doing to the rest of the team and to the fans. They've heard rumours about other clubs before they even imagine that their club are involved.

When one of our players gets sent off, I look over to the spectators because the match fixers are in that section of the ground and the fans are shouting, 'Something's fucking going on. This is shit!' I'm still captain at the time and I look at the players on the pitch who aren't in on the fix and they're looking around at everybody, not just me. No one can work out who is doing what. Confusion reigns.

The moment I know the fans know, the game changes. The pressure increases, people start calling things out. When you leave the pitch or go into training, fans ask, 'What the hell's going on?' Because they want answers.

But I was willing to risk everything for the syndicate, no matter the outcome. As sad as this may sound, I simply didn't care at the time. I didn't think about the fans or anybody else but myself. Fix Nine is the point I think for the first time, 'I can't do this any more.'

Leading into that game, there was a longer two-week plan

from the match fixers. I say to our player, 'This game can't happen unless the keeper's in.'

He has the best relationship with the lads. They drink and go to the pub, plus he stays after games and socialises with the fans and management. His influence is significant as he eavesdrops among the players when I'm not around. He is my trusty confidant. This is why I tell him what is going on.

'You've got a better relationship with the keeper. How much do you reckon we can get him for?'

He says, 'I don't know, man; two and a half times.' The goalkeeper is on about £150, £200 a week. So, he asks him at Thursday's pre-match training session.

'I'll give you two and a half grand if you let in some goals at the weekend.' The keeper says, 'Absolutely fucking not.'

I'm shocked, 'Fuck. Why did you tell him that?'

'What do you mean? You told me to tell him.'

'Not like that, though.'

It's the first time that I'm in a situation when I think, *This could pan out any way.*

If the keeper isn't involved, we're just going to have to do the crazy stuff. When footballers are coming to the end of their contracts at the end of a season, they normally play out of their skin to try to secure a new contract.

They adopt a survival mentality: 'I've got to prove myself day in, day out.'

It's getting harder because more people are aware of the fixing without really knowing what's going on. Our keeper rejecting the proposal is playing on my mind going into the game. But even worse, there's a player in the Bromley team who I really don't want to have to face up to about this – Braveheart.

* * *

The last fix is the hardest. The mythical Golden Goose for the syndicate is the goalkeeper. The one person you never tell. I had more chance of persuading our manager Mark Goldberg to fix.

The Boss sends a Skype message to me and the player, who had done so well for him in the previous Fix Seven. Boss tells us he's made millions this season. To celebrate he wants to invite us both on a five-star trip to Singapore, all expenses paid. First-class flights, accommodation and the Asian women of our dreams. He requests a 'VIP meeting'.

We go to the May Fair Hotel for the last time that season. Hunken attends and the Boss joins via Skype. He appears like a deity wearing a crown, and the light from Hunken's laptop illuminates our faces in the dark room. We are the chosen ones, his loyal acolytes. For the first time, the Boss speaks directly to the other player first and says, 'Can you get me the keeper?'

'Boss, for you I can do anything.'

I elbow him on the bed. Why are you saying that when you know our goalkeeper will bring the whole thing down? The game needs to be another defeat on the back of an already horrible losing streak.

Boss says, 'Confirm the keeper is in and I'll pay you your usual bonus.' We leave the meeting. The following day in training, as we warm up and practise set pieces, I spot our player chatting to the keeper.

* * *

On the day of the match, I pick the player up from his home in Elephant & Castle to drive to Maidenhead. He turns to me and says, 'Moses, he's in.'

'What? I don't believe you!'

'He said no at first but I convinced him. I told him it's for £1,000. I'll pay him directly.'

I'm still not convinced that the keeper really is in for the fix. Let's see.

Then I get a text message from a friend who works in the betting industry.

'Your game today. We've put a red flag on it.'

'Red flag? As in what?'

'No more bets. We think it's dodgy.'

Fuck. It's only two and a half hours before kick-off.

We arrive at the stadium and speak to the few people I trust. I say, 'I think this game's dodgy. But let's see what happens.'

* * *

Fix Nine

The last fix is on. The game kicks off. I see things during the opening ten minutes I've never seen our player do. He's playing like he's got mud in his eyes. He's letting players run past him, trying to get sent off. It's blatant. Exactly the way he did in Fix Seven.

Our other players start to suspect something isn't right and so do the fans. I hear certain players mumble under their breath, 'This is shit!' I feel something die in me in this game. I lose my voice and I also lose my match-fixing composure. I make sure we play with a high line, but the defender decides to do his own thing. The Boss's confidence in him, the power he hands to him to control the destiny of a game, has really gone to his head.

Goal number one. Braveheart and our right back end up in

a tangle after good play from their left winger. I watch the ball coming in and I stop dead in my tracks. I'm playing left side centre half, but I'm so far central and the winger is racing down the left channel. He cuts the ball back in the six-yard box – I make a late, half-hearted effort to track back – and their striker rifles it into the net.

1-0.

The game takes a turn for the worse. Discontent among our fans. I hear one shouting, 'You lot are match fixing. This game is bent.' Me and the player exchange stern words. People are now wagging their fingers at us from the stands. For the first time I can't see where Hunken is.

Then Braveheart pulls a goal back. I accidentally jump for the corner, the ball ricochets off me and Braveheart nods it home. What the fuck am I doing? Braveheart jumps on my back. I don't even celebrate.

1-1.

Another high line and I'm fake running, a stunt I've perfected. Their player races clean through, one-on-one with our keeper and scores.

2-1.

They play a simple lofted ball into the box and my man is half asleep, watches the ball bounce and they get a shot off on the stroke of half-time. Even though they don't score, I hang on to his shoulders as we walk off the pitch.

'You're making this too obvious!'

'Moses, it's payday; I don't give a shit!'

Coming out for the second half, Braveheart holds his captain's armband, sniffs, looks into my eyes as he pulls it on to his sleeve and walks on to the pitch. Straight players like him, who smell something fishy are like, 'Fuck this. Let me play out of my skin.'

The pressure is on; we need them to score again. They get a corner on the left, swing it into the six-yard box. I don't even jump. None of us jump.

3-1. With the opposition's two-goal advantage restored, the fix is back on.

Then Braveheart does the unthinkable and gets sent off with twenty minutes to play. He loses his head and gets involved in a pointless tussle with one of their attackers. Kicks someone, swears at the ref. Straight red card. It's got nothing to do with the actual game. It's got everything to do with what's going on with me and our player.

He points angrily and shouts at my recent match fixing recruit, 'You know what you're doing! This is fucking shit!' He rips his captain's armband off and storms off the pitch. He doesn't come to me. We have a relationship, but he secretly dislikes the other player. This is the moment I know my fixing career is at an end.

As Braveheart does the walk of shame, I get an eerie feeling that everybody in that stadium knows what's going on. Everybody. During the last twenty minutes, I can't help notice Braveheart sitting on the bench having an animated conversation with the Gaffer. He's going berserk. I can hear his voice from the pitch.

The clock is ticking. I think, 'Fucking hell, this is mad. The Gaffer's making subs.' Attempting a fightback. We're down to ten men, but we keep attacking.

With eight minutes to go, guess who goes and pulls the goal back? One of the 'cowards' as the Boss would refer to them.

I half wonder if it's his revenge and a 'fuck you, Moses!' for all the times I didn't pay him.

3-2.

We've agreed to lose by two clear goals, so the pressure is back on.

The last ten minutes of the game are brutal. Like the twelfth round of a boxing bout. We might as well go down swinging. We have a match to fix. I can't say anything to the team any more because I'm thinking, *Fuck it, let me just play a high line. I'm not even going to run back.* All I have on my mind is securing the fix.

They launch another attack down the left. Six minutes to go. I amble into the box leaving their player with a clear run through on goal. It's obvious I make no attempt to stop him. He lashes the ball into the net past a static keeper.

4-2. The fix is in.

The whistle blows for full time. I'm panicking. Nervous, anxious. I don't want to go to the changing room. It's the first time it's been so blatant. I'm scared to face the lads. I don't know what to expect. In the game, lost in the moments, I'm thinking, *Fuck them, fuck everyone, I've got to get this money.* Now when I'm confronted with the stark reality of it all, *I don't fancy this.*

Suddenly, I'm a mouse. It's the moment the bubble bursts. I walk into the changing room and grab a towel. Silence. The Gaffer has his hands on his head and tears in his eyes. A grown man in his fifties, weeping. He looks haggard. It's like every match that was fixed in the whole of the Conference South League is revealed to him in that moment.

I cast my eyes around and everyone is staring at me. I sit

down, and Braveheart stands up. I drape the towel over my head and look at my feet. I feel his presence next to me. His eyes burning into my skin.

I can't physically lift my head to look up at him or anyone. Braveheart says the game was bent. He's losing his shit.

Braveheart lived five minutes from my house. He's the first person I'd pick up to drive to the football. If I can paint a picture of a model pro, it would be him – he's not the most naturally talented, but he does everything by the book. First in, last out, never shirks a tackle, leaps for every header, he'll bust a gut for the cause.

As I pack my bags to leave, Braveheart looks at me and says, 'You're a fucking idiot.' I bow my head again and walk out without collecting my weekly pay packet. No half cheque, half cash for me. Braveheart never swears. It cuts me to the quick.

* * *

Straight after the game, I'm going to Milton Keynes for a night out. I get in my car for the hour-and-a-half drive. Half an hour in my phone rings and I put it on speaker. It's Braveheart. I answer.

'Yo, Braveheart, what's going on?'

'Listen, do you respect me?'

'Yeah, why?'

'All right, cool. Let me ask you a question. Be fucking honest if you respect me. How long has it been going on?'

'Probably a season.'

'Were you involved?'

'Yeah.'

'Why didn't you tell me?'

'Fuck . . .'

He asks again, 'Yeah, why didn't you tell me?'

I hang up.

I feel empty. I'm never going to see him again.

I respected him because he has what I want. I wish I was that pure. I wish I didn't have this pressure, this burden of expectation. I'm living a lie and he is living a good life.

I've amassed riches from my fixing, but he's twenty times happier than I can ever be.

* * *

There are still two league games left of the season to play. Our manager phones me up and says, 'Moses, these rumours, prove to me that it isn't you.' I ask him to let me go into the next game and give my best. I have a point to prove.

I'm racked with anxiety following Fix Nine three days before. Even though this match won't be fixed, my teammates will never look at me in the same way ever again. I walk into the changing room and say nothing. I take my seat and fist-bump some of the mandem. Nobody speaks, not even the Gaffer. No eye contact.

Suddenly, Braveheart emerges dramatically through the steam from the shower area. He grabs me by my face as if he's about to head-butt me. He pulls me into his chest with my arms dangling loose by my side, wraps his arms around me and says in my ear, 'Moses, you owe me one today. Just for today, do it for me. I know there's a player in you. I don't know how, why or what has really been going on, but you owe me.'

He takes a deep breath, sniffing while he jumps up and down. I see the pit bull terrier in his eyes, ready for battle. His intensity triggers something in me; I cry but there are no tears. It's my soul and gut eating away at me. We need a win today.

The Gaffer has been affected most by what's happened. He pulls me to one side. Bear in mind I didn't take my wages after the previous game.

'Moses, what's going on?'

'Nothing.'

I look him straight in the eye with an icy coldness. All I have on my mind is the text he sent on New Year's Eve. Fine me for going to a medical appointment with my pregnant girlfriend? And he hadn't paid us our wages for over two months in the build-up to Christmas? Fuck off. I don't feel sorry for him, nor do I feel any guilt for what I've done.

My plan has always been to avoid this intimate conversation with him. This game will be my last dance.

'OK, you're starting the game and I want you to lead the team out.' He wants me to remind him of the Moses Swaibu he once signed and silence these vicious rumours. Mark is in denial. I know that deep down he knows what I've done. Not the full extent of it . . . and he can't bring himself to believe it. Is my trauma playing out? Feeling let down again by a father figure and me exacting revenge, getting my own back without speaking out? I don't know. Maybe. Part of me wishes this had never happened. The other part realises it's all too late. The last dance is twenty minutes away. I have one more job to do.

My fire is back. I have a point to prove. I play like I should have done from the start of the season. It's my best ever performance in the club's colours. Too little, too late.

The way our team is set up is different. We play with a low block and defend on our box. Our midfielders sit in. The biggest difference in non-fixed games is that the team has a distinct spine and are a tighter, more compact unit. You can hear commands being shouted out on the pitch. We bounce back from an eight-game losing streak to win 2-1. We have grit and team spirit. Braveheart plays like a lion for ninety minutes and our defence is outstanding; everyone does their job.

I play my heart out. I run myself into the ground, I chase lost causes, I leap for headers, I shout, I scream. I get on the ball, I make passes. This is the real Moses Swaibu, the one that made the fans surprised that a player of my pedigree had signed for them.

It's a tight game against a very decent side. They take the lead with twenty minutes to go. We don't panic. Keep our shape, stick to our game plan. Our super sub comes on and grabs an equaliser in the eighty-second minute. But we don't settle for a point. The club's top scorer hits a last-gasp winner on ninety minutes to make it 2-1.

We return to the changing room. My spirits are high but nobody speaks, not even the manager. A deafening silence. No eye contact. Nothing. The Gaffer looks confused. He says something that will stick with me for years. As I'm about to walk out of the changing room for the last time as a player of the club, he says in a faltering voice, 'Moses, if we and you had played like that all season, we could have won this league.'

He finishes off with, 'Why?'

I leave and walk to my car. No messages from the Bosses. No messages from anyone. Only Crystal asking me what time I'll be home. I was trying to win back people's trust, but the trust has been broken by all the other games that were fixed. I was trying to condense redemption into ninety minutes. I don't feel a shred of redemption. After my man of the match performance, I thought I would. It only drove me deeper into my darkness.

It's the loneliest drive I've ever had in football, a fade to black moment. As the evening wears on I disappear into a black hole. I feel light-headed, drunk. For the first time I'm confused. I don't know what to do.

I sit at the wheel of my car; turn the music off. As I drive past Arsenal's Emirates Stadium and Holloway Road Tube station, a tear rolls down my cheek. I'm scared. I feel like a lost boy on his own in the middle of nowhere. The closer I get to home, all I can think about is the damage I've done to my team, my manager, myself. So what that Mark said he'd fine me or not pay my wages! Who have I become?

I approach Streatham Hill thinking about the next steps. What am I going to do with all this money? How do I expand and grow? Shall I create a franchise platform with the Boss and Hunken? Should I fly to Singapore for the celebration holiday? The money needs to move. It can't stay in the back of the Dalston Chinese restaurant any longer.

The next few weeks are going to change my whole life.

* * *

Despite losing ten of our last twelve league games – with five of them rigged – we avoid relegation by the skin of our teeth. After the farce of Fix Nine, reaching the a cup final provided some end-of-season relief.

We win in the semi-final in a penalty shoot-out. Now for the final and, of course, we do it the hard way. Having gone 2-0 up our defender is red-carded. We're down to ten men. Then I hobble off with an Achilles injury.

The opposition claw a goal back, which makes for a nervy finish, but we hold on for a 2-1 win.

The whole team are jubilant. The tears have been replaced with a beaming smile. He pats me on my back and kisses my head. I can't bear to look him in the face. I've never felt so down winning a trophy. Completely deflated. Fixing football matches has really fucked me up. My body and mind are broken. Mentally, emotionally and physically. I have no fight, nothing left in me. I hate what I've become. I got addicted to the gamble and risk. It ultimately came to define who I am.

None of the cup games I played in for the club were fixed. In the run of games at the end of the season, we played fixed games and 'normal' cup games back to back.

The Boss only wanted to fix league games. Not cup games. But there were also league games that weren't fixed – maybe thirty out of the forty-two fixtures weren't fixed. In the games where I was playing normally, other teams were fixing games. There were games that we won that were fixed, but the other team had to lose.

I knew this from the start of the season. I am aware of the overall picture. It goes back to my point when I said to my team-mates, 'This is gonna happen with or without you.' What they don't understand is that there were games we played that we had to win and the other team had to lose.

I was aware of that because the Boss told me he had put money on a specific team to lose a specific game. He'd tell me to make sure our team played well and scored. The opposite is happening. I'm not directly involved with this game that's fixed but I still have to play.

Imagine fans of those other teams are like your team. They can win, lose or draw, but whatever the outcome, the whole system is rigged. The more I began to think, *What the fuck; are other football matches like this?* I get deeper into this thought process leading into Fix Nine and it makes me want to give it one last big hurrah. Realistically speaking, every game this season should have been null and void because of the level of corruption.

But the cup games are pure games. They are supposed to offer me a release, a respite, a return to the joy of playing football. But they have the opposite effect. My sense of guilt is too huge. I want to win the club's first ever trophy because I know the deeper I got into the fixing world, the more intense the battle of love/hate with football has become. I love the game, I hate the game.

I make excuses, but I eventually decide that enough's enough, because I've lost control. Deep down, I want to do well for the team. I'm captain and I want to lead. The problem I have at the club is, even if you thought I was a part of that run to the cup final, to what extent was I actually part of it? Just because Mo got the man of the match or Mo scored a goal? These are games where I'm playing as I should be playing.

But Tan is ever present, dangling a money carrot over my head. In the games they were fixing for other teams, I learned how I could maximise my earnings by understanding how these fixes worked. I used to take pictures of my five-a-side team at a distance so you can't really see their faces and send them to the match fixers. 'Here are the five players.' Because I built up trust, they stopped arranging meetings or even asking for photos any more.

They'd say, 'Moses, just send us the players so we know the fix is on.'

I'd say to Hunken, 'I've got five players. These are their names.' I'd pick a random selection of players and the game would be fixed. I'd arranged the outcome. I'd take all the money. I largely knew how a quarter of the season was going to pan out. The more I tried to understand, the more they'd tell me, the more information they'd share, the more I'd be around them. I'd be constantly learning.

You start to see the patterns emerging. But I still have questions that need answers. Then I get a message from the match fixers: 'Moses, what's next?' I go into the final league game and cup final thinking, *Let me show these guys what I'm all about as a football player.* Then when I finish that last game, I tell Tan and Hunken, 'Guys, I can't fix no more.'

Tan replies, 'Don't worry. We've got a new plan. There's a team called Alfreton Town FC. We're going to send you there. We plan to buy that club. We'll bring players from the Conference South that have fixed with us before. Then we'll expand. Moses, I want you to come and celebrate in Singapore.'

I tell the Boss to let me go and mull it over on my summer holiday in Mykonos with the Ferrari Boys.

CHAPTER 14

HANGING UP MY BOOTS

I'd never heard of Alfreton Town FC in my life. Turns out they play in the Conference North. The small town of Alfreton is in Derbyshire. The Boss has a grand plan to take over the club for a cool £1 million. Set up the whole operation in time for the start of the new season, 2013/14.

He'll use the syndicate's betting company, Red Star, to front the bid. Take control of the club from top to bottom. Install a hand-picked Harlem Globetrotters of match-fixing players. Hire their own manager and coaching staff. Every single element of the club will be corrupted. Players, coaches, kit man, tea ladies, ground staff – everyone is in on the fix. The players will live in accommodation nearby, all expenses paid, a company car and offered a higher average wage than the rest of the league.

The Boss knows that me and one of our players, Duane, are on non-contracts at the club and we both want to leave. That's when he floats the plan to me. I speak to Duane at training, not long before the shit hits the fan at fix number nine.

'Boss wants you to play up top for Alfreton.'

'Who?'

'We're going up there on a trial. Bro, trust me, man. They'll give you a car.'

I don't tell Duane it's with a view to fixing matches. Remember when I told you the Boss had half the league? He already had players in the Conference North and South eager to be part of the new plan. All those players on non-contracts were having trials at Alfreton.

By the end of 2012, I already knew about Tan's plans to take over other teams. As my career at the club unravelled, I'd vent my frustrations to the Boss: 'This current fixing situation won't last, so what's the plan? How does this evolve? Things can't stay the same.' I'm thinking it might be time to hang up both my football and match-fixing boots.

He knew Tan had accomplished all he could in the Conference South. It was time for a change of scene, a fresh, exciting, wildly ambitious opportunity. He tells me the fixing won't be as before as there will be greater scrutiny in a higher profile league. He'll cherry-pick a few games in the season, with particular focus on the FA Cup which he prized so dearly.

The FA Cup is Tan's World Cup. He's infatuated with its long, rich history – the oldest national football competition in the world – and the idea alone has him salivating.

He wants to send a message to his people in Asia. A show of strength, status, control. Plus, any lower league team that reaches the second or third round of the FA Cup will net the players hundreds of thousands of pounds each, not to mention millions for the syndicate Bosses.

It was after the final league game where the Bosses said,

'We're gonna buy you a ticket to Singapore. We want you to go into Asia.' Part of the deal is taking over Alfreton. I'd play for them too. It was almost like I'm getting better terms on a business deal. I think *damn, man, this is extremely tempting . . .*

Hunken pretends to be my agent while cosying up to the Alfreton chairman about the takeover. The Gaffer has no idea me and Duane are appearing in a reserve game for another club as triallists. We even miss a midweek training session to make the three-hour drive to Alfreton.

I'm standing next to Hunken as he speaks openly to Alfreton's club chairman and other staff about his plans. They're looking at me and thinking, *Why is this potential owner with these two players?* It never crosses my mind that it might have looked suspicious. They took Hunken seriously. He showed up with a personal driver and security. He looks and acts the part, as always.

After the match ends, we meet Hunken in the car park. He came to watch the reserve game to get an insight into what I think can be achieved with this team. The layout of their ground means you can see into the car park. I look over my shoulder and I see the Alfreton manager and assistant pointing towards us.

Hunken goes over to speak to them, comes back and says they wonder why he's talking to players.

He tells them, 'We're going to sign them.'

I say, 'Hunken, this isn't how you communicate with football people – that's a red flag.'

He said it was OK but doesn't realise that him and the Boss simply don't understand how football works without a player's insider knowledge. Duane stands beside me and says nothing. I don't think he realises how much ability he has. He's the most valuable but also the most vulnerable player in our squad.

I don't think he realises how much footballing ability he has. The manager has him on low wages and treats him unfairly.

Duane is a go-with-the-flow-type character. Can he fix a match? Absolutely not. When asked to do so he did the exact opposite and put in man of the match performances on a weekly basis. But he is essential to my future plans. Being one of the best strikers in the league makes him extremely valuable to the organisation. Especially when the Boss has market share and control of teams.

* * *

Then I start to realise that these guys are making millions. A hundred grand is nothing to them when they're putting on million-pound bets with a ten million pounds return. I'm getting a little bit ahead of myself. I'm trying to accelerate my earnings when maybe I would be better off just playing it cool.

It goes back to my playing career. I have a tendency to overstep the mark. But football and crime are two different things. Whereas I'll go to the managers I played for and say, 'I want to be captain,' now I'm going to the Boss saying, 'I'm not being paid enough.' The difference is that he isn't a football manager.

I'm impatient because I am the one taking the biggest risk, so why am I not earning what the boss is? My greed for more kicks in. I know what my value is. I thought I had enough leverage. I thought I was a main player. When I'm losing control, I try to calm myself by saying, 'OK, I'm a big player; I'm doing this my way.' The power went to my head.

I begin to understand this shit is much bigger than I anticipated. It's way bigger than me. It's way bigger than this league. When I find out about the attempted Alfreton takeover,

I'm thinking, *Wow, now they're moving on from individual players and are trying to buy entire football clubs!* More players are getting involved. How long will this last before I have to get out, before it all comes crashing to the ground?'

* * *

Towards the end of the season, Delroy phoned me out of the blue. I haven't heard from him since my Lincoln days, over two years ago. The Conference is split between South and North. Del's in the North. He says, 'Yo, what's happening down there?' He's got wind of what's happening in our league.

I feign ignorance, 'I don't know.'

He has no idea of my involvement, never mind that I'm running the show. He says that he's got new investors, looking to set up a new match-fixing operation. Am I interested? I mention it to my Boss, Tan.

He says, 'OK, go on, then; go do business with him.'

During the chat, Del asks if I 'remember that thing'?

Obviously, I know what that thing is. A thing in a Northampton hotel room involving a bag of cash and a big Russian dude.

He says, 'What's happening down there? I hear people are making a killing.'

'Yeah, man. I hear the same thing,' I reply. 'If I find out anything, I'll let you know.'

Then I cut the call.

* * *

A shift in my mentality, a shift in the future. A lot of the conversations I'm having with the match fixers is about their next steps: where they want to go and what they want to do.

They'd virtually taken over the Conference South. That league, those fixtures for the 2012/13 season should have been null and void. I can either join what's happening in the match-fixing world or turn a blind eye to it and still play football. I'm contemplating retirement, but the next best team in the league, Sutton United, are interested in me.

I eventually make my decision. I leave the club and go to Sutton. No fixing is going on during my three months there. The syndicate don't need me. Imagine an employee being burnt out to the max? What they needed from me is firm commitment, one way or another. What am I going to do now? If I'm not playing, not the captain, my career's on the dip, sitting on the bench, I'm no use to them.

I'm no longer a commodity in the eyes of the syndicate. This is my chance to get back to the player I'd been at Crystal Palace and Lincoln City. I can concentrate on my football and fall back in love with the game again.

When I go to Sutton, they have an all-star team for that level of football. They have players from the Football League, players that are experienced, two old centre halves who are really good but also coming to the end of the line in their careers.

Benji Kudjodji does pre-season with me. He had a career-threatening injury when he was at Cheltenham Town, but his level of quality stands out – and his fitness is second to none.

Me and Benji go into pre-season, Boats is there too but not a regular starter. I'm fit, sharp, motivated. I sign a short-term deal. I go to Sutton to try and recapture my love of football. I'm not going to fix there. I want a clean slate. But then I realise too much has happened the year before for me to compete again. I've lost my edge.

My motivation's gone. I'm on £250 a week, but it's not about the money. My heart has gone from the game. Guilt is eating away at me.

I play two games for Sutton and then I tell the Gaffer: 'I can't do this. I'm leaving.'

Boats also leaves and immediately joins Whitehawk FC, another Conference South team. Whitehawk's ground is in a suburb of Brighton and, in Boats's view, far from the heat of the match-fixing scene in London. A club with only a couple of hundred fans at each match, away from the scrutiny of the officials.

At Sutton, Boats is barely getting a game. At Whitehawk it's a different story. He's an automatic first-team pick. Boats knows that getting on the pitch means an opportunity to manipulate and fix games. I know he is under some financial pressure. He owes money on a smart car.

Boats broaches the subject of match fixing with me. 'Mo, show me how to do it.'

'Show you how to do what?'

'You know what, bro. I need to make money, man. Don't you remember the car?'

'Oh fuck – the car.'

That favour Boats did for me to cover the finance on my white Mercedes. Now he's looking for payback.

'How much do you need to pay off your smart car?'

'Three grand.'

If Boats is looking to match-fix, then he must be short of cash. Although my money is still held by the syndicate, he knows I can go and make a withdrawal from my Dalston savings bank any time. This is one of the crazy things about working for an organised crime organisation. They hold on to your match-fixing money for you. And even if you get out, you can still go back at any time and get your cash.

I take Boats to one of the syndicate's businesses near Leicester Square. He waits outside while I go in and make a withdrawal. I hand him five grand and say, 'Here, Boats. Go and pay off your debt and keep the £2k on top of it.'

The Favour has been returned, but better yet, with no debt. Boats has no need to ask anything else about match fixing. About a week later, I realise, I've actually achieved the opposite of what I set out to do. I've thoughtlessly groomed Boats. You don't give someone a two grand gift. So now he knows what I've done, how I've done it. He's looking at it like, 'I ain't really had two grand like that before. How do I get more?' I've given him what Delroy did to me at Lincoln: 'There's sixty grand. Let me dangle it over you like a carrot in front of a donkey.'

Boats sees me now the exact same way I once looked at Delroy. I could easily have said to Boats, 'Give me your bank details and I'll transfer the money to pay off your car?' But what I've done is given him candy and opened his eyes to a tantalising new world.

* * *

Tan tells me to take a holiday. The tickets to Singapore are booked, all ready and waiting for me.

Then he says, 'Be patient because the next club you go to, we'll just pick up again where we left off.'

I tell him, 'It's not the same. I don't have the influence; I'm not captain.'

If I go into a new environment, I'll need six months to

establish myself. I haven't got the desire to go back on the field again. Boats is pestering me to come to Whitehawk to resume fixing there.

'Moses, man, we need a centre half.'

'I can't be bothered.'

'You don't mind if I give the Whitehawk manager your number?'

'Boats, I'm done. I don't want to play football.'

Whitehawk would be my third Conference South club on the bounce. After Bromley, and especially Sutton, I don't need it. The more I tell Boats about match fixing, the more excited he gets. He says, 'Imagine what we can do together at Whitehawk?' He explains the set-up, the team and the players. Whitehawk FC are newly crowned champions of the Isthmian League Premier Division, newly promoted to the Conference South. Does that league sound familiar?

They tried to change their name that summer to Brighton City FC, but the FA Council ruled against it. The Gaffer, Darren Freeman, is a local lad who played in League One as a striker with Brighton & Hove Albion. Boats says he rates me highly.

I have three calls with Darren. 'We're going to give you £350 a week.'

'It's not about the money, bro.' If only he knew the mountains of cash I have at that time. But this guy really wants me to come and play.

'Gaffer, I'm not match fit.' It'll probably take me a few months to get in proper shape. He's unfazed, 'Don't worry about it. Just come in and train.'

He's pretty persuasive and complimentary about my abilities on the pitch. If I'm being honest, it was talking to Boats again that seals it for me. I end up signing for Whitehawk on a short-term contract.

During the first training session, the floodlights blow. Whitehawk is a shithole in the middle of nowhere. Even the showers don't work. We train opposite the stadium at East Brighton Park, a sports ground used by Brighton College, next to a caravan park and the municipal dump. It's depressing.

The truth is I didn't want to come to the club. My little brother Boats wants me to come to fix. I don't have an influence on the team. I'm not captain. I'm on the bench. I'm not fit. I don't know Brighton. The only relationships I have there are with Boats, his best friend, Hakeem Adelakun and a fellow Croydon lad called Danny Mills. They organise a car pool to drive to games and training.

I already know football isn't for me any more. It's not going how I expected. I still have the match fixers and the trip to Singapore and all those grand plans in the back of my mind.

As soon as Boats persuades me to sign, I'm thinking, 'Why the fuck am I here?'

The first few games, I'm confused. I'm on the bench. Darren Freeman brings me on ten minutes before the end of a home game in October. I say, 'Gaffer, I'm not fit.'

'This is where you get your minutes.'

We're ahead in the game. I come on as a sub and the opposition equalise in the ninetieth minute, last kick of the ball. That creates a shift in the dynamics of the team. They're all Brighton-based, a tight-knit group. Some of the lads are best friends. When I come on, no one speaks to me. They probably feel that I'm worse than what they already have.

I start the next game at home to Gosport Borough on

2 November. We're leading 1-0 at half-time. I don't come back out for the second half. I've had enough.

I don't even notify the Gaffer. I sit down and look around the changing room. I listen to the water dripping from the broken shower and realise this isn't for me any more. Not for the first time, I don't collect my wages, I don't have a shower. I pack my bag, say to myself, *'I'll never kick a ball again,'* walk out of the ground and drive home alone.

My football career is done. What am I going to do now?

A week passes and I get another call from Delroy Facey. He has a proposition for me. New investors, a pair of Singaporean match fixers, a plan to create our own operation. This time I don't cut him off.

I say, 'Delroy, to be fair, I've dealt with the higher echelons of that world. This stuff you're telling me doesn't make sense.' I'm also on a kind of match-fixing holiday, winding down before I contemplate expanding my empire into Europe. It's still up for grabs. I'll be discussing this with Tan and Hunken on our break in Singapore.

Del says, 'Oh well, if you know anyone else . . .'

I check in with Boats and he's keen to talk to Delroy. So I bring the two of them together.

CHAPTER 15

WELL GROOMED

Grooming started at home. The one I should have trusted the most – my own father – was the biggest manipulator. There are themes and signs you don't notice, especially when you're young and impressionable. A young boy or man tries his hardest to seek guidance, and nurturing any person requires early involvement in their life. When you're robbed of your feelings, emotions and thoughts, it feels like your head is bleeding. I was full of pain and resentment. What's worse is that I remember feeling love without knowing what it was.

My dad was also my groomer. He once made me feel safe, especially at home. But how could my young mother, with three children to look after, possibly depend on a man who was broken in all aspects of his life? What had my father witnessed growing up in a Uganda torn apart by Idi Amin's violent military dictatorship? What was he exposed to? In my life, I've looked deep into the eyes of those who have done wrong, friends growing up, full of the same emotions and feelings as me.

But then a switch flips and that same loving look turns to darkness. Empty eyes. A person's eyes will always reveal how much pain they carry.

Growing up, not many of my own community expressed their feelings. I never once saw my father cry. All he displayed was rage and violence. Was this an acceptable way to behave with young boys in the house? Ultimately it would lead to a reflection on my own character and behaviour until I found the game of football.

It's a gradual process, but when you're being groomed, things begin to not make sense. I start to see violence on the streets. Back then most of the 'road yutes' made money from selling weed. Jermaine had a ruthless reputation. I heard it but I never saw it until we went to his old estate in Croydon, a five-minute drive from Selhurst Park stadium. He once picked me up late in the evening and told me one of the youngers had skimmed some of the profits behind his back. Jermaine kept a billy bat in his car. It's what you put on the steering wheel so your car doesn't get stolen.

When we got to the estate, he asked me to pull it out of the passenger-side seat. His worker approached the car and we got out.

'Moses, pass me the "ting".' I gave it to him and he held it with both hands before smashing it right in the worker's face. I remember shaking and looking back as we drove off, with his worker lying unconscious on the road. We went back to Jermaine's house and I slept on his floor. I remember crying. Don't ask me why. Tears just started rolling down my face.

My neighbours took the drugs my friends sold. Even at eleven I recognised this was grooming in all its shapes and forms.

Jermaine wanted power, but the burden of peer pressure just kept the flame burning.

It was no different with Delroy and the syndicate. By then I knew it was wrong. But I've never snitched on anyone no matter what they did. All the shit I saw growing up and the emotional and physical abuse made me think bad things equals secrets. Part of me knew – just like that worker – what would happen if I stepped out of line.

Groomers come in all races and sizes. You never know where they might pop up. They understand the codes of the real world or the underworld or the streets or all three. There are so many layers involved and as you're getting groomed, so you then unknowingly become the groomer. The baton is passed on, generation after generation.

I once thought I was doing Boats a favour, just like Del thought he was helping me out, just like my dad thought he was teaching me a lesson, just like my stepmum thought she was on my side, just like Jermaine normalised selling drugs and violent behaviour for an eleven-year-old.

The pattern continues. The groomed becomes the groomer. It's a natural, sinister cycle. And with that comes autonomy over your mind, body and soul, which all get exploited without your knowledge. The power they get can be financial or merely to control.

The syndicate induct you into their family of other groomers. The streets call it gangs but these syndicates are a different breed. It's organised. In real life, they're called mentors, peers or guardians. In the dark world or illegal system, they're called the Boss, or Boss of Bosses. There's a tight structure, a rigid hierarchy, a highly organised system of control.

The ringleaders in street gangs are those who are smart enough to elevate themselves to that position. They grow into the role and eventually do less, but it's all collaborative and collateral damage. Abuse comes in all varieties. The only way out is making money by any means necessary. He who controls the power controls the army and the mules.

Being under the influence of someone older or someone who you once trusted can result in permanent damage. For most, it's too late, but those tough streets of South East London give you a booster pack. It's a dog-eat-dog existence. Survival of the fittest. It's the normal way of being for those coming from the most deprived communities. You can't ever understand it, or get perspective on it, unless you or someone else makes it out the other side. But when they do, who has the capacity to educate those they leave behind?

I went into football with personal targets. But when your identity is compromised, this organised game is the exact same thing that groomed young people. Where is the education at Crystal Palace, the guidance, the counselling, the positive mentorship, when many of their Academy players come from South East London's concrete jungle?

Who was there during my time to oversee this or understand this? Just like I did, young gang members play football for a way out. Football clubs don't do due diligence the way they should. This still happens today all over the world when those who don't make it are released and find themselves slipping through the net without support.

Those who are groomed need stability, guidance, role models, trust, love and belonging. Do you know what a young person will do for you with all of the above? They'll do better in life, have an opportunity to succeed and make the most of their latent abilities rather than just opt for the easy route.

Let's be honest. How many parents or teachers are even paying attention? This may sound controversial but what does the data say from the groups or communities? Look at society and schools. Many parents themselves are still kids, who haven't developed their own life due to these failures in society. How many men are doing prison sentences because life got so hard they had no other way, leaving broken families behind?

Football has failed many. But to the wider public, the world of modern football is money, glitz and glamour. No one cares. Why should they? Is there the right racial diversity across senior leadership or is it still an old boys' club with those in positions of power and responsibility still tending to be older white male figures, over the age of fifty-five, out of touch with modern culture and society?

The root cause in football also coincides with human trafficking. Players come from all over the world for the promise of financial gain. Just like the streets, you either sink or swim, eat or be eaten. That is the condition of grooming. This doesn't happen overnight. It's built up over a long period of time, years and decades without protest or a real duty of care. It becomes normalised once targets are identified and told to hold the weapon of secrecy and truth.

The crazy thing is you think you owe a debt to someone who's helped you. A misguided loyalty without boundaries. The psychological trauma lasts a lifetime.

CHAPTER 16

THE LURE OF FILTHY LUCRE

I haven't spoken to Delroy Facey in nearly three years, but I want to organise future plans, so I call him again. He tells me he has two new match fixers from South East Asia – Chann Sankaran and Krishna Ganeshan – with a guaranteed fixing fund.

'Look Del, I'm out. But I know someone who can sort of take over from me. Let me connect you both.'

Then I text Boats and say, 'I'm going to give you Delroy's number.'

Boats has been constantly pestering me about how he can get involved in fixing matches because he's still playing for Whitehawk. Boats says to me, 'Do you remember that favour, Mo? Bring me in,' which means in slang, show me how to do it. The favour he's referring to is the time he sorted out the finance on my white Mercedes.

'I can't show you how things are done, Boats, but I can tell you.' And so the groomed becomes the groomer.

Boats knew games were being fixed in the Conference South

but he didn't know it was me. When I handed him that five grand in Leicester Square and told him to keep it, I inadvertently revealed how the plan works: how to match-fix, get paid *and* go undetected.

For weeks and months, I try to ward him off, tell him why it's dangerous and why I can't reveal the full scope of what I do. Alarmingly, a few players even got threatened, receiving bullets in the post after a fixed FA Cup fixture didn't go to plan, and I didn't feel that my little brother was ready for that lifestyle.

After I take a break from fixing and quit playing football, I try to leverage everything I've learned to introduce Boats to a new syndicate. I'm the connector between Boats and Delroy. Without me, they would never know each other. This way, I don't need to be so close to it. I can organise things from the periphery. I play middleman and take 70 per cent.

My 70 per cent means I sit down with Boats and Delroy. I understand how to fix football matches, I know the industry and I can bring it all together. If they ask me why am I taking such a big cut, I can explain to them the blueprint of the plan: I'm going to hold Boats's hand, and I'll bring Delroy into the picture and maintain control of them both, because I have the knowledge and the connections to the market and they don't.

As you know, Boats never asked me for any money or any payment when he helped to finance my car.

All he said was, 'Moses, go and buy me a pair of trainers.'

I said. 'You just got me a forty-grand car. Why am I giving you a hundred quid's worth of trainers?'

'Because you're my big brother.'

OK, if I'm your big bro, I'm expecting you to be smart.

If I say you *could* do this, I'm not expecting you to go and do it. Delroy was once my big bro. Even though he didn't make me match-fix, he showed me that match fixing is real on that night in the Northampton hotel.

Boats had never been involved in anything illegal. He was as clean as they come. No criminal convictions. An intelligent young man with a bright future ahead of him. Like Braveheart, because of his purity, I didn't want him to go near it.

I said to Boats that before he thought about match fixing, to let me give him the money first. When he found out I was the match fixer, he saw me as a mafioso, as a John Gotti figure.

He reminded me of myself when I was coming into the game, hence me not wanting him to get involved. But the more eagerness he showed and the more potential I saw in what he could become, I realised that Boats could be moulded into my trusted lieutenant. I could have said to him, 'Boats, look, I'm going to go to Singapore. I'm going to give you £5,000 for the summer. But when I come back, I need you to do one thing; I need you to procure at least a few players across every team in the new league.'

I planned to give Boats the blueprint to everything I'd learned. He was young and impressionable. He had a sense of innocence about him. He came from a good home, he was never homeless, and he wasn't fostered. He was the opposite of who I am. If I teach him the right things, he can take over the UK side of the business while I focus on Europe and the rest of the world.

As long as Boats is paid well the first time around, we can go on to create a partnership alongside Delroy. Even though I know my old Lincoln mucker, Del, is a bit shady and untrustworthy, Boats has the ability to become an underboss.

But then Boats deceived me when he met Chann and Krishna and the investor. This is why I must teach my little brother a lesson. He's let me down. He acted behind my back. Who does he think he is? I've been a student of this criminal enterprise for over a year and he thinks in the space of twenty-four hours he can come in from nowhere and someone's just going to hand him tens of thousands of pounds without informing me about it?

* * *

After I introduce Boats to Delroy, I say to Boats, 'You two exchange numbers, and whatever you agree, I'll work out how much I'll take.'

Delroy's new match fixers, two South Asian guys called Chann Sankaran and Krishna Ganeshan, are asking for information about the game we're aiming to fix – a Conference South game between Arlesey Town and Boats's current team, Whitehawk.

Boats is confused because he doesn't know the mechanics of how it works. I tell him, 'You go along to a meeting and they usually give you pocket money.' He wants to know how much you should ask for. I say, normally no less than £3k.

I give Boats the play and the heads-up. This is what's going to happen: I'll speak to Delroy's investors first, to find out how much money they have and ask which games they want to do. I'll report back to Boats with further instructions.

In my mind, I'm sitting on the top of the food chain and in control. I don't need to kick a ball ever again, but what I can do is sit at home and let everybody else do the donkey work. One of those people is Boats, and the other is Del.

I say to Boats, 'Don't go and meet these people. I'll explain what they want you to do.'

The plan is that we'll tell Chann and Krishna that Whitehawk's away game at Arlesey Town on Saturday, 30 November, will be fixed. They'll put a down payment on it. Because Chann and Krishna are so eager, I'll tell them to provide us with half of the money up front instead of the usual pre-match pocket money.

The outcome of this will be: Boats is going to get paid, I'm going to get paid and Delroy is going to get paid.

Next, we need players and I already have leverage on that front. I'm going to go to my five-a-side football on Monday and take photos of the players in my team. I'll present these players to the match fixers as if they're in the Whitehawk team and in on the fix. They have no reason to question the validity of the photos and names I'll supply them with.

The fact of the matter is, whether it's fixed or not, they're going to pay us. We're going to take the money. I'm expecting a return of £30k – £5k pocket money, £25k for the team, five players each. I'm planning to give Delroy £10k, Boats £5k, and keep the rest.

Days go by with no news from Boats. Something doesn't feel right in my gut. We've gone from planning to fix a match to a complete lack of communication and Boats wants me to deal with everybody except him. Despite it being his first ever fix, he thinks he has all the power because he still plays for Whitehawk, so he has the player relationships and nobody will ever suspect him. Boats has the nice guy role. I'm the bad cop. I start to find Boats's radio silence disturbing.

Eventually, I call Delroy: 'What's happening?' Del tells me that the match fixers have got twenty-five grand and he's gonna get this, and Boats is gonna get that. I thought Boats would've told me. OK, he thinks he's smart. Let me call Boats.

'You ain't met no one have you?'

'Nah, bro, I ain't met no one.'

'All right, cool.'

I sense he's lying to me. I can hear his voice tremble on the other end of the line. He's unusually quiet, tense; this isn't the Boats I know. I ask him, 'Is everything OK with the Singaporeans?'

'Yeah, bro, why? What's wrong? By the way, how much money did you say I'm getting and are you sure you're going to give it to me?'

I reply, 'Yeah, of course; why wouldn't I?'

'Because I know you've got too much money and you might bump me,' he says. Bump means to rip somebody off in slang.

'I won't do that,' I say.

Then Boats surprises me by saying he's already been to meet Chann and Krishna and an investor, a white man, at a Starbucks by East Croydon station. 'Why didn't you tell me before you went?'

No reply.

Then I ask him, 'Did you take money?'

'Yes.'

'Boats, you should never have done that.'

'How much did they give you?'

Again Boats doesn't answer.

I say, 'A white guy ain't fixing no football game.'

I hang up the phone. I'm seething.

At this point, because I know Delroy's characteristics, I sense that if this goes ahead, they'll try to cut me out of the money. They're not being straight with me; they're giving me the runaround.

Boats withheld information and acted behind my back and against my original plan. Why won't he tell me how much pocket money they gave him?

Did they hand him the full amount up front? He didn't exactly lie to me but he definitely deceived me.

I call Delroy. 'Give me Chann Sankaran's direct number. I'm back in the game.'

If Boats thinks he's gonna bag £25k, I'm gonna take that £25k and intercept his plans for the Whitehawk game – the real fix. I want to teach him the same lesson I taught my former Bromley teammates when they said they would fix but didn't fulfil their promise.

Imagine if I told my old Chinese syndicate that Boats had taken the money or not given me my cut? It would have put me in a very difficult position because this is the match-fixing business and I know how it works.

If Lil Bro wants to become Big Bro he needs to learn and learn fast. When the dust settles on all this, I'll tell Boats straight to his face to never go behind my back again.

Between 21 and 26 November 2013, I exchange a series of WhatsApp messages and Skype calls involving me, Delroy, Boats and Chann and Krishna. It's like we're all circling each other, sussing each other out, talking in riddles. There's a lot of avoidance and delay tactics going on. False promises being bandied about.

Del asks me what teams I have. I tell him Sutton, Whitehawk and Staines. He passes on these details to Chann who claims he has the money in place from the investor – €60,000.

Del tells them he can secure the teams but only via me. I'm the Boss and in control. I have all my ducks lined up in a row. Del's impatience makes me realise he's desperate, in need of a fix and my help, therefore the price will be a premium if they are going to buy the game.

Del tells Chann the players are keen to do the business and that he's secured six/seven players in total across the three teams.

Then Del sends me a WhatsApp message accusing me of going quiet on him:

'Mo u say help u out now ya gone AWOL bro, I've sorted it out for u'.

There are plenty of delaying tactics and almost a rat race rush to the money. This needs to happen on my terms. I ignore Delroy and don't take him seriously. Everyone's basically lying to each other, making false promises about meeting players, fixing results. Nobody knows who is saying or doing what.

Chann isn't completely stupid and wants to formally meet the players who are in the photos, at his hotel in Manchester. Del can't possibly arrange this. For starters, he's based in the north of England and these clubs are in London, my territory. Plus, there are *no players to meet*.

Without my knowledge, Del being Del, he starts panicking and goes ahead and plans to meet the fixers in Manchester and tells them he'll bring along the players.

Del asks me which team is the best option. I say Whitehawk. I play five-a-sides every Monday. Instead of an in-person meeting, I'll just take photos of the five players in my team and tell Chann that it's the Whitehawk players. Then I'll send them the names of five black Whitehawk players.

Delroy shares my number with Chann who messages me

on Skype for the first time – 'Hi jon gotti I'd like to add you as a contact.'

I send Del photos of the players and tell him to give Chann the following names – Boats, Hakeem, Danny Mills, Tom Cadmore, Sam Elhab playing for Whitehawk who make up the five black players in the Whitehawk eleven. No one is ever going to Manchester to meet the fixers.

Chann wants more evidence the players are real and I spin him along in text messages, promising to show him the players on a video call, but I never do it. Delroy keeps telling the two fixers that the lads are stuck in heavy traffic on their way to meet them in Manchester. It's borderline farcical – there's a lot of posturing going on.

Del tells me Chann realises the team being presented is not genuine and he threatens to pull out, so I step in and start messaging Chann. We call each other several times on Skype but no one answers. It's a strange game of cat and mouse.

I complain about Chann's avoidance tactics to Del – 'This guy pissing me off del never answers his phone.'

But I'm also not answering calls from Chann, and he's getting equally irritated.

Later that night, I send Chann a video message. I then give him my mobile phone number. Me giving him my private contact details is the biggest turning point in the whole thing, a giant schoolboy error. Because of his lack of knowledge and match-fixing immaturity, I have no option but to speak directly to him.

At lunchtime on 26 November, I text Delroy: 'Del your ppl ain't straight. Can't do business with these guys.'

Chann finally begins to play the game. When I speak to him

for the first time, I can tell that he knows he holds the aces – £60k's worth – and he can try to dictate what he wants to do with it. Chann confirms the money is real in the photos he sends me during the call. This changes everything for me. Now I know these guys are serious.

I decide this is the perfect moment to introduce my new plan to him, separate from the Whitehawk fix. I ask Chann to meet me in London that night. I tell him that I have complimentary tickets for the AFC Wimbledon v Dagenham & Redbridge game – and that I can help them fix the game. I say that I have players on both teams and that I know what the final score will be. It's a bluff. I want to collect some easy pocket money while teaching Boats a lesson, and furthermore, test Chann and Krishna on their match-fixing capabilities. I also reason that this fix will settle everyone's nerves before the main fix – Saturday's Arlesey Town v Whitehawk game.

I also want to meet Chann and Krishna to make sure they know I'm in charge and Boats works for me. I suspect Boats is trying to play all of us off each other, telling Delroy one thing and Chann and Krishna another and putting on a Mr Nice Guy act for me. He thinks because I left Whitehawk and I can't orchestrate the fix as a player on the pitch – and that he still can – that he deserves to take the majority of the money. I won't allow this to happen. You might argue that I'm motivated more by greed than revenge on Boats, but in my opinion he's a loaded gun without any aim, wet behind the ears and I don't answer to him. I'm gonna show him who's really the Boss here.

Delroy knows I've lied to Chann and Krishna about the Wimbledon game being fixed. I'm keeping Boats out of the loop for now due to his deception. But I decide to still give him and Del a slice of the pocket money I'll insist on getting from Chann. This will keep everyone happy.

Chann and Krishna agree to make their way down to London. We arrange to meet outside Wimbledon's ground, Kingsmeadow Stadium. In my mind there's £30,000, give or take a few grand, on the table. They have the funds but not the access. That's where I step in. I tell them I have players on both teams in on the fix and that the final score will be 2-1 to the home side. They seem satisfied enough to place large bets on the correct score at a Ladbrokes in Manchester's Deansgate before they board a train to London. They also relay my information to their Asian bosses to confirm that the fix is on.

However, I also need to be ready for a worst-case scenario; so for the first time I involve someone outside of the match-fixing world. It's Stephen, my old flatmate from Lincoln. I ask him a simple question about what I'm planning to do. I say that there's €60k in cash sitting in Manchester. I might need some muscle if I go there. What's the best way to handle a situation like this in case things go wrong? His brainwave: let's go to Manchester, rob them and take all the money. This is the last time I speak to any outsiders about anything to do with match fixing.

On the evening of the AFC Wimbledon v Dagenham & Redbridge game, I'm at my girlfriend Crystal's house. I put my baby daughter Taliya down to bed and tell Crystal I'll be back in time for her famous chicken curry.

In June that year, I get fined at South London Magistrates for making a false statement to obtain insurance. Then I'm charged with driving my Mercedes uninsured. Bang to rights, and I get hit with a lengthy driving ban.

So I need someone to drive me to Wimbledon's ground in Kingston upon Thames to meet Chann and Krishna. I call my best friend Benji . . .

I kiss Taliya as she falls asleep, say my goodbyes to Crystal and jump in the car with Benji. It's time for a London derby, although it's not exactly the Champions League. This is League Two, AFC Wimbledon v Dagenham & Redbridge, but I'm not there to watch a football match. I'm a man on a mission, focused on my objectives and targets, namely Chann and Krishna, the Singaporean match fixers. I've told them I know the final score, that the game is rigged, and it'll finish 1-0 to the home side. Except, it's not – it's all a bluff to test what these guys are all about. There's potentially £30k up for grabs but I'll take the lion's share and maybe give Delroy and Boats a slice of the pie. Before we get to that part of the deal, I'll collect my £5k pocket money, my standard fee for showing what I can do, organising the fixture.

Now I'm here with the fixers face to face and it's time to teach Boats a lesson, remind him that he shouldn't go behind my back. Little bro, are you crazy?! I brought you in on the business and I can take it away just as quickly.

At Wimbledon's Kingsmeadow Stadium I make sure we enter via the tunnel so the players can see me and I can shout out their names. Before kick off, I exchange a signal – a simple wave of the hand from my ex-Dagenham teammate on the pitch to me in the stands – which shows Chann and Krishna the fix is on

We're five minutes into the game and I turn to Chann. 'Yo, where's my money?' I tell him not to give it to me here, that we must go outside the stadium. Benji and Krishna stay for the second half and it's 1-0 to Wimbledon. My fake fix is on.

Me and Chann exit the ground and head for a nearby curry house to talk business. He hands me a white paper bag in a dark alleyway behind the ground and we walk to the restaurant. I count the cash in the loo, it's two grand short – £3k instead of £5k. This isn't right!

I return to the table and we start to bicker. Suddenly, a classy blonde woman struts through the door, swiftly followed by a man who sits down next to her. Are they on a date, in this dump? Why are they staring at us? Am I paranoid? They've totally thrown me.

We hear the crowd roar, Dagenham have equalised! It's 1-1 and all bets are off. Chann is furious and monitors the action unfold on the in-play betting app on his phone. He goes crazy and demands his money back. He's causing a scene, and I tell him to calm down, but he's not having it. He's freaking out, like he's high on drugs.

Chann's hysteria draws more attention from the date couple and panic kicks in. It's clear something fishy is going on. I text Benji and tell him that we've got to get the hell out of here. He arrives two minutes later with Krishna, and Chann hurls abuse after me as I make for the door. The blonde and her date grab Chann, and me and Benji speed walk to the car park. I turn to my best friend: 'Benji, something weird is happening!'

Yells, screams, chaos, confusion, a crowd of people suddenly swarm round us. What is going on?! I hear shouts of 'Stop! Stop! Stop!' We're surrounded. 'Moses Swaibu – you're under arrest.'

My head is spinning and all I can think about is that final text of Tan's: 'greedy man, no see clearly'. I catch a glimpse of Chann's twisted grin in the moonlight, a knowing wink as he gets taken away and before I know it, I'm in handcuffs, getting bundled into the back of a car. NCA? Who are they? Where are we going? Birmingham?

All that money, Dalston, the Chinese takeaway. It's too late. I'm done. The whistle blows for full-time. My match fixing career is over. Do not pass 'Go', do not collect £1 million, go directly to jail.

CHAPTER 17

TRANSFER TO BIRMINGHAM

I reach to pull on my seat belt and the plastic cuffs slice into my wrists. I'm trying to make sense of it all. I can't get my head around my eagerness to teach Boats a lesson. Greed put me in a position I wasn't expecting. No anger, no fear, just a deep dark sadness and a black hole I felt I was sliding into. Had Boats set me up?

The driver flicks on the blue and white flashing light on the car roof to accompany the wail of the siren as we head north out of London. I sit in silence until the police officer in the back strikes up a conversation: 'So who did you play for?'

'Crystal Palace and Lincoln City . . .' I try to respond but my words fizzle out to nothing. I'm struck dumb, and I feel sick to my stomach.

The first realisation of what I've done hits me hard. Tan's greedy man text echoes in my head again. I'm a naughty schoolboy who's just been summoned to the headmaster's office for bad behaviour. In a halting voice, I start telling the officer about playing in the FA Cup. One thing I'm certain about: I'm not speaking to a regular football fan. These people are driving me to my final destination, in the back of beyond.

'Where are we going?'

'Cannock.'

I've never heard of it, never mind know where it is.

My mind turns to just how damning the mobile phone can be. I think of every contact on there, of the call register, of every incriminating text message, every voicemail, every email, every WhatsApp and every photo. I know with every fibre of my being, right to the core of my body, that from this instant, my life has entered a downward spiral. I can't see any way out of it. Yet, for some reason I'm not scared. Maybe it's because of everything I've already been through.

Torrential rain beats down on the roof of the car. The windscreen wipers flap furiously from side to side, trying to beat off the cascades of water. No radio, no music, no chit chat. These officers mean serious business. Unmarked cars. This is not normal police.

'We're the NCA,' this same officer tells me when I ask.

'I don't know what that is.'

'The National Crime Agency.'

'We're a new police force, the UK equivalent of the FBI.'

'The FBI? What are you talking about?'

I roll my head back and look down at the plastic handcuffs. I look out of the window at the yellow lights flickering by as we speed along the motorway. The noise of the car engine sparks a flashback in my mind. I'm in the Porsche 911 Turbo S and my white Range Rover, cruising through the City of London with the Ferrari Boys. Falling out of a Mayfair nightclub in the small hours of the morning. Switching cars. Racing to see who can get to Waterloo Bridge first. Scenes.

I'm thinking of Crystal and her chicken curry. She'll be frantic. I go out to watch a football match with my best friend and don't come home. And Benji's been arrested too. Nobody knew what I was up to. Nobody.

There's a strange kind of stillness when you're trapped in a car on a cold November night, handcuffed to the seat, staring out of the window at nothing. It's as though time itself has folded into some dark crevice, leaving me suspended in the limbo of what's been and what's still to come. The road is endless; the white streaks of light pass by like ghostly reminders of the life I once had. My body is numb, but my mind is alert, reliving everything that brought me to this moment.

It wasn't supposed to be this way. None of it. Was my destiny to end up in the back of an NCA car wearing the weight of my mistakes like an albatross around my neck? I imagined myself different, better. I remember when football was pure – when it wasn't about money or power, but about the joy of the game. I remember the first time I stepped on to a pitch in front of a crowd, the first time I knew I could make a difference, that I could be something.

The early days felt like a dream. My studs sinking into the soft grass, the sound of the ball at my feet, the rhythm of it all. I was part of something bigger than myself. My first professional contract, my first goal, the first time I heard the roar of the crowd. I was Moses Swaibu. I was someone. The promise of a better future was in front of me, shining so bright I could almost touch it.

But somewhere along the line, that promise slipped away.

The passion turned into business, the beautiful game into a dirty one. How did I get here? How did I end up as the guy who fixes matches, the one whose name gets whispered in dark corners? It didn't start out that way. It wasn't about the money at first, not really. I was just trying to survive in a world that doesn't care about you unless you're giving something back. Then came the whispers, the opportunities. Little things at first: a conversation here, a handshake there. It was easy to ignore, easy to convince myself I wasn't really in it. Then it started to snowball.

And soon enough, the lines blurred. Fixing matches didn't feel like a crime. It felt like I was just playing the game by different rules, rules that didn't matter any more. A wink here, a little nudge there, and before I knew it, I wasn't just playing football – I was fixing it. I'd become part of a world that had no place for men like me, a world where everyone was either bought or sold. And I sold myself.

My body tenses as the car hits a bump. I'm pulled back to the present – the sound of the officer's voice breaks the silence. He's been quiet for a while, but I can tell he's watching me in the rear-view mirror, gauging my reaction. I'm not in the mood for small talk but the officer won't stop. He wants to know more about my playing days.

'So, Moses,' he says, his voice too casual, too probing, 'you played in the FA Cup, didn't you? Must've been something special. Bet you thought you were going to make it big then, huh?'

I don't answer immediately. The question lingers in the air, hanging between us like a phantom from a past life. The FA Cup? I almost laugh, but it catches in my throat. It seems so far removed from who I am now, from what I've become.

The kid who thought he could change the world with a pair of boots and a dream.

'Yeah,' I say finally, my voice flat, 'it was a good experience. A decent run.'

It seems like a lifetime ago. My mum was so proud. What will she think of my arrest? I can't bear for her to ever find out. The shame of it will crush her. 'Every boy's dream' is how players and managers and pundits on TV always describe football success. For a few years, I lived that dream. Now it was turning into a nightmare.

I can feel the officer's eyes on me, but I won't give him anything. Not now. Not after everything. The man in the mirror doesn't see me for who I am, just for who he thinks I was.

The car slows down as we approach some indistinct place. I don't know where we are. I don't care. All I can think of is how easy it is to tell myself that the game is over. But I've been lying to myself for a long time now.

Hours later we get out of the car in the back of beyond. The police station looks like it's landed from outer space, as if it's been custom-built just for us.

It's pitch dark and looks closed. I've been arrested before, but this is completely different. While I get fingerprinted and photographed, I catch a glimpse of someone walking past me. They look oddly familiar. Panic rises inside me. Hang on? What the fuck! Is that Hakeem? Boats's best friend. What the hell is he doing here?

My paranoia increases as I take off my shoes. They've got laces. I'm not allowed them in my cell. *bang!* The door is slammed shut behind me. Hakeem?! Why is he here? Where's Boats? Who else has been arrested?

I only knew Hakeem as Boats's mate. He was at the Crystal Palace Academy. He's always been a quiet boy. I never once spoke to him about match fixing. As far as I knew, neither did Boats. I was already on an emotional roller coaster, so to see him in the police station sent me into a spiral. Why is he here in this particular police station, all the way up in Cannock?! It didn't make any sense. It kept me awake all night. I couldn't sleep for thinking about it.

Just like Benji, Hakeem had nothing to do with any kind of match fixing. He was collateral damage in the path of Boats. I paced around my cell. I sat down. I got up again. I was wracked with anxiety. The lack of clarity was driving me mad. It was like the good and bad side of my brain had started glitching. There's a Pixar film called *Inside Out*. In the mind of a young girl, Riley, are her five personified emotions that influence her actions: Joy, Sadness, Fear, Disgust and Anger. I was wrestling with all five at once.

There is an irony in those plastic handcuffs. The police give you them when they value your level of criminality. It's like you earned the right to special treatment.

I spent so much time climbing, whether that was in life to avoid the abuse and trauma I survived as a child, or navigating a pathway to fulfil my deepest dreams: making it to the top of football. This journey would be my last climb. Was I chasing the snake's head or was I trying to establish something I never really saw an end to?

Tan's voice rang in my head like a Jay-Z album. I held on to every word and teaching; the pitfalls he warned me to avoid. It was like he saw me crashing before I could blink. My hard head and drive for some form of top spot gave me boss status but for all the wrong reasons. All I thought about was prison. Can I survive the years I could potentially face inside? Trust me, growing up, I did everything I could to avoid jail. I always got away with being smart and sensible enough to keep my distance from any type of fire. I felt like a man graduating when I first entered the world of match fixing.

On the drive to Birmingham in the back of the police car, there were moments of laughter mixed with sadness. I think deeply about the changing room. The best place. Every former professional will miss that camaraderie for eternity. While I enjoyed those big moments before a game or hearing the fans chant and the white noise before kick-off, I also did the opposite: match fixing. I had no soul. You had to be soulless. I'd made a deal with the sporting devil.

CHAPTER 18

LOCKED PIN

The phone! Fuck. The phone!

They release me from Watling Street Police Station that same evening.

The custody officer allows me to call a local cab firm to book a taxi. They don't return my bank card. I didn't expect them to. Luckily, the long number and the expiry date are somehow lodged into my brain. I recite it to them over the phone and state my destination: London. I spend the entire three-hour journey sprawled across the back seats of the black cab. My head is a mess. I've been released on bail pending trial. It's like being set free but still trapped. How the hell am I supposed to process that? I've always hated the feeling of being controlled. This is next level.

I don't know the gravity of the arrest. I'm in trouble. I don't quite yet understand how much trouble. I've apparently been done for conspiracy to defraud the betting trade. I keep thinking about Hakeem. Why is Hakeem all the way up here in the same police station as me? I have playback in my mind as I wrestle with the five empty seats in the back of the cab.

I reflect on yesterday's interrogation by the police. I took my chances in the interview. I went in knowing I was going to say 'No comment' to every single question. Then halfway through I realised the police didn't have much to pin on me so I gave them what they needed to hear. I concocted a story on the spot. I told them that Chann was a licensed FIFA football agent who got my phone number from the Professional Footballers' Association website. I'm a semi-professional footballer looking for a new team after leaving my last club, Whitehawk. I said I got Chann and his football agent colleague, Krishna, tickets for the Wimbledon–Dagenham game and invited them to meet me and my mate Benji at the stadium in London. The money I had on me? It had come from a variety of sources. Had Chann ever handled it? No. I told them I paid for the match tickets from my wad of notes.

I said I left the stadium to get something to eat and the stewards wouldn't let me back in. That's how I explained why I went to the Indian restaurant with Chann. To grab some food and have a proper chat to this agent about finding me a new club. I told them Chann was getting agitated about the score in the game because he'd put a bet on the result. He was a gambler. I described Chann banging his hands on the restaurant table in frustration. I say to the police interviewers that their undercover officers could vouch for this. They could also vouch that I got up and left Chann in the restaurant. I said I was on the phone to my girlfriend Crystal when I got stopped in the car park . . .

It was mostly improvised nonsense. I made it all up as I went along.

I'm restless, fidgety as we drive south on the M1. I manage to sit in every seat trying to work out who the protagonists are in this conspiracy. I move around so much in the back of the taxi the driver must think I'm a mad man. He picks me up from a police station in a field outside of Birmingham then goes on a £400 road trip to London. WTF. He keeps looking at me in his rear-view mirror trying to strike up a conversation.

My mind is spinning. Has Tan been arrested? Has the money been recovered? Even worse, have they arrested Crystal or raided her flat? Have they gone to my mum's or my place and issued warrants in the middle of the night? I have £50k in Crystal's attic, £25k on top of the money counter in the wardrobe of my bedroom. And please God do not let them go to the Dalston Chinese.

My mobile phone is the ultimate lethal weapon. In among the whirling mess of thoughts it's the main thing on my mind. Once opened, it could bring down the whole syndicate and its associates. It links everyone internationally to an even bigger conspiracy. Chann and Krishna are small fry compared to what's on that phone.

Our whole system, from top to bottom and back again, is on there. Details about the money funnelling from Singapore through Eastern Europe and the Balkans to players across Europe. Information about the Asian markets where the huge bets are being placed on games.

When the cash comes in, the Boss of the Far Eastern syndicate ships the cash to criminal gangs via a network of couriers. Let's say each courier gets more than €2 million to use to bribe players. Bribes can reach up to €100,000 per match. Players are bought. Couriers pass the money on to corrupt players – sometimes even match officials – to ensure that the result, or another facet of the game, is fixed. Then the bets are placed. Groups of intermediaries place bets for syndicates with bookmakers in Asia. The odds are usually low, so to win big, huge amounts of money are needed. It's easier to hide the bets on the Asian markets, where the volumes of transactions are enormous. Winnings are shared. If the fix succeeds, the money flows back to the syndicate and everyone takes their share of the profits. If the fix fails, then the losses are shared. Each member of the syndicate bears the loss. The criminal gangs put huge pressure on the players to ensure a favourable outcome.

Once a bet is fixed and manipulated on the Asian market, especially with Asian handicaps, millions are made. Half our league is involved. I'm not even privy to the extent of what players have done or who's been paid in full. I read that there are more bets each day on Asian sports markets than deals on the New York Stock Exchange.

All this shit is on my phone, and much, much more. Text messages to the Boss, Hunken, corrupt players, contact details, online pseudonyms, locations, meeting points, pick-up points, the runners and cash couriers who look like teenagers, addresses of casinos, restaurants, locations of car parks, details of hotel reservations, apartment bookings, football fixture lists, photos of bundles of cash, money-counting machines, every payment made, the names of everyone I've spoken to, messaged, the masterminds behind what would have been a global network connected directly from Asia to Europe. A self-made casino incriminating the heads of the syndicate over and over again.

There's information on all the betting companies in Asia that hide the money. The casinos that give you the perfect paper trail.

'Hey, Mr Police Officer, I have a gambling habit,' or 'I hit it big in the casino!' This is the script if we're caught.

Will they crack the code of my text message alias, 'Jon Gotti', a play on the name of the notorious mobster, John Gotti, boss of the Gambino crime family in New York City in the 1980s? What if they know who he was or who I was making out to be? Have they seen the movie? I close my eyes, but I can't escape the images flashing behind my eyelids. My life, my choices, the endless descent. The people I've hurt. The promises I've broken. The doors I've walked through with no idea where they were leading. I thought I could outrun it. I thought I could disappear. But this – the charges, the upcoming trial – the net is closing in on me.

I watch the digital meter ticking, slow but steady, the numbers flicker in the dim glow of the taxi, hypnotise me, sending me in and out of an uneasy sleep, my head a mad jumble of paranoid thoughts. Is this all a crazy dream?

One thing is certain: I *cannot* let the police get hold of the PIN to unlock my mobile phone. If they pull the PIN on my phone it will explode like a grenade, blow the roof off the whole operation. I *cannot* incriminate the syndicate. From the very start of my involvement, they gave me the most subtle summary of their gambling – it's like joining a cult or the Mafia. 'If you get caught, you heard nothing, you saw nothing, we don't exist.'

I knew what I was signing up for. What I didn't expect was for me to end up like this. Especially after what Dom the French did on day one. I was aware of their capabilities when they sent bullets to players. And the Boss was obsessed with catching the French. He put a bounty on his head just for information.

I'm not scared; I'm petrified. I've put everyone I know –

especially those closest to me, family and friends – in extreme danger without their knowledge. Truth be told, I feel that I've played with the devil. These people have the capability of killing me softly without leaving a single trace of who did it.

What if the Bosses don't know I've been arrested? They soon will if it hits the media outlets. Maybe it already has?

I risk being killed. I could lose my life and the money or worse. Pointing the finger at the syndicate, spilling the beans to the police. Imagine if Hunken gets arrested? Or the stash houses are compromised? Or the casinos are put on a red list? The next thing I know I'm on the front page of every newspaper in the country.

I've been dealing in hard-core cash. No crypto, no exchanges. Just the right brokers who can change the money for the best rates. Our one-stop shop was a bureau de change in central London, opposite McDonald's on the corner of Tottenham Court Road. Do they have CCTV cameras? Have they got footage of me coming out with sports bags full of cash? Did they see me with the Ferrari Boys? Have I tied them up in this conspiracy? Have they arrested Dave at Tower Bridge car rentals because of all the cars and money that was spent? Am I going to be charged with money laundering?

Nothing makes sense. Nothing. First Ben is put in cuffs, then Hakeem. Both completely innocent. Why are they arresting them? I can't get my head around what's happening. It's a massive head fuck. A massive fuck-up. For the first time in my life, I feel like running away. But I can't. I want to wake up and be a normal person. But there is no time for tears or feeling sorry for myself. I must face the music.

As the meter adds more digits to the already enormous fare,

we hit London, and that's when I think, *Bingo! Follow the money!* I go straight back to Crystal's and crash out until the early hours of the morning. I wake up and put on the TV. My eyes are on the screen, but it takes me a moment to focus, to comprehend what I'm seeing. Sky News. A huge breaking news story. The biggest match-fixing scandal in English football history. I just stand there frozen in shock.

The yellow news ticker rolls along the bottom of the screen: 'Six men arrested for match-fixing-related crimes.' My face flushes, my body goes hot, especially as I'd seen Boats's friend, Hakeem, at the police station. He must be one of the six. Boats too? Chann and Krishna. Delroy is the first to be named. I don't realise the severity of the charge until I watch the news bulletins. I'll be on bail for seven months before going to trial. The next few days are awkward and strange. I'm plagued by paranoid thoughts. Delroy has gone AWOL. I quickly realise I'll be getting charged too.

I freeze when I first see that my name is out there too. All the people I've dealt with, all those names are on the TV screen. Delroy's face hits hardest. I thought he was a friend. I thought we were in this together. But now, he's one of them.

I sit down, not knowing how to feel. My phone buzzes. I don't pick it up. I already know who it is. It's Delroy, but it feels like someone from the past. People I used to know. Now, they're just ghosts. The world keeps turning, the city keeps moving, unaffected. But I can't escape what's coming. Everything is falling apart.

A few days after I get home, I call Boats. His tone has changed. He makes me think he's the reason I got arrested. Our phone call is full of one-liners, one-word word sentences, awkward silences. Boats mumbles non-committal replies, 'Yeah, hmm, hmm, yeah.' I'm thinking, could he be feeding the police confidential information? Maybe his phone's being tapped? Then I start hearing things through our mutual friends.

I hear rumours about Boats. He's saying stuff like, yeah, man, it ain't my fault. It's Hakeem. This is what he's telling people on the street. I'm thinking, *Hakeem?* To this day, they don't speak because of that. When you live a lie, it's very funny how that lie will eat you up.

It made me realise that someone that had a pure heart became toxic. In his mind, it's survival of the fittest. I've always been in a state of survival. You can trigger that survival mode at any time. Someone may pass away and you have to survive. You've got to be strong for your family and your friends. Boats is in that survival mode. Unlike him, I know what to do because of my childhood. When I'm in that mode, it can be a blessing and a curse. This is the end of everything. The end of the game. The end of me.

One thing remained certain: I can't let the police unlock my phone.

CHAPTER 19

THE TRIAL

The daily trips from London to Birmingham wear me out, both physically and mentally. The early mornings and long train rides feel endless. Each day, I walk into Birmingham Crown Court with a weight on my chest. The pressure is different from football. This is like a constant mental battle with myself. The hardest part is sitting through the long, painful deliberations of the lawyers. The prosecution demonises me as a player who fixed matches, someone who betrayed the sport I loved. It hurt to listen to it, knowing how the trial would end, but still having to face it.

I tell the court that Hakeem has nothing to do with this crime. The reason why I've done that is I could have taken the years. Boats, it's his first time, but he knew what he was doing. If Hakeem goes to prison, that's on me. As much as there was a plot and a twist, this is someone that's blind to what's going on. He didn't know anything. It made me realise that you can go to jail for some shit you ain't even done.

The verdict comes in the next day and it looks like I'm in the clear. I think to myself, *I could have got away with this shit.* That's crazy. The NCA is the FBI of the UK, and I could have got away with it.

I told Robert Drake, the officer who arrested me, 'Damn, you didn't get me this time.'

'No, but you'll be back.'

I don't know what he means. He repeats it, 'You'll be back.'

I don't know what a hung jury is. Boats is going to prison, Hakeem is cleared of any wrongdoing and the jury is discharged from reaching a verdict on me. I'm granted unconditional bail pending a retrial. By giving me a new trial a year later, it gave them more time to investigate and link everything together. And it gave them a new prosecutor. I knew the day that I got cross-examined, that this prosecutor – Robert Davies – doesn't know what he's talking about.

His first question was why are you getting paid in cheque and cash? And I was like, go and ask Bromley. The jury can clearly see that they're avoiding tax. For a whole season, half cheque, half cash, I'm going into the bank every month to deposit cash. Then I'm putting in a cheque a few days after and I'm explaining that this is what happens in lower-level football. And he's saying, no it doesn't. His knowledge of football was non-existent. He didn't give a compelling argument as to why I'm guilty.

What am I guilty of? Am I guilty because the club that I'm playing for hasn't been transparent with money? When I go and take money from match fixers, where's the crime in that?

If I'd found that money on the street, I may have put it in my pocket. I think I gave the jury a lot of food for thought.

If they find me guilty, what am I guilty of? The night I was arrested, I met some men that claimed the match was fixed. There's no evidence of a match being fixed. No players have been involved. There was a lot of lies being told by everyone. He's going to do this; he's going to do that. The *Daily Telegraph* has given Chann money.

Chann has given me money. I've predicted what the score will be, knowing they didn't have all this information before. I'm not being arrested because of what I've done. I'm being arrested because somebody else has been caught. When I shook the officer's hand, he said to me, 'You know what, you're unlucky, man.'

The scariest thing is I could have got away with it. The reason why I say scary is because if I had got away with it, what would have been my next steps? I was on an ego and power trip. I was willing to get on a plane to Singapore. As the trial wore on, I was thinking, *What the hell? I might actually get away with this.*

I pleaded not guilty and I realised, if I hadn't gone to the AFC Wimbledon v Dagenham & Redbridge game that night, I would have got away scot-free. I could have gone to Dalston and withdrawn my money. Closed my secret savings account. Throughout the trial I was thinking, I call the syndicate – look, I've got 'not guilty'. I don't know how that message would have been received. Ultimately, I may have been so solid to this organisation.

Maybe they would be thinking, he's been arrested. We know what he's done but he's got 'not guilty'. Let's now increase the risk. What else do you want to do? But in the back of my mind, I keep thinking, *Shit, my daughter* – what's going to happen to her if I'm not around? It brings the severity of my situation into sharp focus.

* * *

Can you imagine this flaky little character Chann in court taking the stand? That's how I knew Wilson probably wasn't what people made out. This was his trusted lieutenant? Sending him payments from the *Telegraph* sting money? Chann really wanted to impress me by telling me that he was close to the Big Boss, the notorious Wilson Raj Perumal. Perumal didn't strike me as the boss of all bosses. It's only when you're on the inside you find out the truth.

Chann acted in such a strange, unprofessional way. But he fooled enough people. What the hell was Chann's incentive to do this? What was Wilson's urgency to get involved? I knew that England and the UK was the devil's playground when it came to match fixing. Chann said he had no intentions to come to the UK since nobody was able to penetrate the markets here. The UK was thought to be too pure, above the threat of fixing. Even Tan knew the risks – the police, the potential sentences. The damages it would do for the business if anyone was caught.

Chann thought the €60,000 came from the middleman. He didn't know it was an undercover police officer. When I spoke to him about it, he said it was an investor, but the money was too clean. I could instantly tell when I counted it in the toilet of the Indian restaurant. It hadn't been touched by human hands. Why does this guy Chann from Singapore have smooth, crisp banknotes?

He came across as a clown with a desperate attitude, trying to impress Wilson, wearing his Manchester United jacket every day. In addition to him never handling that kind of money, he sent me photos of the bundles of cash. That's how excited he was. Throughout the whole trial I sat thinking, *Chann is an idiot.* Worse, he was a big kid. A total liability. He claimed he knew the business. But he didn't. His erratic, excitable behaviour immediately set off alarm bells for me.

The crazy part is that it also shows the *Daily Telegraph* investigation was a flawed one. They were also desperate. Are these two really match fixers? They couldn't rub two pence together, but everyone, including us and them, behaved rashly. The *Telegraph* wanted to nail these two guys to suit their story.

When I began to understand how badly this was investigated, I really believed it would be impossible to convict me beyond reasonable doubt. The evidence they had against me was flimsy. I felt sorry for the jury, to be honest. They must have thought this was a big circus. A prosecution relying entirely on WhatsApp and Skype messages. You can see why it's so difficult to prosecute match fixing. Even bribery. Who was being bribed? That was everyone's defence.

I was unlucky to get caught up in this newspaper investigation. But the other side was, more money, more greed, more power.

* * *

During the trial, I was thinking, *How can I bribe if I've not got the money?* I'm not actually saying, 'Take this and do this.' Someone's given me the money to pass over to someone and say, 'You go do this.' In my naivety, I didn't know about conspiracies and all the other stuff that comes with it. I thought to myself, if you do get caught, what are they going to do? Can you get caught if someone says there's ten grand or you pick that up off the floor?

If I'm outside a bank and I say, let's go and rob this bank for two million, we drive off, the bank gets robbed and the police get that information out of a phone, is that conspiracy? How can you say these players conspired to fix a game when there's no evidence of a fix?

Everyone's trying to get the upper hand on everyone. The police have set up a sting. Boats tried to take money that he never had the capabilities for because there's no evidence. How can you say that's conspiracy? Then I realised, when you go to court, it needs to be proven beyond a reasonable doubt that this crime was committed.

If you think Moses may have committed the crime, that doesn't prove the burden – that's not the burden of proof. I was thinking, so I can get away with this because as much as I am guilty, what am I guilty of? That's what I couldn't figure out. I was told to plead 'not guilty' because there's a lack of evidence. But because of that lack of evidence, they tried to change their indictment several times.

The indictment that they were changing was that we were first arrested for conspiracy to defraud the betting trade. When I heard that, it sent shivers down my spine. I couldn't get my head round it. Betting trade as in the UK betting trade? Because that's how it sounded to me. I'm thinking, *Fucking hell, we're in trouble.*

I was on trial for a crime that was conspiracy. I wasn't on trial for match fixing. That was completely separate. Let's just say that if they did have the evidence, what would I be tried for? Because in order to arrest people, you usually need a top and you need the bottom. You usually need someone that's forthcoming, who says, here's a witness. There were no witnesses to this. The witnesses, the people, don't even live in the UK.

Am I being put on trial for all these businesses that are generating millions of pounds and dollars across the world? Or am I being put on trial for taking over a league because I've been receiving money from this big, organised crime group that no one can see? Because if I was on trial for that, then it's me versus ghosts.

* * *

Throughout the court proceedings, I know that if they get my phone PIN, I'm toast. The evidence is damning. Players, money, locations, games, distribution networks, named individuals and the heads of the syndicate. They even threaten my legal team since I gave them the wrong phone PIN countless times. The courts give them an ultimatum. I still say, 'No!'

I'm strangely comfortable taking the stand, just like at my previous trial in Guildford. After hearing prosecutors fall short countless times on evidence and opening arguments, by the time I get on the stand I'm asked why I have so much money in my bank account. My reply is savings and half cheque, half cash.

They can't understand why I was paid like that and painted me out to be a liar. The truth is that's how non-league teams paid their players. It's a can of worms the prosecution does not want to open. Imagine the national scandal? English football teams in tax avoidance wages scam!

I admitted some form of guilt and knowledge especially when it came to Hakeem and Boats. They weren't match fixers or didn't have the capabilities. The jury were confused, as was the prosecutor. I was telling the truth. The prosecutor relied on my police interview. First time round I gave a 'No Comment' answer to every single question. After a quick confab with my lawyer at

Cannock police station, I offered them another version of events that I thought they wanted to hear. Completely improvised. Mostly nonsense.

In court, I state that I changed my mind to tell the truth even though it was white lies. There are elements of the truth hidden within my second police interview, they just didn't know where to find them. After coming off the stand I feel more than confident. Then I watch Boats crash and burn. Imagine not fixing one match but acting like the Big Boss and sounding and appearing arrogant? I knew he had a one-way ticket to jail.

Luckily for us, while everyone went back and forth from London to Birmingham, Del would be tried separately. Nobody understood why, but his case was due to follow on from ours. Later, I discover that they want to buy themselves time to further investigate his movements. Due to his travels to Grenada on international duty, they think he might have manipulated matches abroad.

My phone was a bomb. The following factors helped me. Match fixing was not recognised as a crime in the UK. It fell under the charge of bribery, but who was being bribed? The police never arrested Tan or Hunken. They got the Singaporeans, Chann and Krishna. No money was ever recovered. It vanished into the darkness, just like I did that evening.

In the court, I swore on the Quran. Some of the jury members were Asian and women. There is no way they would have found me guilty. Plus, the day before, I saw all the jury members and the white jury members went to lunch together. Something didn't feel right, but it worked out in my favour.

At least I thought it had. Hakeem and his family are over the moon. Boats's face is blank. He leaves the dock in tears.

The jury delivered its verdict by a majority of eleven to one. There are unanimous verdicts against Chann Sankaran and Krishna Ganeshan – described as the 'central figures' in the plot to fix matches – on the same charge of conspiracy to commit bribery.

And then came the deliberation. Fifteen hours. It felt like an eternity. They couldn't come to a verdict. They couldn't decide what to do with me. The weight of it was unbearable. For all those hours, I sat there wondering if I would be going home that day, or if they would send me away for good. Would they find me guilty? Would I walk away free?

In the end, the jury was discharged. No verdict. The pressure, the anxiety, the stress – it all just melted away into nothingness. I was granted unconditional bail, pending retrial. But it didn't feel like a win. Not really. Not after everything I had gone through.

Being granted bail meant that I could leave, but I knew I wouldn't be free. Not yet. Not until the retrial. The same questions lingered. What would happen next? Would they charge me again? Would I spend the rest of my life fighting this? It felt like a never-ending cycle.

That first trial – it didn't end the way I thought it would. It didn't bring the closure I was looking for. Instead, it was just the beginning. The beginning of a longer fight, a battle that would continue to tear at me until I couldn't tell where the fight ended and I began.

There was no peace. Only the looming shadow of what came next. And in those moments, with the trial now over, I found myself wondering one thing: *How the hell did I get here?*

One last twist in the tale: I'm told I'll have to face the retrial with ... Delroy Facey. Oh, Del, so we meet again.

CHAPTER 20

THE STING

I find out in the first court hearing about a mysterious character called Terry Steans. This big, burly, straight-talking guy takes the stand. He's introduced as an independent sports anti-corruption consultant and a former Global Investigations Coordinator for FIFA's security department. Turns out he's been working with not only the NCA but also a *Daily Telegraph* investigation into match corruption, led by a journalist called Claire Newell. It's all news to me.

Steans and Michael Pride, another former FIFA anti-corruption investigator, had got wind of plans by a Singaporean match fixing syndicate attempting to set up a fixing network in the UK. Chann Sankaran was working with Wilson Raj Perumal – a convicted match fixing overlord – on an alleged plot to infiltrate English football – long assumed to be above corruption.

Singapore was known as the centre of a suspected web of fixers thought to have manipulated the outcome of football matches around the world for years.

I hear pennies drop in my mind at the prosecution's opening statement, disclosing the evidence. They rely entirely on a chronological order of events built from WhatsApp messages between Boats, Delroy, Chann, Krishna and me.

I'm gobsmacked when I see all the text messages I'm not part of until they get to me passing on Boats's number to Delroy. This was my downfall moment.

The messages between Chann and Terry Steans are almost comical. Chann couldn't even afford a burger from room service, let alone pay for his hotel in Manchester. He seems amateurish and panicky from the start.

Nobody knew who was saying what. We only found out at the trial what the hell was going on – the how and why of my arrest. My suspicions and paranoia were right. It was a bizarre and shocking experience sitting in the dock and hearing all these revelations I had no idea about. How the hell had I got arrested in the car park outside AFC Wimbledon's stadium on 26 November 2013? Was there a snitch? Was that snitch Boats or Del? It all came tumbling out over the course of two trials. It was like a punch to the gut to hear all these bombshells dropped.

I was arrested for conspiracy to defraud the betting trade, then charged for conspiracy to commit bribery. I never understood why we weren't standing trial for anything related to match fixing. There was no law for such a crime, eight? How did they manage to arrest and charge us with no Russian or Chinese or Singaporean crime bosses in the dock?

This is how 'The Sting' went down. For five days, National Crime Agency detectives were all over Chann Sankaran and Krishna Ganeshan, following their every move. On 22 November

2013, an undercover NCA officer, posing as a potential investor, met Chann and Krishna through a 'middleman' (Delroy Facey) at the Great Northern Warehouse in Manchester.

A hidden recording device picks up Sankaran boasting about the lower league teams he has in his pocket – Bromley and Whitehawk. He claims he can arrange a three- or four-goal defeat for Whitehawk FC on 30 November if the players are bribed.

On 23 November 2013, Chann and Krishna make this seemingly random trip to Hyde, a small town in Greater Manchester. They show up at Conference North football team Hyde FC's ground and pose as FIFA football agents, offering players a chance to play abroad. It's all pretty weird.

Two days later, they head south to Croydon to rendezvous with the fake investor. This is the meeting Boats and Hakeem also attend at a Starbucks in an East Croydon shopping centre. The undercover investigator/investor quizzes Boats, asks him if he's up for it. Boats agrees to do everything and anything. No hesitation.

Then, the undercover guy gives Chann and Krishna a bag with €60,000 in cash – all marked notes, courtesy of the *Daily Telegraph* newspaper, who were helping fund this whole sting thing.

Later, the two Asians give Boats €450 'pocket money' to keep him 'onside'. Boats changes it into sterling at a bureau de change and gives Hakeem £100, in the process incriminating his best friend.

On 26 November 2013, Chann and Krishna meet another player who police say is volunteering his services as a 'middleman' between players and the businessmen. This player is me, Moses Swaibu.

Unbeknownst to us, the NCA had been bugging Chann's Manchester hotel room, recording everything we'd discussed earlier about fixing the game that night – AFC Wimbledon v Dagenham & Redbridge.

Afterwards, Chann and Krishna were spotted making phone calls to contacts overseas, including the notorious Perumal, telling them the fix was on.

Chann said he had control of clubs in English League Two and that he'd text them details of the exact scores, encouraging them to stick bets on this specific League Two game. Big money was at stake. . .

Chann and Krishna even place their own wager at a Manchester branch of Ladbrokes, a gambling and betting shop, putting more than £1,000 down. They're fully convinced the fix is happening.

On the day of the match, Sankaran and Ganeshan – still being tailed – travelled to AFC Wimbledon to meet me and Benji outside the ground. Together, we watched the first half, which ended with Wimbledon leading 1-0. Benji and Krishna stayed on for the second half while me and Chann went to a nearby curry house. Dagenham & Redbridge equalised. The fix was not going according to my plan. That's when the NCA swoops in. They arrest us as we finished our meal.

Chann's got £3,000 on him, Krishna had £250. As you know, I also had £3k in cash on me. Talk about getting caught in the act.

* * *

We also hear in court about an organisation called Sportradar that keeps an eye on suspicious betting patterns in betting activity. If a ton of bets are put on a game, they flag it as a sign that something dubious might be going on. Sportradar Integrity Services also keeps tabs on the people who play in these matches

In July 2013, there was a newspaper article about an English player who had moved to Australia. Sportradar's antennae pricked up – according to them this guy had a potentially dodgy playing history. He'd played in a bunch of matches pinpointed as being fixed. Sportradar was tracking a few players in my league. I wasn't one of them and neither were any of my teammates. Then this same guy moves from England's Conference South to join a club in Australia's semi-pro Victoria Premier League called Southern Stars.

His name was David Obaze, a former Bromley teammate of mine. I didn't know him personally but after what happened to me at Lincoln, I found out on the news that players from the UK had gone to Australia and been lured into rigging games. My heart sinks when the prosecution mentions Australia and the former English players who were tempted Down Under to fix games.

I knew those players had come from our league. I also knew at the time, simply because of what they were posting online, and some of the stuff that they were doing, that they were hot. They probably would have gone under the radar had they not blown their cover with flashy posts on Instagram about 'living the high life'. Expensive holidays in Bali, extravagant purchases, glitzy nightclubs, living a lifestyle that didn't fit the norms you'd expect of an amateur footballer.

These players go to Australia, and they get caught up in fixing. Sportradar investigate it. They monitored their games during that season and turns out they performed much worse than expected. Worse than the betting markets predicted. They were losing by three, four, five goals multiple times. Sportradar spotted increasingly fishy-looking betting patterns in the Asian betting market.

The Football Federation of Australia and the Victoria Police were contacted. During the matches, a Sportradar staff member was on the phone with the police relaying live information about what they were seeing across the Asian bookies. The police stuck wiretaps on the players and even planted microphones in the goalposts so they could hear every word the team said. The hidden mics picked up players chatting to people off the pitch about bets and exactly what had to happen on the pitch to fulfil the fix.

The joint investigation bagged five convictions – four players who were previously from the English Conference South, plus Segaran 'Gerry' Subramaniam, the fixing ringleader. But the police were confused. They could see the players had been making calls to a number in Hungary, and some of them had been talking about a Singaporean man they called the King. So, who was that?

They got 'Gerry the Malaysian', but they didn't get Wilson Raj Perumal, who was really running the show.

In 2013, Terry Steans worked for the International Centre for Sports Security. His job was rooting out corruption in football on a global scale. He also worked as an investigator for FIFA with a similar remit.

He was tracking the movements of Wilson Raj Perumal and his worldwide match-fixing operation, At the time, Perumal was in Hungary. Terry had a source in the Hungarian police who said Perumal was still trying to orchestrate fixes. They mentioned a guy called Chann who had paid him a visit. Terry devised a plan to target Chann to get to Perumal.

Of course, Chann is Chann Sankaran, one of the two guys Delroy introduced me to. Terry Steans and his investigative team set up a honey trap using Facebook to get to Chann. Terry posed as a fake football agent promising quick money and big investment.

The Facebook agent started approaching Chann's friends asking if they know anybody that can put them in touch with the fixer? They tell them that they've got a big businessman with money to invest.

Chann took the bait. They asked him what games he could provide. Pretty much anything – international friendly matches, some major tournament games, even fixtures in the UK, albeit the lower leagues.

The plan was to entice Chann to the UK and let British police take over from there. Chann agreed and asked for them to pay for his flight to Manchester.

He also needed other expenses such as cash to pay off players. He wanted £60k for that and expected Terry to stump up the cash.

Terry didn't have that kind of money, so he called Claire Newell at the *Daily Telegraph*. He made a deal with Claire: if the newspaper helped to fund the operation, then they could publish the exclusive story in return. A good deal but a complicated one. It's not so easy to get hold of €60,000 cash and get it to Manchester in the space of twenty-four hours. Also, there are all kinds of hoops to jump through to make sure you're doing it within the law. Risks are attached to it for the journalists, and for Terry.

Once it had been signed off, the *Telegraph* bought flights and hotel rooms for Chann and his sidekick, Krishna. They had to book it in a way that wouldn't obviously be connected to the newspaper.

They book rooms under a fake company that the *Telegraph* used for these kinds of scenarios. With Chann on a plane to Manchester, it was game on. Claire Newell was the chief investigative journalist at the *Daily Telegraph* – a well-spoken Bond-girl look-a-like who gave an impressive testimony in court. She hopped on a train from London to Manchester to get together with Terry. An undercover meeting was meticulously planned for the bar in the Great Northern Warehouse Hotel. Chann joins Terry and they start the meeting. The investigative journalists positioned themselves at tables all around for a clear view if any documents or money changed hands. The encounter was being recorded.

Chann was super confident about his plans to fix matches. But the tricky part was getting him to show he could deliver players. Terry and Claire needed proof that Chann wasn't just all talk. To properly nail him, he had to produce the players. The next day there was a phone call between Terry and Chann where Terry asked to meet the players. Chann agrees but is reluctant to show his hand so the Sting operation has to apply pressure on him.

This back and forth between Terry and Chann goes on for a while. They reach a bit of an impasse with Chann, who almost flies home. They've got this person who they believe is a match fixer, but they can't prove it because he won't give them the players. And if he won't give them the players, they're not giving him the money. This explains why Chann was so anxious for me to supply him with photos and names.

But then a breakthrough. Chann mentions someone called Delroy and says that he's involved in the fixes. Terry works out this must be Delroy Facey because of the description that Chann has given him. Claire and Terry were playing a risky game. If they stepped across a line, like paying money over to a match fixer, then they were part of the crime. Terry contacted a friend of his, an assistant commissioner with the Metropolitan Police who told him he was simultaneously one step away from glory and one false move from prison. He said the police should take over the operation. It was a job for the National Crime Agency. The NCA picks up the ball and runs with it.

In the UK, the NCA is a special police agency that leads investigations into organised crime. Match fixing falls into their area of activity. Terry tells Claire that they've got to give up their own sting operation and defer to the criminal investigation. Although the NCA was going to take over the reins, they still needed Terry. He was the guy Chann had been talking to up to this point, so he couldn't just suddenly disappear. Terry worked with the NCA to put them in place next to Chann Sankaran.

The NCA told Terry to wait for a phone call. Terry's burner phone started to ring. It's Chann asking him where he is, that he's late. Chann is getting twitchy waiting for him.

Terry needs to hand the operation without raising any suspicions. So, he tells Chann he can't make it to the meeting, but he's sending someone else instead. He's the money man. He's the businessman they've been talking about all this time. Terry warns Chann not to upset him because he's the man giving him the €60k.

Now the NCA have their 'in'. They send their own under-cover man in Terry's place, posing as the businessman, and snare

Chann and Krishna, show them the money. They fall for it, hook, line and sinker.

That was as much involvement as Terry had. Then the whole operation was taken over by the NCA. They followed the Asian fixers down to AFC Wimbledon. They had them bang to rights. Then these three guys – that's us! – get nabbed because of Chann and Krishna bringing the cops into the mix.

That's how they got me. Remember Boats and Hakeem had gone to a meeting with a middle-aged white guy? He must have been an NCA officer. And the meeting I had with Chann in the Indian restaurant next to AFC Wimbledon's ground? The NCA was all over that with the glamourous blonde woman and her 'date'.

And although he wouldn't be arrested until later, the NCA knew all about Delroy's part in this too. Maybe Wilson didn't get caught in the trap, but two of his foot soldiers did. Chann Sankaran and Krishna Ganeshan, along with the four of us – me, Del, Boats and Hakeem – were royally stung. We all wound up in court, and I was going to a retrial with Del.

* * *

The Retrial

I had an extra year to prepare for the retrial and the very real prospect of prison, which helped me mentally. My daughter, Taliya, would have been two years old. She had chickenpox for a couple of weeks before I went in. Up until the month of me going to prison, all I could think of was trying to do my best to not see her as much and get used to the fact that this could soon be my reality.

The retrial started with a different tone. Twelve white jurors who all looked like ex-police officers or retired armed forces. The opening speech from the prosecution was immaculate. They were not like the other jurors, lazy and tired, not wanting to be there. Each jury member had their own handbook and notepad. Every time our names were brought up they all looked at us in sync. After the first morning session I said to Del, 'D, you know we're going to jail?'

By the time the retrial came, I was expecting the worst. When Judge Mary Stacey delivered her verdict, sixteen months in prison, it didn't shock me. I had already prepared myself. I wasn't begging for mercy. I just stood there, numb. No one can really be ready for jail, but I had already made peace with it. I knew the consequences were coming, and I was exhausted from fighting it.

The hardest thing about the retrial was the judge's summary. That was the bitterest pill to swallow. I've never had a moment like it. I've never had someone who said something so chilling. It makes your whole body go cold. It was so powerful.

'It's about the fans of the teams involved, the families who follow the fortunes of their teams with passion, loyalty and devotion,' Judge Mary Stacey said.

'They assume that all the players in those teams will be sharing in that and playing their hardest and best.

'It's also about the employees and staff, groundsmen, coaches, the cleaners, even the owners and shareholders, the match stewards – many of whom will have been volunteers. You have betrayed all that trust, all that confidence, and it's like a cancer at the heart of football.'

She talked about the people affected by our actions. I never really thought about that up until the time she'd given us our sentence and her summary. She called it a 'fall from grace'. It was a sobering moment. It made me question everything. What the hell's going on? What have we done? What was I a part of?

It wasn't a public humiliation because there weren't a lot of people in court. I'll say it was more of a drowning effect. I felt like I was drowning in myself.

The last time I stood up like that was when I had to speak in front of the whole school. That's what it felt like. I'm standing up straight. The judge spoke with a conviction that was cutting, like invisible bullets.

On 20 April 2015, I was convicted of conspiracy to commit bribery by fixing football matches in the Conference Premier League. I was jailed for sixteen months.

The first thing I did was shake the hand of the NCA officer who arrested me. We had a little bit of banter. I said to him, 'Look, man, no hard feelings.'

The judge stopped speaking. I turned and was ushered downstairs into the holding cells for the formalities and to get my mugshot taken. I was told to 'look up' and you can see I'm totally washed out.

I'm fatigued. I'm drained of all emotion or feeling, beaten down, crushed. It's like I've been stripped naked.

After I shook the officer's hand, they asked if I wanted to call someone. My mum didn't know the verdict. I called her and there was a harrowing scream. I've heard that sound twice in my life. The other times were from Mum again when Oliver's brother, Herve, died. Two hours after Oliver was killed, I went to the place where he was killed and I heard the distressing wail with different mothers, not just one.

That's what I heard from my mum. A sound you never want to hear, one that will definitely keep you up at night.

In this story, nobody died, but I felt like I was already dead. I got the same feeling of me being locked outside the house. It was like I'd been there before. I was emotionally stripped bare when I was locked out of the house and sitting on the doorstep in the cold. This path went all the way round in a full circle and back to the same feeling.

Judgement day had come. I shook the NCA officer's hand and said to Del, 'Let's go down.'

The holding cells were horrible. Del's black shirt and red tie combination made me feel like we were both in secondary school detention. Del looked like he'd lost weight in his suit, a diminished version of his former self. The world came crashing down after we got our mug- shots and headed into the police van to take us to HM Prison Birmingham.

* * *

Choices. Tired. Fatigue. Ready.

I had to go to prison. Getting away with this meant options and once more a feeling I could have got away with it. But now, the money was gone. I'll never see the syndicate again. I was burned and so were my relationships. I could always start anew but the stumbling block is that I am hot. I'm damaged goods. Everything is fun and games until you get caught. I guess the picture I'm trying to paint is that it was all a big gamble, something I'd ridden my luck on for over a year. Now I had nothing left in the tank.

And I would finally find out about the real Delroy Facey. Del was connected to a wider international syndicate directly linked to big-shot match fixers, Wilson Raj Perumal's global network of mules, including Chann and Krishna.

Del also played international football and had a gambling addiction. He owed money to some very unpleasant people. Every-thing made sense from the day I met Del right up until him being my co-defendant.

Del was collateral damage due to his habits that were bigger than him. His own pressures were passed on to me and many others. The scary thing was the web of players directly involved. Part of me thought if I had let Delroy in, we could have had the whole of the UK under our control. But Del couldn't be trusted.

Another part of me felt sorry for him. He had a daughter and a family who had to watch him go to prison. I couldn't inflict my own mistakes and failures on anyone. I had to take my punishment like a man.

Del couldn't even see any of it. He carried this deep-rooted sense of denial. Some of the things that were said in his defence made me realise how sloppy and confused he was. He thought he did nothing wrong and even tried to blame it on racism. Even I was shocked.

They made me believe in the power I had and created. They spoke of this character I made up, 'Jon Gotti', Mr Untouchable avoiding conviction like a Shakespeare play, not really realising this was me. I turned to look at Delroy in the back of the van and his eyes just glared back at me.

The judge telling us how we have ruined the experience and trust of football and its community. That was the knife to my heart, the moment I had the flashbacks. My legs felt weak, and my body turned cold. I needed cleansing.

CHAPTER 21

GOING TO COLLEGE

My stepmother screams when she hears the dull thud of me hitting the floor. I fumble for a toy horse. My dad kicks me again. If I can just reach this toy horse, grab it, raise it above my head and hit him with it . . . Suddenly, everything is black.

I have school the next day. I wake up, still lying on the floor. Groggy, a dull ache in my head. I look in the mirror. I have a cut and a black eye.

* * *

It's dark again. We go into our cell for the first time and I stand over the sink. I look up and see a spot on the wall with broken glass. The glass is meshed. It looks like someone has put their fist through it. I look into this little cracked mirror and I see a reflection of fragments of my face.

When you have life-changing moments, it's funny how you remember all the bad things that have happened to you. In that instance, I have a feeling like I've been here before. Screams. Kicks. A toy horse. Everything is black.

What would Andy Brogan, my first football manager as a kid, say if he saw me in here and he knew the reasons that brought me to this place? Andy saved me, but now look where I am.

The weather is turning spring-like and the drive from the court to the prison reminds me of when we would travel to our cup final games. Andy had us spray-paint our hair different colours, he played music on the old-school open-top bus. The thought of him reading the news about me is frightening. What would his reaction be to my story?

I'm taken to a waiting area and then leave the court as I board a minibus, which is almost like a cage on wheels. You don't know where you are; it's disorientating. Suddenly it stops. We're outside the prison. You troop off the bus and are taken to another waiting area. Then they check you in, take your personal details, take photos, provide you with basic information about prison, what you need to do, etc. They hand you a little breakfast pack and simple toiletries.

By the time we get on to the wing, it's getting late, around six or seven.

Me and Delroy look at the bunk beds: 'What do you want? Top or bottom?'

Big Del and his 95kg hulk of a body had no choice but to take the bottom bunk.

I look at the dirty, half-shattered mirror. Even when you try to clean it, it's still foggy. My reflection is the perfect metaphor – my face is broken, I'm broken.

The cell is cold but we don't have bedsheets so we both have to sleep in our clothes. Del slept in his suit and I slept in the tracksuit I'd worn to prison. I experience a similar sensation to when I was locked out of my childhood home. But this time

I'm not with my brother, Ayub – I'm with a football teammate. It feels mad.

As me and Del climb the stairs of the prison wing, it's like walking up the stairs in my dad's house. When you reached the first floor, you faced the neighbour's door and ours. The prison space is literally the same – from the cell door to the toilet.

I say to Del, 'This is so weird, bro. I have this strong sense of déjà vu, like I've been here before.'

It's an unsettling feeling and I have a restless, fitful night in the bunk. The vivid memories and flashbacks return. Often in my cell, I have these moments of almost delirious, comedic recollection. I remember the good times, funny occasions, nice moments with family and friends.

Prison doesn't feel real, at least not for the first two weeks. It's hard to adjust your brain and it's all overwhelmingly surreal. You know what you're getting into – but you don't know what to expect. The first proper day locked up seemed to last an eternity. It's the biggest waste of time in my life.

* * *

The grim reality of prison hits me hard. It's nothing like the movies – this is real life. The walls are high, the doors heavy, and the air is filled with the scent of metal and sweat. I had been sentenced to sixteen months, and for the first time in so long, I am out of control. There is no football to distract me. Only the cold reality of being held captive. The first few days are the hardest.

Everything I took for granted, my freedom and choice, is gone. I'm locked in a small, dull room and time seems to crawl. The silence is deafening. I start questioning how I'll survive.

After a few weeks, I visit the prison therapist. It's not about confession. It's about trying to live with my situation. The pressure of being in prison has me replaying my mistakes on a constant loop in my head. The shrink asks tough questions that challenge me to face my anger and regret. I'm not even sure if it helps.

Prison football becomes my escape. It's not professional, but it gives me a break from the walls. These prison football games are different, but for ninety minutes, I feel semi-normal again. Not perfect, but it allows me to regain a semblance of control.

I captain the jail prison team, which means I get to pick the best players on our wing. The highlight of every week is the Sunday fixture of the prison football tournament. Bragging rights are essential. Of course, we win many games, but on the occasions we reach the final we have something to talk about for the whole week.

The prison officers are tough to deal with. Some are fair, others make our lives harder. I learn quickly who to trust and who to avoid. I try to stay out of trouble, but the constant scrutiny wears me down. Then, of course, you have to deal with your fellow inmates. Respect isn't given; it's earned. Some stay out of your way, while others test you. I have to figure out how to survive. Delroy is there too, and while he understands what I'm going through, our shared situation creates tension between us.

The hardest part is dealing with my own conscience. The guilt is unbearable. I can't escape my mistakes and the people I've let down. At night, it feels like the walls are closing in on me. It's just about serving my time; it's about coping mentally. I have to push through. Time drags. Every day is the same: wake up, eat, work out, play football, and repeat. I have to confront, unflinchingly, what I've done and what has happened to my life. Prison isn't only about the sentence; it's about who I become in here.

* * *

I'd been arrested before, but that was nothing compared to being in prison. At least when you're arrested, you know you're coming out at some point. Here, you lose track of time. You lose sight of who you are. Everything's a number. It's designed that way, isn't it? A kind of sensory deprivation chamber. It can reach a point where your senses are so confused that you have no concept of time.

You know how I tell the time? Television shows. I know when *The Chase* comes on it's lunchtime. Saturday night is *Ant and Dec's Saturday Night Takeaway*. I hear those theme tunes today and still associate them with telling the time in jail. *Police Interceptors* – I probably watch every single episode. Sunday is *EastEnders* omnibus. You can tell when something good is on TV because everyone on the wing bangs on the wall. We have Freeview TV in our cell. There's no HBO or Netflix, but people had USBs and Fire Sticks. There are ways around it.

One time, someone has a phone which they let me borrow, so I ask them if I can call home. I ring my brother while he's on holiday. I speak to my friends. I tell them I ain't doing that shit again. They ring me and I ask where they are right now? They say, 'I'm in Marbella, man – we wish you were here.' Damn . . .

Crystal brings our young daughter, Taliya, to see me. This innocent little girl comes running into the visitors' hall, as two-year-olds do, and wraps her tiny arms around me.

She doesn't say anything, she just holds me tight and doesn't want to let go. For the next two hours I can't speak. After I see my daughter, I don't want to see anyone else. No more visitors. No more phone calls. It's too much knowing what is happening in the outside world.

* * *

Was I angry when I went to prison? Absolutely not. I know that there's a fine line between what is and what isn't the law. I was prepared for that. I wasn't angry. I was more upset and disappointed in myself than anything else.

I've never really been someone who gets angry and blows their lid. If I am angry, I don't like showing that emotion because whenever I am angry and I can't handle the scenario I feel out of control of my body. I wouldn't say that I'm an intense person. I can be if I believe in something, but that belief pattern can come from different things. Am I passionate about my community? 100 per cent. Across any platform or anything that I may do internally and publicly, it's important to remember who I am and where I'm coming from. This is something I'll never forget no matter what I'm doing, and I see this as a real positive.

However, in a negative way, I understand those levels of anger and intensity. It's about me understanding that I'm still trying to learn and grow and be a better person.

I can be withdrawn especially on areas of focus and that comes with discipline and a tunnel vision about what I want to do and achieve.

I don't have distractions across anything I do in my life because I'm able to protect that space. I learn a lot about myself in prison. When I go through therapy, I learn how to create values and not allow others to scornfully influence or negatively impact who I am and the values that I have.

I do wear my heart on my sleeve and when I love, I love hard. That's especially with my family, my daughter and people that I really care about. I'll go to bat for them. I think it's important to remain resolute, but intelligence is something that can be projected in various forms as well.

* * *

Sharing a prison cell with Delroy Facey adds another layer of complexity to the experience. On one hand, I have someone I can talk to, who has a mutual understanding of what we're both going through. But on the other hand, being around him also means dealing with the fallout of our shared situation. He and I had both been caught up in something that destroyed our lives. We were both trying to make sense of what happened, but there are times when we clash. The tension between us is hard to ignore – two men trapped in a system that neither of us can control, both trying to figure out what to do with the rest of our lives.

Delroy is an imposing physical character with a massive personality. They say you can't teach an old dog new tricks. But the old dog sitting in the corner is very wise because he doesn't need to move any more. It's the young puppies that want to run around and impress, but Delroy's been around the block. He's seen it all.

In this environment I see how the racial slur, 'I'm a big Black man' can be adopted and twisted, as Del demonstrates, to win favour, status, respect. It infers that you can't question me because I played in the Premier League. Everything is taken at face value. It's only when you spend time with someone that you can figure out whether their heart is hot or cold. If your heart is cold and you're soulless, you can see the coward in that person. I've shared a cell with Delroy. I'd mentally prepared for the environment, but he hasn't. He'll say things like, 'Hey, Moses, let's go out together.'

I reply, 'Bro, I'm trying to make new friends. Get the hell off! Let me go and get my lunch.' We're not the same age, so our conversations with people are not going to be the same. This is a new environment and he's kind of a shady character. He may have ripped someone off who's in here too. They might know him because the Midlands of England is his neck of the woods.

So Delroy plays the big Black man role when we go inside and he's the reason we get enhanced – we receive special treatment and extra privileges – because everyone's a football fan.

Initially we're on an induction wing at HM Prison Birmingham but we get moved straight to an enhanced wing because one of the officers is a West Bromwich Albion fan – one of Del's former clubs. When we arrive at our new cell it's got two single beds.

On our first night, there's a knock on the cell: 'You're Delroy Facey, ain't you? You lot are the footballers?'

'Don't worry, Del, we're going to look after you.'

Not Moses Swaibu. Delroy perfects his act where he can pick and choose when to turn it on and off.

Birmingham is dominated by gangs. You're either in the Johnson Crew or you're one of the Burger Bar Boys. The city reminds me of London, but it also reminds me that a lot of gang culture and prison culture is passed on through generations.

In Birmingham, I was on a general pop (population) wing along with about 100 people. Prisoners are moved to my wing because of good behaviour. Being enhanced is like winning a golden ticket. Me and Del were on the best wing in the whole place.

Many prisoners on my wing are in the frame of mind to reflect back on their lives and try to understand what they've done, try to use their time and the prison experience to reform themselves. Think about it all.

They speak to me and ask, 'Why are you here? You're footballers.'

I sit down and I reason with them. Then I start to speak to the OGs, the older prisoners. I'll be like, 'Yo, OG, give me some game,' which is give me some advice. They're much older than me – fifty, sixty, sixty-five years old – but they talk like they're in their teens. Their minds have not developed. Or their minds have become fragile because of being confined to this block for so long.

In the cell next door is a 55-year-old Black guy who owns pubs in the outside world. He tells me he used to get into scraps, little fights.

Education is compulsory, so I sign up for maths classes, my worst subject at school. This guy is in my maths class so we go there together.

There's a group of English Defence League (EDL) racist types. They're sitting in a corner minding their own business. I'm walking back to the wing from education and I see my neighbour having a confrontation with them. I want to mind my own business and not get involved, but the Black guy calls out my name, 'Moses, come, come, come.' I'm not going there. I'm going back to my wing. When he returns, I say to him, 'Yeah, man. I ain't Mo.'

He says, 'Tomorrow when we go to education, we'll go do this and that to the EDL.'

And I say, 'OG, I ain't doing nothing. That's on you.' This guy is fifty-five years old. Just because we look the same, there's a feeling of entitlement from him. That entitlement comes from us not understanding each other. Young Black boys don't have these conversations.

Dad's not in the house. Dad's abusive. Dad cheats on Mum. Son sees violence. Dad's in and out of prison. No positive male role models. When we interact, unless we're talking about music, sport, entertainment, women, partying and lifestyle, what have we really got in common? When I meet young Black boys in and out of prison, they are a reflection of what I could have become.

When I'm serving my time, the English prison system is privately run. This means I can request to switch jails. I immediately ask for a move south to be closer to home. Two months into my sentence, I transfer from Winson Green, Birmingham to HM Prison Onley, near Rugby, which is like a London resettlement.

At Onley, I have a cellmate who is in his early twenties. I'm twenty-six. All he ever talks to me about is gang life. We have arguments about this and I try to understand his perspective, rather than offer him advice. We become friendly.

He's trying to become a better person but he can't escape his past. One day he leaves the wing and bumps into a stranger, someone who doesn't know him but knows his family. This person has revenge on their mind.

When he returns to our cell, he's acting weird. I say, 'Bro, are you drunk? What's wrong with you?'

I think he's been stabbed or something because I see blood. But I don't realise he's bleeding from the back of his head. Then he collapses on the cell floor. I don't know what to do. I ring the prison buzzer, bang on the locked door and shout for help. It takes them five minutes to arrive. He could've died in the cell in front of me. I find out the next day that he got blindsided. Someone punched him and he fell on to a cone and injured his head.

Someone had quickly picked him up off the ground, rather than let him lie there knocked out. This person has then run back into their cell. But no one really helped him.

He left Onley and was admitted to prison hospital. When he came back, he had bruising on his brain.

* * *

For the duration of my prison time I was either rooming with Delroy – for the first two months – or someone else. It wasn't until the last stretch of my sentence that I picked up a book from the library.

'Damn, what am I gonna read?'

I had this cellmate who is Bitcoin mad and everyone thought he was crazy. His name was Wretchy. He would say, 'Oh my God, Moses, I'm telling you – cryptocurrency is gonna be the next big thing!' Everyone thought he was a madman. Before you know it, look what's happened?

How does this young Black Nigerian boy fleece banks? It was extreme. He was a talented cyber hacker. He'd been in prison for eight years. The FBI came to see him. My goodness, I thought I had a life story!

At the prison library with my cyber hacker friend, I pick out a book – Mike Tyson's memoir, *Undisputed Truth*, and I was completely hooked by the first page.

Even though I'm only in there for a short period of time – four months – I think, how can I come out of this situation and not give something back to the world, knowing what I know now? In my mind I'm an Avenger having absorbed all this information and experience of prison life. It injects me with a new lease of life to help people. You don't have to listen to me. But whether you listen or not, it will hit home.

I spend a lot of time in my own head, thinking, contemplating, mulling it all over. No one's here with you. No family, no friends, no girlfriend, not even a TV, just a book. I read *Undisputed Truth* for two months and I identify with Mike Tyson because of what I am going through. There are inspiring, iconic sports stars like Cristiano Ronaldo and Lionel Messi, but Mike Tyson is now my ultimate sporting hero.

When I was a young footballer, Tyson was someone who I didn't really understand. One minute the lion can be happy, but in battles, the lion can rip your head off. But the lion's still a human. Reading his book and thinking back to what I remember seeing of him on TV, makes me realise even more that life is such a complex journey. Tyson is a supremely complicated character. When I think of Mike Tyson I don't just think of the animal, I also think of the tender fragility of that man. He has an aspect of femininity about him.

There's a scene where he has all the money in the world and he crashes his Rolls-Royce. He gets out of the car, hands the keys to someone at the side of the road and they drive off. A $300,000 car! I'm thinking to myself only an empty person would do that. He has no value for anything any more. No value for himself.

He's a husk. It's a very a sad moment for him, and I can relate to what he was experiencing at the time.

* * *

In many ways, this was always going to happen in one shape or form or another. I had to experience what success felt like to know what the highest version of myself was like. Then I had to see what the lowest version of myself felt like. Once upon a time, people said I could have been a Premier League player. But I wasn't one. I could have extended match fixing, but I didn't.

So now I'm here. Which way do I want to go? I have so many conversations with myself over my four months of incarceration. It's like I'm whitewashing the evil. I think Christians do this, ask for forgiveness. I'm not even asking for forgiveness. I'm trying to seek new forms of guidance. Up until prison, I hadn't prayed since I was ten. But I want to try and revisit the good things that happened in my childhood. I remember going to prayers (Jema'ah) on a Friday and there was always a good energy, an almost physical sensation as if I was being cleansed. I want to experience that feeling again.

* * *

I'm not saying I would ever wish my prison experience on other people, but it should almost be prescribed. We go through life never being completely alone, in a place of solace where we can properly stare into the abyss, look into the heart of ourselves and work out who we truly are. We're constantly being told how to live, instructed how to behave by society. We're on a conveyor belt from childhood, going from birth to school, family life confronted with all the different combinations of challenges, problems and obstacles that we have got to overcome. We never get that opportunity to clear our heads and to think with clarity. We're on a hamster wheel, relentlessly running forward to keep the wheel spinning, trying not to fall off.

Towards the end of my sentence, I'm thinking that prison is like a Cambridge or Oxford University for criminals. When you go to prison, everybody wants to connect. If you connect to the drug dealer, you connect to the fraudster or the white collar criminal or whoever, and ultimately, by the time you come out, you inherit their network. It's like LinkedIn. But instead of LinkedIn it's called LockedIn.

When my time comes to be released, I don't want to tell anyone. I notice those who tell other prisoners their release dates are summoned to a goodbye initiation for fun. What happens to them? I can't tell you that. All I can say is that despite being in their thirties, many of the men in jail still act like teenagers, with childlike tendencies.

My release day is getting closer and closer. How am I going to hide the date? I pack my bags and leave everything behind: clothes, books, magazines, and I hand them to a prison officer with a few people's names written on them – parting gifts from me.

Everybody is banged up. Leavers are the first people in prison to have their doors open. I walk out of my cell for the last time and head to the security exit gates. No goodbyes. I simply walk away and never look back.

CHAPTER 22

FIXING THE GAME

We had a right back in our Bromley team whose name was Pedro. He was also at Crystal Palace with me. During lockdown, around mid-2020, I was playing football at an open space in London and afterwards I walked to my car.

I spot him in the car park, 'Yo, Pedro! What's going on?'

'Hello, Moses.'

But it's a cold 'Hello'.

I think, all right, cool. He's kind of got a weird character anyway. We're walking back to our cars together and I'm with my teammates. He's alone and there are four of us.

Then Pedro pipes up, 'Yo, Swai . . . what's going on, man?' He looks at me and says, 'Bro, see when you were doing the match fixing, yeah? Why didn't you tell me?'

'I didn't tell you because you would have ended up in jail too.'

'Yeah, but other people knew.'

'That's on them, innit.'

'You don't even know that what you did, it had a big effect on me. I couldn't get a club.'

I'm shocked. I don't react. I just listen.

'After you left, they thought I was match fixing, simply because we played together on the same team.'

Then he says, 'You could have told me and I could have made some money too.'

When he says that it brings back all the decisions I'd made.

I say, 'If you wanted to do it with me then we both would have gone to jail, because that's what it would have come down to in the end. It's easy to say you wanted to do it just to make a bit of money. But even if the offer was there and you decided not to do it, the fixing is happening with or without you.

'Without you realising it, bro, if I didn't match-fix it wouldn't have mattered. The league was rigged anyway.

'In the nicest way, Pedro, it had to happen, because that's the way it was. That was the play.

'Let's just say I didn't fix any games. They would have found another person who would've said yes. I don't control this. Someone approached me, bro.

'Do you get it? Someone gave me the opportunity.

'Bro, that's what I have to live with. Do you understand? I have to take that.'

* * *

In August 2015, I'm released from prison after serving four months of my sixteen-month sentence. Next up: four months on home tag – wearing an electronic ankle monitor – otherwise known as Home Detention Curfew (HDC) followed by weekly probation meetings with a curfew of 7pm every day at my home address. The final eight months of my sentence will be completed without the tag and back living in the community.

When the prison gates close behind me, I don't feel free. It's not a celebration. It's more like realising life has to move on, even if I'm not ready for that scenario.

Being in prison makes me feel like I was born again. I have a fresh new opportunity to share my experiences. Throughout my sentence I was maturing each day. I used my time productively. I saw a therapist in jail. I spoke many times with prisoners on lengthy sentences.

I have to remind myself about my beginnings. There are still elements of my life I need to explore. What better way to start a fresh chapter in my life than with my first love, football.

I never imagined I'd be in a position that made me question how this evolves. How do you go beyond match fixing and not only heal but repay a lifelong debt? I want to clean up football. I don't know how or when to begin. After prison, I don't look at newspapers or go online. I'm just so happy to be home.

My brother, Ayub, picks me up from the prison gates. I can't sleep the night before. My cell is the last door at the back of the landing. When inmates check out, other prisoners traditionally have the opportunity to take what they leave behind, stuff such as phones, clothes, food, the simple things.

As the gate opens, I take one look back and walk to Ayub's car. I can't get words out of my mouth. I'm so filled with joy. The things I once took for granted, drinking fresh water, or going into a shop to buy chocolate and sweets, even seeing other people and smiling. It feels so pure.

One thing is still on my mind as I'm leaving prison – the contents of my mobile phone which was never recovered or presented in the course of two criminal trials. It has absolutely everything on it, like a little black book of all the match-fixing secrets, payments, bribes, distribution channels, clubs, managers, coaches, players and the whole illegal betting system. I know it's valuable but I don't want to do anything with it.

At a Football Association tribunal in November 2015, I'm issued with a global lifetime ban from football. It's here that I first meet Ian Ryder, at the time the FA's integrity and anti-corruption manager. As an ex-Metropolitan Police officer, he was once part of Operation Trident, a specialist crime unit, dealing with organised crime groups.

He sits me down with a thick wad of paper, possibly 1,000 pages, with my name printed on the front of the file. I take one look, and I know what it is. The complete download of the contents of my phone.

Ian then tells me his plans. He explains that the FA plan to help young people and wish to enlist me to the cause. 'Moses, can you help me so this never happens to anyone again.' I instantly agree.

From my experiences, I already know what the next phase of match fixing will be: targeting young players at Academies, especially those being released, not quite making it at the top level. Since betting companies and illegal sponsors have a foothold in this market, the FA have no clue where to start. I give Ian a tip and ask him to follow my lead. I tell him if this gets out it will not only ruin football but also poison these players behind the scenes and nobody can stop or deal with it.

'Ian, go to Alfreton Town FC and ask them if they were ever approached by a company called Red Star, who were a front to purchase them for a million pounds? If they say "yes" and tell you everything, then you'll believe me.

'Do you know how I know? I was sent there and have insider

knowledge of the whole front and back end of exactly how they were planning to do it.'

Ian follows the lead and gets back to me a few weeks later, verifying what I've told him is true. For the next few months, I help the FA, Premier League and the PFA deliver integrity sessions that become compulsory every season. My lifetime ban is downgraded to a fifteen-year ban due to my accountability. The work I do with Ian allows me to be able to be involved again in the game.

I deliver my first integrity session at Manchester United in 2017. I can't believe it when international and Premier League players start to open up to me that they were also approached in various ways – in person and online – by match fixers.

I say that the match fixers are ten steps ahead of everyone else. They'll be at the forefront of technology and innovation until they're caught.

At every club we visit, one or two players come up to me and skirt around the issue but eventually confess to me their own revelations. It is even bigger than I thought. Because of this, the FA and PFA see this as significant progress being made. But this is the sum total of their work at clubs – go in, do an hour's presentation, spread the message, then leave.

I can't believe what betting is doing to kids in the under-18s and under-23s squads.

I voice my opinion, tell it like it is, and send my knowledge up the food chain. It starts with players then clubs and leagues, then federations all the way to governing bodies. Next on the list is government entities, lawyers and the law, schools and institutions, data companies and the wider betting world.

At the PFA, Simon Barker and Terry Angus both lend a

generous helping hand to me. They always put me forward and enable me to speak truth to power; encourage me to get my message across to the right people. That included Ian Ryder at the FA and Gordon Taylor, chief executive of the English footballers' trades union, the Professional Footballers' Association.

I become more and more vocal until the penny drops. I tell these important football figures that their help needs to go beyond ticking boxes and patting themselves on the back thinking that they're doing all the right things. It's not enough.

I start to educate myself even more, to study what integrity means. While the FA, Premier League and PFA bring on board players who have no expertise on the subject of match fixing, spot fixing or any other form of match manipulation, I know I have gained the support of the players. My ambition is to take this beyond the clubs and explore creative ideas and innovative, imaginative ways to make the proper impact that is badly needed. This new generation of footballers are different; they're online, they have phones, they need to see information on the internet and social media platforms and app-related content.

Then I experience the doors being closed in my face and kept shut by the gatekeepers. They use people that look like me to come and deliver subtle messages. I understand this to an extent – after all, I've just come out of prison – but that is not what integrity is all about.

I have a handful of impactful people who fight my corner, both at the FA and PFA. Unfortunately, Ian Ryder leaves his post to become an agent. Gordon Taylor, who first spoke to me and helped me after prison, and Simon Barker, were both phenomenal.

However, I have a gut feeling that something still doesn't

feel right. How do I use what I know to reach out to FIFA? Will they listen? How do I connect with UEFA? How do I bridge this to other sports? Everything leads to the same road, which is education.

When the Covid-19 pandemic hits the world in early 2020, I can't physically go into football clubs any more as the whole country is in lockdown. But I know everyone, including the players, are reachable online. Despite this, the FA inform me that someone else is delivering this content now. Eventually I figure out that the biggest platform I have is my own voice. My most powerful asset is me and my life experiences. I become a one-man campaign utilising my voice. It brings me back to the only thing I loved in school – writing and reading in English class.

I've written my whole life and I've always been creative. Then I did an article with the *Guardian*, followed by *Forbes*, Crystal Palace's website, and other major media outlets. My voice in this space became bigger. I began to attract those people who share the same story but in different areas, such as education, betting, gambling, HR, compliance and business.

I increase my studies and become obsessed with using the knowledge that I have to help educate people. Match fixing isn't Moses Swaibu; match fixing wears the face of billions of dollars in revenue from betting. Tan, the Boss who I once worked for, is prominent. I recognise it all. Then it clicks! I tell myself, 'I need to become an expert. I need to speak to every policymaker and stakeholder.' Then I meet Chris Eaton and everything changes.

Just before lockdown, I wanted to explore the world of match fixing on a global scale, so I hired two people for research and development. I knew I wasn't the only one with this story and wanted to understand the industry in its entirety. Who were the major players? Where did the money go if you followed the paper trail?

They eventually tracked down Chris Eaton, the godfather of anti-corruption in sports. Chris had previously worked at the highest levels of Interpol and Europol and was FIFA's head of security during the South African World Cup – a real-life superhero in this field.

Getting a meeting with Chris came with conditions: I had to take the first train to Paris, then head to Lyon. He insisted on meeting in person. So, my journey into the world of match fixing investigations began – two hours to Paris, two more to Lyon. The only French I knew was *bonjour*, and I found myself lost in the metro, ducking and diving through the stations.

I met Chris outside Lyon's main station. As we walked and talked, I realised we only had an hour. He exuded an air of high-level security, like something straight out of an action film – his sharp moustache and dark shaded glasses adding to the effect.

He pinpointed what I already knew about match fixing, easing my paranoia, before diving deeper into his lifetime mission to eradicate this poison. He explained everything – from the highest levels of government to the darkest corners of the underworld, where my journey had to stop.

Through our shared experiences, I felt like he was passing me a torch, much like the Olympic flame. With his mentorship, I was set to embark on my own redemption journey, carrying forward a mission to protect the future of sports.

My purpose has turned into something bigger than I could have imagined. Since prison, I begin to surround myself with mentors and people involved in the business world.

I feel that I have to recruit a team of Avengers who want

to effect the same changes I do. Our mission is built around integrity – to take on this multi-billion-dollar industry but this time to do it the right way. Not only empowering players but law firms, insurers, stakeholders, government officials, clubs, federations, leagues, data companies and bookmakers.

Football is in a perilous state with many more higher profile cases on spot fixing and match fixing. I've seen it from the inside out. Match fixing isn't just a threat to the game, it's a direct attack on its soul. In 2025, it's bigger, more sophisticated, and harder to track than ever before. The fixers have evolved, going beyond cash-in-hand deals to digital manipulation, cryptocurrency transactions and AI-driven betting models. It's no longer just about bribing a player or players: entire leagues and competitions can be manipulated globally through algorithms, fake data and dark web syndicates.

The scariest part is that the authorities are still playing catch-up. Law enforcement and sporting bodies don't fully understand the scale of what they're up against. Even if they do, they're still trying to work out what works and how it all connects together. Are they moving at the same pace as the fixers? Or are they just hosting more events and panels, making sure that betting operators, or at least the illegal ones, are still able to keep the lights on but use 'integrity' as a throwaway catch word? While match fixers are operating in a whole new dimension, the authorities are fighting yesterday's battles with outdated tools. The fixers are far more sophisticated, miles ahead of the authorities in an unbalanced race. The cops can't keep up with the robbers.

The underground networks I encountered in my past are now more connected, smarter and bolder, with their hands reaching into every level of the game. This isn't just about football, it's about organised crime, money laundering and corruption at the very highest levels across all sports. Illegal betting markets are worth billions, and for those who control them, football is just a means to an end. It's about power, influence and control. And if we don't act now, we'll wake up to a sport that no longer belongs to the people. It will be owned and run by criminals.

The FA, FIFA, UEFA and other governing bodies may have integrity units, but from my own experiences, some still rely on outdated box-ticking methods. They hold educational workshops, issue bans and make statements without going deep enough into the root causes. FIFA have been prominent in trying to identify the sources of the problem and to implement the correct framework for its 211 member associations. I have been a part of their intention to change the cultural structure by empowering integrity officers with the tools required. FIFA are currently at the vanguard of tackling corruption in sport.

The problem is that match fixing isn't just about individuals making bad choices; it's systemic. Vulnerable players, particularly younger ones in Academies and those at lower league clubs, are targeted because they're desperate. Worldwide, there's not enough financial security in football's lower tiers. This is where the fixers target first. Until that changes, match fixing will always find a way in, especially as it's also used to fuel other crimes. There is a lack of significant legal framework in most countries. If convicted, it's for bribery or elements of fraud and money laundering, nothing to really strike fear into the hearts of any individual caught or the organised crime group behind it all.

The sporting authorities and the miscellaneous stakeholders are not doing enough of treating this like a proper organised crime issue. The same way anti-doping authorities go to extreme lengths to catch drug cheats, we need forensic-level investigations into match fixing. Data companies, betting firms, clubs and governing bodies must work together instead of operating in silos governed by politics and bureaucracy.

What do we even mean by 'real integrity'? The truth is, while there's money, power and corruption, there will always be people trying to cheat the system. Human greed isn't new, but what can change is how we defend sport.

Integrity isn't only about rules and regulations, it's about culture. It's about players, coaches, fans and clubs refusing to accept corruption as part and parcel of the game. If we can educate, empower and protect the next generation, we can create a football culture where integrity isn't just a word; it's a way of life.

In many cases, betting sponsorships are being stripped from the front of football shirts as in the UK. It's a conflict of interest on every level. When the same companies profiting from bets are financially supporting clubs and leagues, how can we trust that the game is being played fairly?

Worse still, this normalisation of betting is harming young people. When I go into clubs, I see youth players addicted to gambling before they've even made a first-team appearance. They grow up seeing betting logos on shirts, on stadium billboards, on pitchside and TV adverts, and before they know it, they're hooked. The game is selling its soul for short-term financial gain, and the long-term damage is devastating. Clubs need money, yes, but there are ethical ways to earn it.

I've learned that mistakes don't define you; it's how you respond to them that does. I went from a promising football career to a prison cell, but I refused to let my story end there.

Prison humbled me, taught me the value of time and made me realise my true purpose.

I've seen the best and worst of football. I've witnessed corruption at the highest and lowest levels and the resilience of those fighting to clean it up. I've learned that speaking out comes with consequences, but silence is far worse.

* * *

I don't mean to seek sympathy, but I'm thirty-five years old now, and it's taken half of my life to understand it and to not have an emotion where I'm sad or I feel like I want to cry.

It isn't just about match fixing. When people ask me, 'How do we know you're telling the truth?' I respond by saying, 'If I share with you what I've been through in my life, and I've hit the lowest point – hearing a Crown Court judge destroy my character, shaking a police officer's hand before being sent down, revealing my soul to a prison therapist, flashbacks to violence and turmoil in my early life – trust me, I'm telling the truth.' I had to change my life. Because the change would never have come if I had continued on that path. And I'm so happy I caught the cancer. I caught it at an early stage.

The only time I allow myself to revisit difficult memories is when I take time to reflect in order to impact people in a positive way. When players say to me, 'I've been approached by match fixers,' I don't think about the act of match fixing itself. I think of the worst-case scenario and how it goes beyond the pitch and poisons your life.

If you make a decision to get involved in match fixing, I want to know who you were as a kid. I want to know about your childhood. Because I can tell anyone in the world – stakeholders, betting companies, whoever it is – if you have a child that's had similar experiences to me growing up, I can almost guarantee there's a 99.9 per cent chance they are going to go ahead and be involved in some form of manipulation or organised crime.

If you look at the statistics, and you speak to every single person who has embarked on taking the wrong path or turn in life, there's always a reason behind it. It's usually trauma-related and it comes down to one fundamental thing: people think match fixing happened yesterday, that it isn't a problem in modern football. But it's happening now, under our very noses – and it has to be stopped.

It's the right time to do these things because we're now going through the second wave of sports corruption and match fixing in a new digital world. If we can catch the second wave and build the right tools or put the right assets, books, or whatever it may be, in place, then there's always somewhere people can go for guidance and education.

If I could give advice to my twenty-year-old self, I'd say: 'Be careful who you trust. Stay focused on your craft. Money will come and go, but integrity lasts forever. Don't take shortcuts; they'll cost you more in the long run. And most importantly, always stay true to yourself. Because one day, your daughters will look up to you, and the man you become will be their role model.'

GameChanger360 isn't just a project, it's a movement. Our company's vision is to enhance the game using cutting-edge technology and digital tools to reach parts of the world like never before. Quicker and faster than ever. The goal is simple: protect young players, protect the sport and educate the football community. I want to make sure no player goes through what I did, that no young talent is exploited by match fixers, and that the game we love is safe from corruption. Integrity isn't a choice, it's a responsibility, and it's about building a new foundation for football's future.

I want people to understand that match fixing isn't a side issue, but instead a disease eating away at football. It's bigger than one player, one club or one league. If we don't take it seriously now, we risk losing the sport we love to those who see it as nothing more than a money-making machine.

But there's hope. The same way match fixers evolve, so must we. Football belongs to the fans, the players and the communities, not to criminals. If enough of us stand up, speak out and demand real integrity, we can take the game back.

This is bigger than just football. This is about the future of sport itself.

Looking back, I see how my circumstances shaped me. I recognise how the pressures, the influences and the desire to make it in football made me vulnerable, open to the wrong kind of influence. The game was supposed to be my escape and my way out. But even football isn't immune to the same temptations that exist on the streets and that's the reality. Being at the top of the tree isn't always as cosy and rosy as it seems. Your foundation needs to be solid and that starts with family, love and care. That's a bare minimum.

I don't believe in fate, but when it comes to these things, there were moments in my life when I could've made different choices and I own that. But I also know that for a lot of kids from similar backgrounds, the system is designed to push you in a certain direction. If you don't have the right mentors, the correct guidance or a strong sense of self, it's easy to end up on a path you never intended to walk.

EPILOGUE

My tears have turned into love and realignment. Nothing is more important than your blood.

Being reborn on Friday, 14 February 2025 wasn't planned. Maybe it happened in ways beyond my understanding? Valentine's Day, the day of love, and also a day of reconciliation. For the first time in over twenty years, I hear my dad speak on the phone.

'It's Moses,' I say, followed by a 'Wow!' from Bashir and a smile I find myself familiar with. My father's voice makes me feel so young, and yet at the same time, so old.

There was a special film in the late 1990s called *Life* starring Eddie Murphy and Martin Lawrence. At the end, they stage a fire at their care home, pretending to die, only to fake their own deaths so they can meet up again and watch their last ever Yankees baseball game together as old men.

Reconnecting with my dad, after the 'Wow', I heard a big sigh and then a long, heavy exhalation, a breath of release and freedom. It almost felt like we were Ray and Claude in the movie – just two old men who loved each other and never saw eye to eye, until one of us finally broke the ice.

My daughter had just finished school. I'd cooked her favourite pasta for her. As we sat on the sofa she came over and hugged me, whispering, 'Dad, I'm proud of you.' I smirked, saying to her for the first time in her life, 'I'm on the phone to your grandad!'

Time stood still and was followed by vivid flashbacks: my dad taking me to work at his car wash, early morning deliveries in Coulsdon, or my dad meeting Andy Brogan for the first time with all the other football dads. Nothing mattered in this moment. I began having more flashbacks of memories I can now cherish forever. The two of us bonding and going away on a family holiday to Butlin's, me and my brother Ayub in our Team USA tracksuits.

Don't ask me why, but I just felt so happy and free. Love isn't always spoken. It doesn't really come in warm embraces or the way we imagine or dream. Is love a sunrise or an illusion? I had that conditioned into me for life and I didn't really understand. It showed me how to stand on my own two feet, persevering in the face of pain and adversity, going through the hardest times and the biggest battles and challenges.

Yet I'm still here, living, breathing, healthy and full of life. Knowing who you really are comes with many challenges, but seeing who you are comes from within. That's the moment you find out who you truly are. My past has completely reshaped my future, even if it took me twenty years. Peace brought me closure, the opening of a new beginning and the burying of the past.

For years I carried with me questions without answers and wounds that wouldn't heal. I took these on into my relationships

EPILOGUE

and reflected the pain and the struggle back on to myself, using football as my tool to paper over the cracks. But listening to my inner voice allowed my mind to settle into something softer. This isn't just a conversation, or a journey: I've fixed myself for a beautiful homecoming.

ACKNOWLEDGEMENTS

This book is more than just words on a page, it's the story of my redemption, my resilience and the unwavering belief that transformation is possible.

To my beautiful daughter, Taliya Swaibu, you brought me back to life. You found the core of my soul and reminded me who I truly am. Because of you, I stand tall in my purpose, knowing exactly what I represent for today, for tomorrow and for eternity. Integrity lives in all of us.

To my mother, my queen, Mama Bella, your strength, resilience and kindness have been the foundation of my existence. You taught me what it means to stand firm in the face of adversity, and for that, I am forever grateful.

To Ayub Swaibu and Sarah Swaibu, our journey has been one of trials, tribulations and triumph. Through it all, we stand as one – unbreakable, unshakable, a living testament that no challenge is greater than the bond we share.

To my nieces and nephews, never let the world tell you

otherwise: the sky is not the limit. Dream bigger, push further and know that your potential is limitless.

To my brothers in 'The Big Dreams Club', our loyalty, ambition and alignment make us unstoppable. There is real power in unity, and together, we move mountains.

To Monique, your love, patience and unwavering support have been my anchor. Through every storm, you have been my rock, and I am endlessly thankful.

And finally, to the incredible team who helped bring this book to life: Oscar Janson-Smith, my agent, and everyone at Bonnier, especially my editor, Joe; your dedication, hard work and belief in this story have meant the world to me. This book would not exist without you.